DATE DUE

JE 4'02			
NO 20'02			

DEMCO 38-296

America in the Age of Soviet Power, 1945–1991 is the first post–Cold War analysis of the origins of the Soviet-American confrontation and its extension from the central arena in Europe to the periphery in the Third World, particularly East Asia and the Middle East. It explores the conditions in the international system at the end of World War II, the American determination to provide leadership, and the "security dilemma" each superpower posed for the other.

Although Professor Cohen perceives the American-Soviet conflict as systemic, he points to the nature of the Stalinist state, its secrecy and its brutal dictatorship, to explain the course of the confrontation. He also contends that the character of the American political system, the separation of powers and the role of interest groups, prompted American leaders to exaggerate dangers abroad to enhance their power at home. Using information recently released by Chinese and Soviet sources, he provides fresh insight into Chinese and Soviet actions during the Korean War, the Taiwan Straits crises of the 1950s, and the Cuban missile crisis of 1962. His chapter on the war in Vietnam is easily the best brief history of that tragic encounter. The author explains the rise and fall of détente in the 1970s, describes how imperial overreach strained both the United States and the Soviet Union in the 1980s, and ultimately reflects on what the Cold War has meant for the world, and what "victory" has meant for Americans in the 1990s. The book includes a valuable bibliographic essay on the large historical literature on American foreign relations during the period.

The Cambridge History of American Foreign Relations

Volume IV
America in the Age of Soviet Power, 1945–1991

THE CAMBRIDGE HISTORY OF AMERICAN FOREIGN RELATIONS

Warren I. Cohen, Editor

Volume I: The Creation of a Republican Empire, 1776–1865 – Bradford Perkins
Volume II: The American Search for Opportunity, 1865–1913 – Walter LaFeber
Volume III: The Globalizing of America, 1913–1945 – Akira Iriye
Volume IV: America in the Age of Soviet Power, 1945–1991 – Warren I. Cohen

THE CAMBRIDGE HISTORY
OF
AMERICAN FOREIGN RELATIONS

Volume IV
America in the Age of Soviet Power, 1945–1991

WARREN I. COHEN

CAMBRIDGE
UNIVERSITY PRESS

Published by the Press Syndicate of the University of Cambridge
The Pitt Building, Trumpington Street, Cambridge CB2 1RP
40 West 20th Street, New York, NY 10011-4211, USA
10 Stamford Road, Oakleigh, Melbourne 3166, Australia

© Cambridge University Press 1993

First published 1993

Printed in the United States of America

ataloging-in-Publication Data

1, Warren I.

can foreign relations / Warren I. Cohen.

>. cm.

nical references and index.

epublican empire, 1766–1865 – v. 2. The

5–1913 – v. 3. The globalizing of America,

the age of Soviet power, 1945–1991.

ISBN 0-521-38209-2 (vol 1). – ISBN 0-521-38185-1 (vol 2)

1. United States – Foreign relations. I. Title.

E183.7.P45   1993

327.73 – dc20   92-36165

CIP

A catalog record for this book is available from the British Library

ISBN 0-521-38193-2 hardback

FOR NANCY
HER TURN

Contents

Maps

General Editor's Introduction

My goal for the Cambridge History of American Foreign Relations was to make the finest scholarship and the best writing in the historical profession available to the general reader. I had no ideological or methodological agenda. I wanted some of America's leading students of diplomatic history, regardless of approach, to join me and was delighted to have my invitations accepted by the first three to whom I turned. When I conceived of the project nearly ten years ago, I had no idea that the Cold War would suddenly end, that these volumes would conclude with a final epoch as well defined as the first three. The collapse of the Soviet empire, just as I finished writing Volume IV, astonished me but allowed for a sense of completion these volumes would have lacked under any other circumstances.

The first volume has been written by Bradford Perkins, the preeminent historian of late eighteenth- and early nineteenth-century American diplomacy and doyen of currently active diplomatic historians. Perkins sees foreign policy in the young Republic as a product of material interests, culture, and the prism of national values. He describes an American pattern of behavior that existed before there was an America and demonstrates how it was shaped by the experience of the Revolution and the early days of the Republic. In his discussion of the Constitution and foreign affairs, he spins a thread that can be pulled through the remaining volumes: the persistent effort of presidents, beginning with Washington, to dominate policy, contrary to the intent of the participants in the Constitutional Convention.

The inescapable theme of Perkins's volume is presaged in its title, the ideological commitment to republican values and the determination to carry those values across the North American continent and to obliterate all obstacles, human as well as geological. He sees the American empire arising out of lust for land and resources rather

than for dominion over other peoples. But it was dominion over
others – native Americans, Mexicans, and especially African Americans – that led to the last episode he discusses, the Civil War and its
diplomacy. This is a magnificent survey of the years in which the
United States emerged as a nation and created the foundations for
world power that would come in the closing years of the nineteenth
century.

Walter LaFeber, author of the second volume, is one of the most
highly respected of the so-called Wisconsin School of diplomatic
historians, men and women who studied with Fred Harvey Har-
rington and William Appleman Williams and their students, and
were identified as "New Left" when they burst on the scene in the
1960s. LaFeber's volume covers the last third of the nineteenth
century and extends into the twentieth, to 1913, through the administration of William Howard Taft. He discusses the link between
the growth of American economic power and expansionism, adding
the theme of racism, especially as applied to native Americans and
Filipinos. Most striking is his rejection of the idea of an American
quest for order. He argues that Americans sought opportunities for
economic and missionary activities abroad and that they were undaunted by the disruptions they caused in other nations. A revolution in China or Mexico was a small price to pay for advantages
accruing to Americans, especially when the local people paid it. His
other inescapable theme is the use of foreign affairs to enhance
presidential power.

The third volume, which begins on the eve of World War I and
carries the story through World War II, is by Akira Iriye, past
president of the American Historical Association and our generation's most innovative historian of international relations. Japanese-
born, educated in American universities, Iriye has been fascinated
by the cultural conflicts and accommodations that permeate power
politics, particularly as the United States has confronted the nations
of East Asia. Iriye opens his book with a quick sketch of the international system as it evolved and was dominated by Europe through
the seventeenth, eighteenth, and nineteenth centuries. He analyzes
Wilsonianism in war and peace and how it was applied in Asia and
Latin America. Most striking is his discussion of what he calls the

"cultural aspect" of the 1920s. Iriye sees the era about which he writes as constituting the "globalizing of America" – an age in which the United States supplanted Europe as the world's leader and provided the economic and cultural resources to define and sustain the international order. He notes the awakening of non-Western peoples and their expectations of American support and inspiration. In his conclusion he presages the troubles that would follow from the Americanization of the world.

Much of my work, like Iriye's, has focused on American–East Asian relations. My friend Michael Hunt has placed me in the "realist" school of diplomatic historians. Influenced by association with Perkins, LaFeber, Iriye, Ernest May, and younger friends such as John Lewis Gaddis, Michael Hogan, and Melvyn Leffler, I have studied the domestic roots of American policy, the role of ideas and attitudes as well as economic concerns, the role of nongovernmental organizations including missionaries, and the place of art in international relations. In the final volume of the series, *America in the Age of Soviet Power, 1945–1991,* I also rely heavily on what I have learned from political economists and political scientists.

I begin the book in the closing months of World War II and end it with the disappearance of the Soviet Union in 1991. I write of the vision American leaders had of a postwar world order and the growing sense that the Soviet Union posed a threat to that vision. The concept of the "security dilemma," the threat each side's defensive actions seemed to pose for the other, looms large in my analysis of the origins of the Cold War. I also emphasize the importance of the two political systems, the paradox of the powerful state and weak government in the United States and the secrecy and brutality of the Stalinist regime. Throughout the volume, I note the importance of the disintegration of prewar colonial empires, the appearance of scores of newly independent states in Africa, Asia, and Latin America, and the turmoil caused by American and Soviet efforts to force them into an international system designed in Washington and Moscow. Finally, I trace the reemergence of Germany and Japan as major powers, the collapse of the Soviet Union, and the drift of the United States, its course in world affairs uncertain in the absence of an adversary.

There are a number of themes that can be followed through these four volumes, however differently the authors approach their subjects. First, there was the relentless national pursuit of wealth and power, described so vividly by Perkins and LaFeber. Iriye demonstrates how Americans used their wealth and power when the United States emerged as the world's leader after World War I. I discuss America's performance as hegemon in the years immediately following World War II, and its response to perceived threats to its dominance.

A second theme of critical importance is the struggle for control of foreign policy. Each author notes tension between the president and Congress, as institutionalized by the Constitution, and the efforts of various presidents, from 1789 to the present, to circumvent constitutional restraints on their powers. The threat to democratic government is illustrated readily by the Nixon-Kissinger obsessions that led to Watergate and Reagan's Iran-Contra fiasco.

Finally, we are all concerned with what constitutes American identity on the world scene. Is there a peculiarly American foreign policy that sets the United States off from the rest of the world? We examine the evolution of American values and measure them against the nation's behavior in international affairs. And we worry about the impact of the country's global activity on its domestic order, fearful that Thomas Jefferson's vision of a virtuous republic has been forgotten, boding ill for Americans and for the world they are allegedly "bound to lead."

WARREN I. COHEN

Acknowledgments

My thanks go first to Akira Iriye, Walt LaFeber, and Brad Perkins for joining me in this project and to Frank Smith and Martin Dinitz for shepherding it to the point of completion. The first three read my manuscript and suggested improvements, some of which I effected. Don Lammers, my regular critic, performed his usual role with the patience of a great teacher. Mel Leffler and Nancy Bernkopf Tucker examined my first draft with excruciating care. They failed in their efforts to intimidate me. Mel will probably never understand Dean Acheson or American policy toward China. Nancy will have to settle for the dedication.

Most of the work for this book was undertaken during a sabbatical leave from Michigan State University. I am grateful to MSU for its consistent support over the thirty years when I taught there. I am especially grateful to John Eadie, dean of the College of Arts and Letters, who did all that was possible to make the years of commuting between East Lansing and Washington painless, and to Gordon Stewart, chair of the Department of History, who tolerated my frequent absences.

I was a fellow at the Woodrow Wilson International Center for Scholars, 1990–1, where Mary Bullock, Rob Litwak, Sam Wells, and Lindsay Collins looked after me, providing all the support one hopes for from a residential program. Sergo Mikoyan's comments on a paper I presented at the Center in June 1991 were most helpful.

A work of this kind rests heavily on the research and writing of many other scholars, most of whom are mentioned in my notes and bibliographic essay. I benefited also from conversations over the years with many of those cited and with British, Chinese, German, Japanese, Korean, and Soviet colleagues at a wide range of international conferences. Equally rewarding has been the teaching of my students. Listening to Qing Simei probably delayed completion of this manuscript by a year.

Finally, I regret to note that on the day I finished revising this manuscript, I lost my most faithful reader and most gentle critic, my uncle, Raphael Avin.

Prelude

The late 1940s marked the origin of what the journalist and political philosopher Walter Lippmann called, in 1947, the "Cold War," denoting the emerging confrontation between the United States and the Soviet Union. [1] The term remained in use as a shorthand description of Soviet-American relations and an explanation of most of American foreign policy until 1989 or 1990. Culminating in the reunification of Germany, the events of those two years signaled the Soviet Union's surrender of much of what it had struggled to achieve, allowing the United States to proclaim itself the victor — and requiring American leaders to find a new rationale for the use and abuse of American wealth and power.

World War II ended in the summer of 1945, and the Korean War began in the summer of 1950. The United States and the Soviet Union spent much of the intervening five years defining their postwar relationship. Each nation pursued its vision of world order, exploring the possibilities of cooperation in achieving its goals, and testing the limits of the other's tolerance in pursuit of unshared goals. Each exploited the extraordinary opportunity to extend its influence in the vacuum created by the defeat of Germany and Japan and the decline of British power. Each found important allies, although much of the rest of the world proved less malleable than leaders in Washington and Moscow had imagined. They succeeded, nonetheless, in achieving most of their principal objectives, including a rough settlement of the major issues that divided them, and they provided for themselves whatever might pass for security in a world over which hung the shadow of nuclear holocaust. They maintained an uneasy, but hardly threatened, peace between them. And

1 First use of the term *cold war* is usually credited to Herbert Bayard Swope, a publicist employed by Bernard Baruch.

1

they might well have devoted their energies in the 1950s and afterward to much needed internal improvements, had Soviet adventurism in Korea not intensified the fears and reinforced the arguments of those American leaders who insisted that preparation for a military resolution of Soviet-American differences was essential.

1. At War's End: Visions of a New World Order

Allied forces returned to France in June 1944 and were soon battling their way inland from the Normandy beaches. In Washington, President Franklin D. Roosevelt knew that the defeat of Germany was on the horizon, the fall of Japan not far beyond. His thoughts and those of other American leaders, in and out of government, turned increasingly to the postwar world: What legacy would he leave the American people? How could he and his associates ensure an enduring peace and a prosperous America? What lessons could be learned from past failures, especially those that had followed World War I, the inability to stop the economic misery and aggressive violence of the 1930s?

Roosevelt and his colleagues expected the United States to emerge from the war as the greatest power on earth. And after this war, unlike the aftermath of World War I, they were determined to assert American leadership. This time they would create a world order conducive to the interests of the United States, which would allow it to increase its wealth and power, and carry its values to every corner of the globe. There would be no shirking of the responsibilities of power. The United States would provide the leadership necessary to create a liberal international economic order, based on free trade and stable currency-exchange rates, providing a level of prosperity the peoples of the world had never known. The United States would provide the leadership necessary to prevent the resurgence of German or Japanese power or the rise of others who might emulate Hitler and the Japanese militarists.

Typically, Roosevelt left the details of implementation to others, especially technical economic details. The balance among his economic advisers had shifted from the nationalists who had dominated in the dark days of 1933 to Cordell Hull at the Department of State and Henry Morgenthau at the Treasury. Hull, Morgenthau, and

3

their aides were committed to the vision of the French philosophers of the Enlightenment, as explicated by Woodrow Wilson: Economic nationalism led to war; free access to markets and raw materials removed a major obstacle to peace. The beggar-thy-neighbor practices of the 1930s, the economic warfare practiced by the Nazis, had produced untold human misery, much evident even before the shooting started.

As early as 1936, Hull and Morgenthau had begun redirecting American foreign economic policy toward cooperation on currency exchange rates and nondiscriminatory trade patterns. They steered the United States into a tripartite agreement with Britain and France to stabilize currency values – a course Roosevelt had rejected in 1933. Hull's reciprocal trade agreements were designed similarly to open doors and expand international commerce.

In August 1941, as Roosevelt and Winston Churchill produced the Atlantic Charter, ostensibly an eloquent description of the aims of those who resisted Hitler, their aides fought below decks where the Americans attempted to force their desperate British friends to surrender the system of imperial preferences that favored British trade, discriminating against all other, within the British Empire. Similarly, when the terms of the Anglo-American mutual aid pact, or "lend-lease" agreement, of 1942 were negotiated, American negotiators remorselessly pushed British supplicants a step further toward the multilateral, nondiscriminatory postwar economic order Hull and Morgenthau were determined to create.[1]

The apotheosis of the American vision emerged from the Bretton Woods (New Hampshire) Conference of 1944. In July of that year the representatives of forty-four nations agreed to the outline of a postwar monetary system. American officials, specifically Roosevelt, Morgenthau, and his principal deputy at the Treasury Department, Harry Dexter White, perceived the conference and the agreements they sought as the economic basis for the postwar operation of the Grand Alliance. Economic interdependence, a shared stake in a

1 Roy F. Harrod, *The Life of John Maynard Keynes* (New York, 1951), 510–14; Richard N. Gardner, *Sterling-Dollar Diplomacy,* expanded edition (New York, 1969), 40–53, 56–68; Gabriel Kolko, *Politics of War* (New York, 1968), 248–50.

postwar economic order, would bind Great Britain, the Soviet Union, and the United States in peace, as fear of Hitler had brought them together in war. The cooperation of the British, the world's leading traders, whose pound sterling, like the dollar, constituted a basic currency of international trade, was perceived by American leaders to be essential. The Bretton Woods Conference quickly became a negotiation between White for the Americans and John Maynard Keynes, representing Great Britain. Officials of the Soviet Union participated but, as a nation committed to state-controlled trade, the Soviets were less interested in the details of the agreement than in demonstrating their great-power status and their willingness to work with their allies to eliminate trade and currency issues as causes of international tension. Eager to keep them on board, White indulged them from time to time, but the Soviets were peripheral to what was primarily an Anglo-American show.[2]

The principal goal at Bretton Woods was the creation of mechanisms for assuring stable exchange rates to facilitate the expansion of international trade. The participants created an International Monetary Fund (IMF), designed to provide member nations with assistance whenever their balance of payments (the balance between funds coming in through exports, services, tourism, remissions, etc., and funds expended for imports of goods or services, overseas travel and investments by one's own nationals, etc.) was in deficit. A second institution, a bank for reconstruction and development, which came to be known as the World Bank, was intended to provide or guarantee loans in situations private bankers might find unattractive. In addition, beyond the scope of the conference, the planners envisioned an international trade organization that would gradually eliminate restrictive trade practices. The United States, as the wealthiest nation in the world, with an economy that had rebounded from the Depression and manifested extraordinary productivity during the war, would provide much of the funding required by these institutions – and maintain a proportionate share of control

2 Gardner, *Sterling-Dollar Diplomacy*, 11–12; Alfred E. Eckes, Jr., *A Search for Solvency: Bretton Woods and the International Monetary System 1947–1971* (Austin, Tex., 1975), 139–64; Harrod, *Keynes*, 525–85.

over their activities. There was never any doubt, in Washington or abroad, that the Bretton Woods system was designed to serve the long-term interests of the United States, at least as perceived by the New Deal coalition, the combination of economic forces prevailing in Washington at that time. In general, however, in a willing suspension of disbelief, the leaders of other nations accepted the idea that the system that was good for America would be good for the world; that the world would benefit from the responsible and generous position to which the United States had committed itself. Lord Keynes would have done things rather differently, but he was not distressed by the outcome.

On the other hand, Keynes and White, the other participating planners, and knowledgeable bankers and economists who had not been invited to Bretton Woods, understood that the new liberal international trading order would not materialize the day after the war ended. They were committing their countries to a goal whose realization would have to be postponed until the exigencies of reconstruction had been met. In retrospect it seems clear that the Americans, at least, had underestimated the damage war had inflicted on the British economy, the general problems and costs of postwar reconstruction, the needs of developing countries, the opposition to an international trade organization designed to dismantle protectionist structures. Certainly few if any among them imagined that it would be 1958 before anything approximating full currency convertibility could be instituted — and even then for only that part of the world that looked to the United States for protection.

Roosevelt, Hull, and Morgenthau were very much aware that their plans for multilateral free trade would face opposition at home; that free enterprise ideologues would resent this further intrusion of the government into economic affairs; that bankers would be apprehensive about government competition for overseas loans; that protected industries and especially those which had long since lost hope of comparative advantage would oppose trade liberalization, and might well be supported by some labor organizations; that men and women uneasy about American involvement in world affairs would be unwilling to accept the leadership role projected. In fact, the Bretton Woods agreements constituted a classic case of preemption, of an attempt to commit the nation to the desired role, to a particular international economic regime, before the opposition had the opportunity to act. For all its power internationally, the American government could be thwarted relatively easily by domestic special-interest groups, each with its own conception of what was best for the nation. Indeed, however successful Roosevelt and his colleagues were in committing the United States to their vision of an international economic order, they failed to persuade Congress to create an international trade organization, and settled for less funding and less altruism than they had hoped.[3]

Although their success was incomplete, their timetable askew, with the general ratification of the Bretton Woods agreements by December 1945, American leaders had succeeded in launching the world on a new order of their design, based on what the historian Michael J. Hogan has called the "New Deal synthesis."[4] The stalwart forces of economic nationalism had been driven back and much of the trading world committed to the liberal program. The emphasis would be on increasing trade, increasing productivity, on a larger share for everyone rather than a struggle to redistribute existing wealth. Government, business, and labor would work in tandem to realize the new order. When the deadline for ratification was reached, the Soviet Union held back, but its trading role was minor, its interest in the Bretton Woods regime never more than marginal, its absence regretted, but not enough to spoil the party.

If Roosevelt left much of the economic planning to lesser figures in his administration, he was deeply engaged in the political and strategic planning for the postwar world — although attention to detail was not his forte here either. Central to his thoughts was the conviction that a condominium of the great powers, the United States, Great Britain, and the Soviet Union, was essential to keep the peace, to prevent future acts of aggression. He committed himself to the United Nations Organization, to an international organization, primarily to soothe public opinion and the Wilsonians

---

3 Eckes, *A Search for Solvency,* 165–202; John H. Williams, *Postwar Monetary Plans and Other Essays* (New York, 1947); Gardner, *Sterling-Dollar Diplomacy,* 129–44.
4 Michael J. Hogan, *The Marshall Plan* (Cambridge, 1990), 12–18.

around him – to demonstrate American willingness to accept participation in and leadership of the postwar world – but he had few
illusions about a future in which the Big Three did not cooperate.
He knew the British could be difficult: Keynes had been tenacious in
protecting the pound and British markets, Churchill no less so when
prodded on freedom for the colonies. But Churchill and Roosevelt
had developed a personal friendship and their countrymen drew
deeply from a well of shared values. Stalin and the Soviet Union
were more of an enigma. Soviet and American statesmen were still
circling each other warily, mistrustful after a generation of enmity,
which Hitler had forced them to shelve. But the Soviet Union and
the United States had no vital interests in conflict, cooperation
would be nearly as urgent after victory, and Roosevelt was confident
that he and Stalin could find a way to sustain it.[5]

When the Big Three met at Tehran in November 1943, and
throughout 1944, Stalin's anxieties had been evident, his fear of a
resurgent Germany palpable. Roosevelt shared Stalin's apprehensions and unhesitatingly offered his assurances that the steps necessary to prevent a postwar resurrection of German power would be
taken: Germany would be subdued, pacified, and perhaps even dis-
membered. Stalin's security concerns in Eastern Europe were marginally more troublesome. Certainly he was entitled to a buffer of
not unfriendly nations on Soviet borders, to what some would call a
"sphere of influence." The Soviet desire to rearrange Poland's geo-
graphic position, to move the country some distance to the west, at
Germany's expense, and to the advantage of the Soviets who would
annex a slice of eastern Poland, would surely upset the Poles. It
would likely upset Cordell Hull and a host of other Americans
religiously committed to the principle of self-determination. But if
some modest rearranging of the map was all that was necessary to
bind the Big Three in peace, it was hardly too high a price to pay.
Certainly Roosevelt would not scruple to barter German for Polish
real estate, though he had title to neither, in the name of world

5 Robert Dallek, *Franklin D. Roosevelt and American Foreign Policy, 1932–1945*
(New York, 1979), 282–4, 317ff.; Herbert Feis, *Churchill, Roosevelt, and Stalin*
(Princeton, 1957), 121–4, 269–79, 596–9.

peace. The Poles, to be sure, had the right to self-determination, which was still possible, albeit with minor territorial adjustments. On the other hand, the Soviet Union had won the right to secure borders. Rather than a case of right versus wrong, Roosevelt saw a matter of conflicting rights, in which the Soviet need took precedence, especially while the Red Army bore the burden of the battle against Hitler's Wehrmacht.[6]

The Polish question posed a domestic political problem for Roosevelt, which he assumed he could finesse. If Polish Americans concluded he was betraying Poland, they might well desert the Democratic party, hurt his reelection prospects in 1944 and the prospects for his party for a generation after. Ideologues might harass him and hamper his efforts toward a just peace, as they had used territorial concessions to Japan made at Versailles in 1919 to savage Woodrow Wilson and his peace treaty. Opponents of his conception of America's role in the postwar world order or of cooperation with the Soviet Union might distort the issue to their advantage. He conveyed his concerns to Stalin at Tehran and in the months that followed – and he depended on Stalin to arrange affairs in Poland in a manner that would be acceptable to the American people. It was important that Stalin understand that even a strong president in the most powerful nation the world had ever known faced restraints and could use a little help from his friends.

Roosevelt had been in politics too long to believe in sure things, but he was reasonably confident of realizing his vision of the great powers working together after victory to maintain a just peace. He was reasonably confident that he could manage both Churchill and Stalin. But he was also a prudent man who hedged his bets. By fiat he declared his Asian ally, China, to be a great power, to share in the condominium that would rule the postwar world, to sit in the Security Council of the United Nations and, as Churchill complained, be a "faggot vote" at America's side. China's hostility to British imperialism in Asia might be useful if the British became unruly. Should the Soviets prove less cooperative than he hoped,

6 John L. Gaddis, *The United States and the Origins of the Cold War* (New York, 1972), is most persuasive on this issue.

Roosevelt had another, more awesome weapon up his sleeve, the atom bomb. Urged by one of his scientific advisers to deny critical data about the bomb to the British and on another occasion by a group of atomic scientists to share its secret with the Soviets, Roosevelt chose to share the information with his British allies and to withhold it from the Soviets. The United States would not be without resources should the Soviets revert to being as disagreeable as they had been prior to being invaded by the German Army in 1941.[7]

We are far less certain even today – and likely will never be certain – about Stalin's vision of the postwar world. There seems no reason to doubt his indifference toward the liberal international economic order the United States wanted. He saw no place in that system for the Soviet Union, with its command economy and state trading organizations. It might have been vaguely threatening, but Stalin gave no indication that he was much troubled by it before 1947. The lessons he drew from the 1930s – everyman his own historian – had little to do with exchange rates and tariff barriers. The Soviet Union strove toward autarky and would risk economic dependence on no foreign power. No, the Soviet Union had suffered because the capitalist world, led by Great Britain, had been implacably hostile, and, having failed to prevent the success of the Bolshevik Revolution, had encircled and attempted to destroy its heirs. Ultimately, the enemies of the Soviet Union had unleashed Hitler. Shrewdly, Stalin had bought nearly two years with the Nazi-Soviet pact, but Hitler had attacked nonetheless – and come dangerously close to toppling the Soviet regime. More than twenty million Soviet citizens had lost their lives. The country had been devastated by the Nazi invaders. Grudgingly, the British and the Americans had joined forces with the Russians against Hitler, providing modest but essential material support. For two and a half years, however, Roosevelt and Churchill had rejected Stalin's pleas for a second front in France, leaving Soviet troops to engage 80 percent of the German

7 Kolko, *Politics of War*, 218–21; Dallek, *FDR and American Foreign Policy*, 389–91; Martin J. Sherwin, *A World Destroyed* (New York, 1975), 90ff.

Army. Like Roosevelt, Stalin saw no harm in the United Nations Organization, provided the Soviet Union had multiple votes in the General Assembly (he thought sixteen would be adequate) and a veto in the Security Council to protect its interests. But he was no fool: He would rely neither on the goodwill of his newfound friends nor the efficacy of the United Nations to provide for Soviet security. German power would have to be broken, its wealth used to repair the damage the German military had inflicted on the Soviet Union. Germany would have to be occupied. The so-called Baltic republics would have to be restored to the Russian empire, as would territory the Poles, Finns, and Romanians had taken. No Eastern European country could be allowed to become a springboard for a new aggression against the Soviet Union: All would have "friendly" governments, responsive to Soviet requirements. Optimally, there would be adjustments to the south, at the expense of Iran, Afghanistan, and pro-German Turkey. And when the time came for Soviet forces to participate in the defeat of Japan, Stalin had ideas for buffers and bases in East Asia, not only in what was now the Japanese empire, but in China, where both Nationalist and Communist contenders for power had displeased him, as well. Stalin even had occasional dreams of extending his reach into Africa, of being awarded some of Italy's former colonies on that continent by his grateful allies.[8]

Curiously, Churchill had proved relatively easy to deal with. He sat at the table with Stalin one night in the autumn of 1944 and in a matter of minutes the two men had achieved an equitable division of influence in Eastern Europe. Roosevelt was more elusive, apparently more sympathetic to Soviet aspirations, even suggesting the possibility of Soviet-American collusion against British imperialism, but unwilling to make firm commitments about giving the Soviet Union a free hand in Eastern Europe, forever blathering about the need to appease public opinion in the United States, dallying with anti-Soviet Poles. And then there was the evidence Soviet intelligence had brought Stalin that the United States was working with

---

8 Feis, *Churchill, Roosevelt, and Stalin*, 26, 510–11, 550–5; Dallek, *FDR and American Foreign Policy*, 389–91; William Taubman, *Stalin's American Policy* (New York, 1982), 75–82.

the British on a secret weapon, an atom bomb, about which Roosevelt said nothing to his loyal Soviet ally. Clearly, satisfactory postwar relations among the victors were by no means assured. It was a time for caution – and however ruthless he was, Stalin had not survived in the Soviet system of his day without being a very cautious man.

In East Asia, a very different set of circumstances prevailed in the closing months of the war. Chiang Kai-shek, the tenacious Chinese leader, sat in Chongqing (Chungking), husbanding his forces, waiting for his American allies to rid his country of the Japanese invaders. His concerns were, conceivably, even graver than those of Roosevelt and Stalin: The survival of his regime was still very much in question. In 1944 the Japanese were still capable of – and did in fact launch – another offensive. Within his government, there were several prominent figures, mostly military men, ready and eager to succeed him if he faltered. Off in Yan'an, in the northwest of his country, Communist forces hostile to his regime controlled an extensive area and were primed to expand as soon as the Japanese retreated. Indeed, Chiang, to the irritation of the Americans, had posted half a million of his best-equipped forces as a barrier to Communist expansion rather than risk those assets against the Japanese. Increasingly, the Americans were pressing him to engage the Japanese more, threatening to align themselves with other forces in the country more willing to fight. Inevitably, the Americans would expel the Japanese, but then what? Resumption of civil war with the Communists was inescapable. An increased Soviet presence on China's borders was certain – and a victorious Stalin, unchecked by Japan, would be a demanding neighbor. And the British imperialists would return to Hong Kong. With limited control over his own country, with China no match for the allegedly friendly great powers moving in on it, Chiang had to count on his own demonstrated ability to manipulate Roosevelt and Stalin. He had to rely on the traditional Chinese practice of playing barbarians off against each other, to China's advantage.

Chiang had not been allowed to confer with the Big Three at

Tehran in 1943, but Roosevelt had agreed to enhance China's great-power status by meeting him in Cairo before and after the conference. Part of the time, the two men met alone, with Chiang's American-educated wife serving as translator. Chiang, as always, wanted more aid from the United States, wanted more action by American forces in China. Roosevelt, as always, made vague promises, and asked for more action from the Chinese. Promises of post-war assistance to China may have been offered, but there were no witnesses to support some of the later claims by Madame Chiang and her husband.

In 1944, Roosevelt lost patience with Chiang's inaction and demanded that he send his troops into battle under the leadership of the American general, Joseph Stilwell, an abrasive infantryman with whom Chiang had fenced unhappily for two years. Chiang refused, demanded Stilwell's recall, and forfeited a major role in the liberation of China. Roosevelt turned to the Soviet Union to help do the job the Chinese were not going to do themselves. At the Yalta Conference, in February 1945, Roosevelt bought Soviet participation in the war against Japan by agreeing to support Soviet imperial claims in China.[9]

Stalin had feared – and much of the world had expected – a Japanese attack on Soviet East Asian territory, but the Japanese had turned south instead, after crippling the U.S. fleet at Pearl Harbor. So long as Hitler's army battered the gates of Moscow and Leningrad, Stalin's attention was riveted on his European front. Stalin nonetheless had claims on Chinese territory and, when the Germans had been turned back in 1943, and Soviet forces took the offensive, he remembered Chinese intrusions into the sphere of influence he had fashioned in Xinjiang (Sinkiang) in Central Asia. No longer needing Chinese forces to engage the Japanese, confident the Americans could manage that, he attempted in 1944 to drive the Chinese from territory he considered his domain, reminding Chiang

9 Herbert Feis, *The China Tangle* (Princeton, 1953), 166–201; Barbara Tuchman, *Stilwell and the American Experience in China, 1911–1945* (New York, 1970); Charles Romanus and Riley Sunderland, *Stilwell's Command Problems* (Washington, D.C., 1956). For a view from a perspective close to Chiang's, see Liang Chin-tung, *General Stilwell in China, 1942–1944* (New York, 1972).

that the Soviet Union was not to be taken lightly.[10] And, as the months passed, he perceived new opportunities for the Soviet state to rival the achievements of tsarist imperialism, regaining not only territory from the Japanese, whom he would attack in due course, but a sphere of influence from the Chinese whom he would soon help liberate. At Yalta, Roosevelt was not troubled by Stalin's aspirations. No price was too high to save American lives – when it was paid in other people's currencies.

In Yan'an, Mao Zedong, the Chinese Communist leader, struggled to maneuver against the Japanese and Chiang, uncertain of what to expect from the Americans or the Soviets. The Japanese had interrupted Chiang's efforts to exterminate the Communists during the 1930s; Chiang would certainly resume his effort at war's end. The Americans, however, had been friendly throughout the war, Mao's trusted emissary, Zhou Enlai, had spent much of the war years in Chongqing successfully wooing the Americans and alerting them to the seamier side of Chiang's activities. Concerned primarily with defeating the Japanese, the Americans had enlisted Communist support and appeared determined to prevent Chiang from precipitating a civil war. Progressive forces seemed to be in control in the United States, cooperating with the Soviet Union. Mao and Zhou wondered whether the Americans would remain friendly after the war and what role the United States might play in China.

Mao could not count on a benign Stalin. Stalin had betrayed the Chinese Communists to serve his own ends in the past. He had tried to impose upon them leaders amenable to his control. He had tried unsuccessfully to use, perhaps even sacrifice, the Chinese Communists, in suicidal attacks on the Japanese, to protect the Soviet Union in the late 1930s. He had chased Chinese Communist forces out of territories Mao considered Chinese. And the intensely nationalistic Mao was aware of Stalin's plans for Mongolia and perhaps suspected other Soviet claims on Chinese soil. It had taken a great deal of

10 John W. Garver, *Chinese-Soviet Relations, 1937–1945* (New York, 1988), 153–81, 196–230; Allen S. Whiting and Sheng Shih-ts'ai, *Sinkiang: Pawn or Pivot?* (East Lansing, Mich. 1958), remains useful. See also U.S. Department of State, *Foreign Relations of the United States, 1944, China* (Washington, D.C., 1967), 758–823.

ingenuity and good fortune for Mao to rise to the top of the Communist party and for the party to survive the misfortunes of the 1920s and 1930s. Mao and his colleagues would need all of that – and perhaps more – to prevail after the war.[11]

Elsewhere in East Asia, war had brought the usual unpredictable turmoil. Throughout 1944 and on into 1945, as the Japanese fought ferociously to stave off defeat, the peoples they had oppressed and the peoples who perceived them as liberators – Koreans, Malays, Burmese, Filipinos, Vietnamese, Javanese, Sumatrans, subjects of the Japanese, British, American, French, and Dutch empires – waited, some passively, some armed and ready, to learn what peace would bring them.

Franklin D. Roosevelt, four-time president of the United States, died in April 1945, on the eve of victory in Europe. Before his death, at Yalta in February 1945 and in the weeks that followed, he tried desperately to secure the enduring peace toward which he had labored so valiantly. At Yalta, discussions with Churchill and Stalin had gone well. Roosevelt found the other allied leaders frank but reasonable in their demands. Toward his own requirements, they were remarkably responsive. Roosevelt's primary objective was to get Stalin to agree to abrogate his nonaggression pact with Japan, due to expire in 1946, and attack Japan's Kwantung Army in Manchuria. The Chinese had demonstrated their inability to do the job and Roosevelt did not want American lives lost on the mainland. He would call in the Red Army and let the Chinese pay the piper. Stalin agreed, with the understanding that the Soviet Union would be allowed a sphere of influence in Manchuria. Next, Roosevelt sought assurances that the Soviet Union would join the United Nations, without sixteen votes. Stalin settled for three. Finally, Roosevelt wanted Stalin to set aside the puppet government he had established for Poland and respect the principle of self-determination. Stalin

11 Garver, *Chinese-Soviet Relations*, 58–80; Benjamin I. Schwartz, *Chinese Communism and the Rise of Mao* (Cambridge, Mass., 1958), 172–88; Charles B. McLane, *Soviet Policy and the Chinese Communists, 1931–1946* (New York, 1958), 29–34.

would not dismiss the "Lublin" government, composed primarily of Communists long absent from Poland and Communist sympathizers, but he offered to prettify it by giving more posts to non-Communists and he presented vague assurances about democracy and free elections in Eastern Europe generally. Roosevelt accepted. No agreement was reached on Germany, although the United States and Great Britain accepted the Soviet demand for extracting $10 billion in reparations as a basis for negotiations. Afterward, Churchill praised Stalin's loyalty and cooperativeness effusively before the British Parliament. There seemed to be no issues to divide the Big Three. The war was going well, thanks to Stalin's agreement to launch his spring offensive in February, rescuing British and American soldiers savaged by Hitler's Ardennes offensive, and peace seemed well in hand. But Roosevelt lived long enough to see his hopes for Big Three postwar cooperation begin to unravel.

Perhaps because of fatigue or the imminence of death, Roosevelt blundered seriously in March 1945. Uncharacteristically insensitive to Soviet anxieties, he authorized American intelligence operatives to meet secretly in Switzerland with senior German officers to discuss the German surrender in Italy. Stalin immediately suspected the worst: a deal between the Germans and his Anglo-American allies, which would allow the Germans to concentrate their resistance against the advance of the Red Army. At Munich in 1938, the British and French had tried to redirect Hitler's demonic energies against the Soviet Union, but Stalin had outsmarted them. Very likely they were trying again, this time under the leadership of his self-proclaimed American friend. Outraged, Stalin protested without pretense of diplomatic niceties. Roosevelt in turn was offended by Stalin's accusation, conceivably unable to imagine himself capable of such a betrayal. Stalin, clearly, was more imaginative. The incident passed, but not without abrading the thin veneer of trust that might have existed between the two men. Unquestionably, the atmosphere was less conducive to an amicable resolution of the differences that resurfaced over Poland.[12]

12 Feis, *Churchill, Roosevelt, Stalin,* 583–96; Kolko, *Politics of War,* 375–9; Taubman, *Stalin's American Policy,* 95–6.

Reports from Poland, underscored by a cable from Churchill, indicated that Soviet control was being inflicted on that country with less subtlety than that of the American machine politicians whom Roosevelt had expected Stalin to emulate. Opposition to the Soviet-imposed Communist-dominated regime was being suppressed ruthlessly and blatantly. Roosevelt probably had less sympathy for the Poles, who had behaved badly in the 1930s, than did Churchill, whose nation had gone to war to defend their country. He was reluctant to allow the intransigence of non-Communist Polish leaders to jeopardize his hopes of Soviet-American cooperation. Nonetheless, he could not acquiesce in the Soviet denial of any semblance of self-determination to the Poles. It would be wrong, opponents of his conception of America's role in the new world order would exploit the issue against him, and the American people would be angered. Roosevelt's last days were roiled by the disagreeable task of trying to redefine the concessions he had offered Stalin at Yalta – a redefinition that Stalin could hardly see as less than a reversal of American willingness to grant the Soviet Union a sphere of influence in Eastern Europe and the assurance of a friendly government in Poland.

Roosevelt died and Harry S. Truman became the thirty-third president of the United States. Truman had few illusions about his knowledge of world affairs and understood full well how poorly Roosevelt had prepared him for the position. As the Third Reich crumbled before the combined forces of the United States, Great Britain, and the Soviet Union, and as American forces in the Pacific positioned themselves to strike the fatal blow at the Japanese homeland, he, the onetime Kansas City haberdasher, would have to preside over victory; he would have to make the decisions necessary to gather the fruits of that victory and to preserve the peace that followed. He was appropriately awed and, quite reasonably, looked to the men who had advised Roosevelt for guidance.

Truman was untroubled by any of Roosevelt's goals or commitments, as he understood them. The Hull-Morgenthau plan for a liberal international economic order was consistent with Democratic party programs he had supported as a senator. Doubtless there would be trouble with Congress after the war — time enough for that. The German surrender came only a few weeks after he took office, without much need for presidential direction. Accelerated planning for the defeat of Japan required more of his attention, including consideration of the range of options to minimize American casualties. The most immediate problem, according to his advisers, was smoothing out the kinks that seemed to be developing in Soviet-American relations.[13]

In a typical off-the-cuff remark years before, Truman had expressed satisfaction at the Nazi invasion of the Soviet Union, suggesting that the weakening of both regimes was equally desirable. He had no sympathy whatever for communism. But in 1945, Truman evidenced no hostility to the Soviet Union, perceived that nation as a loyal ally, and accepted, without apparent reservation, Roosevelt's conviction that Soviet-American cooperation was essential to the vision of a just and peaceful postwar world. Like most Americans, however, Truman was inclined to measure Soviet cooperativeness by the degree of deference the Soviets accorded the United States.

Immediately after he became president, Truman was apprised of the disagreement that had arisen between Roosevelt and Stalin over Soviet behavior in Eastern Europe. The issue was not whether to continue cooperation, but how best to achieve it without sacrificing American ideals or interests. Several of Roosevelt's advisers, most notably his White House chief of staff, Admiral William Leahy, and W. Averell Harriman, ambassador to the Soviet Union, argued that difficulties had emerged because Roosevelt had been too generous with the Soviets, that he had encouraged them to be demanding, to take American support for granted while offering little or nothing in return. They argued that the Soviets rather than the Americans were reneging on the Yalta agreement regarding Poland. And Harriman, in particular, pressed for a policy shift, for tougher bargaining by the American side, for a carrot-and-stick approach, a quid-pro-quo

---

13 Gaddis, *US and Origins of the Cold War,* 198–206; Deborah Welch Larson, *Origins of Containment* (Princeton, 1985), 150–8.

approach. If the Soviets wanted something, economic aid for example, require them to yield something to the United States in return. If the United States was to help finance Soviet postwar reconstruction, the Soviets in return could ease their control over Eastern Europe, allow free elections, refrain from incorporating Poland, Hungary, Romania, and Bulgaria into a Soviet-controlled political and economic bloc. Again, the idea was not to give up on collaboration, not to be unfriendly, but to find a course more likely to lead to a mutually satisfying Soviet-American relationship, one consistent with the preeminent position of the United States. [14]

Truman accepted the advice to be less gentle with the Soviets and gave Soviet foreign minister Vyacheslav Molotov an undiplomatic dressing-down at their first meeting. Not normally a sensitive man, Molotov protested against Truman's tone, but he had little difficulty understanding the message: American policy had changed. What he could not discern was whether American objectives had changed. Molotov and his aides readily assumed that Roosevelt's death had resulted in a seizure of power by recently dormant anti-Soviet forces in the United States. Truman's language showed little respect for Molotov and the country he represented. With victory in reach, the Americans had apparently concluded they had no further need to cooperate with the Soviet Union. Were the Americans unwilling to concede that the Soviet Union had contributed mightily to the allied cause, that it was now the second greatest power in the world, entitled to the perquisites of that status? Truman probably raised more questions in the minds of Soviet leaders than he had intended. They would be increasingly wary in the months ahead. [15]

In July 1945, Truman went to Potsdam where, amid the ruins of Hitler's Reich, he met with Churchill (and Clement Atlee, who succeeded him as prime minister) and Stalin in the last major conference of the war. Initially uneasy given the importance of the issues to be resolved and the stature of the other two men, Truman's confi-

14 Kolko, *Politics of War,* 390–403; Gaddis, *US and Origins of the Cold War,* 200–5; Larson, *Origins of Containment,* 66–125.
15 See, for example, Andrei Gromyko, *Memoirs* (New York, 1989), and the "Novikov Telegram," in Kenneth M. Jensen, ed., *Origins of the Cold War* (Washington, D.C., 1991), 3–16.

dence was greatly bolstered by word that America's secret weapon, the atom bomb, had been tested successfully and would soon be available for use against Japan. He had never doubted that the United States would emerge from the war as the world's leading power. Now that power would be enough to finish the war alone, if necessary, to maintain the peace alone, should that prove necessary. The atom bomb ensured imminent victory in East Asia and seemed likely to gain the United States additional leverage in postwar international politics. Casually, he mentioned the new weapon to Stalin, who seemed uninterested.[16]

In general, Truman responded favorably to what he saw of Stalin at Potsdam and came away from the meeting persuaded that like his early Missouri political mentor, Boss Pendergast, Stalin was a man with whom one could do business.[17] Indeed, neither Roosevelt nor Churchill — or even Harriman — doubted that a reasonable agreement could be reached with Stalin if the right man (e.g., Roosevelt, Churchill, or Harriman) conducted the negotiation. For all his brutality, Stalin was not to be equated with the maniacal Hitler. Moreover, ideological differences seemed irrelevant. Fundamental security issues between the United States and the Soviet Union did not appear to exist. Disagreement over Poland persisted, but Truman recognized that Poland constituted a vital Soviet interest and was, at most, a secondary concern of the United States. The minor adjustments the United States required would be granted ultimately to the world's only atomic power, to the nation on which the Soviet Union would have to depend for reconstruction financing. He and his advisers were confident he and Stalin could work things out. Truman set sail for home, ordered atom bombs dropped on Hiroshima and Nagasaki, and World War II was over.

16 Herbert Feis, *Between War and Peace: The Potsdam Conference* (Princeton, 1960), 172–9; Gar Alperovitz, *Atomic Diplomacy: Hiroshima and Potsdam,* expanded and updated edition (New York, 1985), 198–204; for a superb historiographic essay, see J. Samuel Walker, "The Decision to Use the Bomb: An Historiographical Update," *Diplomatic History* 14 (1990): 97–114.
17 Larson, *Origins of Containment,* 132–6, 178, 197.

2. Origins of the Cold War

The end of the killing brought enormous relief to peoples all over the world – and a new set of problems. For the Germans and the Japanese, the years ahead promised to be grim, their well-being, their very survival, dependent on the whims of the victors, including those who not long before had suffered, sometimes terribly, at the hands of German and Japanese troops. For most of the allies, a daunting task of reconstruction awaited. The Soviet Union had lost at least twenty million, perhaps as many as forty million of its citizens before the Nazi onslaught. France, Belgium, the Netherlands, Denmark, Norway, and Great Britain had to rebuild severely damaged industrial infrastructures and recover the means to feed and clothe their people. In China, civil war loomed and the task of regaining even the marginal living standards of the prewar era was gravely threatened. And in the colonial world, millions stood poised to end the age of imperialism, violently if necessary.

By comparison, conditions in the United States were glorious. Relatively few Americans had died in the fighting. Only an occasional shell from a submarine or hostile balloon reached the shores of the continental United States. American industry was intact, prosperous on war contracts. American agriculture was ready to feed the world's starving masses. Across the country, the call was to "bring the boys home" and return to what an earlier president, Warren Harding, had called "normalcy."

But nothing is ever so simple. Much as the United States might have been the envy of the rest of the world, it was a nation riddled with grave problems that would have to be faced when the euphoria of victory passed. In the early 1930s, Americans, too, had endured the misery of the Great Depression. Millions of able-bodied men, skilled as well as unskilled workers, had been unemployed. Millions of Americans had lost their homes, watched their children go hungry. Yes, Franklin Roosevelt's New Deal welfare programs, resisted bitterly by most wealthy Americans, had alleviated the suffering, but it was the war that revitalized the economy and brought full employment. Now the war was over and the millions of men and women who had fought for their country would come back — and be looking for work. Would they be forced to the streets to sell apples, as had the veterans of World War I? What would happen to the factories that produced tanks, ships, planes, munitions? What would they produce now? Who would work in them? Who would buy their products? And what would happen to the millions of black Americans who had been drawn to the factories of northern cities during the war — and whose presence had created explosive racial tensions in the midst of the war? And to "Rosie the Riveter" and other women who had taken jobs traditionally held by men? In short, the richest and most powerful nation in the world would be forced to confront profound structural problems in its economy and economic and social issues likely to prove deeply divisive. With Roosevelt gone, in what direction would Harry Truman lead the country? Could Harry Truman lead the country?

To most Americans, in and out of Washington, the creation of a sound peacetime economy was the highest priority. With Hitler gone, the attack on Pearl Harbor avenged, external affairs were of marginal importance to them. The professional diplomats and military officers, and others in and out of the bureaucracy who earned their living worrying about the rest of the world, could not ignore the public and congressional clamor to bring the troops back, to release millions of young men from military service, and to leave the world's problems to the United Nations.

Those responsible for American foreign policy scoured the horizon, calculating its overseas interests and requirements, ever vigilant against potential threats. Most immediate was the need for troops to occupy Germany and Japan and funds to maintain them and the civilian-military administrations that would oversee the pacification and rectification of the people of those countries. Contingency plans for the next war had to be developed and steps taken while American power was supreme to secure the bases and other assets that would make America invincible. Funds had to be obtained to preserve the massive military power the United States had created in the course of the war, power that could now be used to deter would-be aggressors in the future. Civilians involved in implementing the Bretton Woods agreements and working toward the international trade organization and other instruments of the new liberal international economic order could see that reconstruction aid was not going to be sufficient. But at war's end, requests for money for the military or for erstwhile allies – let alone those nations that had started the war – were not welcome. If there was ever a time to put America first, this was it. The message from the people was clear enough and, in a democratic society, government ignores the people at its peril. In 1945, the foreign affairs specialists, the nascent national security bureaucracy, had to step aside.

The boys came home from war in one of the most extraordinary demobilizations the world had ever seen. Discharge from the military was granted democratically, on an individual basis, depending on time in service, wounds, and medals – rather than unit by unit. A ship might be left without a navigator, a tank crew without a gunner – the combat efficiency of units decimated by the loss of key personnel. What was left was far less than the sum of its parts. A mighty military force became a shambles. But who needed it?

When the men came back, the women returned to the home, and many black workers were shunted aside. This time veterans would be cared for, given priority for jobs, for homes. The GI bill enabled millions of them to learn new skills, to obtain educations they might never have been able to afford; it enabled them to buy houses for themselves and the girls who had waited for them – and together they produced the "baby boom" that shaped American demography for the rest of the century. Issues of race and gender seemed peripheral in the closing months of 1945 – at least to the society's dominant white males.

The struggle over the parameters of the welfare state, over how America's wealth would be distributed, reemerged at war's end. Labor unions, their activities protected by the Roosevelt administration in the 1930s, generally accepted his demand for restraint during the war. Some, like the CIO, were more eager to take on corporate America than ever. All were determined to improve the lot of workers, to obtain a fair share of the profits. The country was hit hard by strikes in the last months of 1945 and labor tensions continued to run high. Many employers, eager to exploit a presumed surplus of workers, were determined to reverse some of Roosevelt's prolabor reforms, to break the new power of the unions. Political analysts wondered whether Truman could hold the New Deal coalition together, whether the United States could escape intensification of class conflict.

Much of the outcome of the economic and social tensions in American society would be determined by how the economy performed as it shifted from war to peace industry. The auspices were splendid. With little available for them to purchase during the war, American consumers were eager to spend their savings. It was quickly evident that for the immediate future, before European and Japanese industry was rebuilt, there would be no shortage of overseas markets for American goods, few nations that could compete with the United States for the control of needed raw materials. As in the 1920s, the domestic market flourished and American exports flooded out of the country. Trade and currency agreements engineered by Hull and Morgenthau facilitated the efforts of American businessmen to seize the unusual opportunities of the first months after the war. Increased production and increased profits allowed for more jobs at increased wages, without class warfare. The pattern could not last forever: Sooner or later, without anything to sell to the United States, foreign buyers would run out of dollars with which to buy American goods. If and when that problem was solved, the industries of prewar competitors would eventually be restored and the struggle for markets, even the domestic American market, would resume. But in 1945, that all seemed very far away.

The handful of Americans still focusing attention on world affairs would have noted a number of trouble spots in the Soviet-American relationship during the months immediately following the war. The Soviets, like the British, needed reconstruction funds and wanted low-interest loans from the United States – which neither Congress nor the public were eager to provide. There were disagreements about the amount and disposition of German reparations. America's allies, especially the Soviets, were displeased with the imperious manner in which the United States monopolized the administration of the occupation of Japan. American journalists and diplomats reported comparably arbitrary behavior by Soviet authorities in Eastern Europe. In Poland, in particular, Soviet actions were brutal. In New York, where diplomats and technical specialists of the Preparatory Commission worked to create the operative arms of the United Nations, Soviet and American negotiators found each other difficult, sometimes unpleasant, especially those assigned to develop the UN's military peacekeeping apparatus and those working for international control of atomic energy. [1]

Soviet suspicions angered Americans. American arrogance, bordering on contempt, infuriated the Soviets. Americans could not understand why the Soviets did not accept the benign preeminence of the United States. The Soviets could not understand why the Americans refused to treat them as equals. Cultural differences aggravated the mutual irritation. The loss of the common enemy left both sides free to remember past differences, allowed the luxury of recalling earlier, ideologically tainted perceptions. A deep undercurrent of anticommunism in the United States survived wartime cooperation, as did Soviet apprehension about British and American intentions. Certainly the Soviets could never feel secure so long as the United States retained its monopoly of nuclear weapons. In the absence of a common enemy, of shared values, peacetime cooperation would not be easy. With perhaps declining enthusiasm, Soviet and American diplomatists kept at it.

Across the Pacific, there were other problems tugging at American leaders. For a brief moment, it looked as if the situation in China might get out of hand. American forces had been providing transportation to facilitate the movement of Chiang Kai-shek's government troops into regions threatened by the Chinese Communists. U.S. Marines denied the Communists access to urban areas liberated from the Japanese, holding the cities until Chiang's forces could

---

1 Thomas G. Paterson, "The Abortive Loan to Russia and the Origins of the Cold War, 1943–1946," *Journal of American History* 56 (1969): 70–92; interview with Dean Rusk, April 1977; Warren I. Cohen, *Dean Rusk* (Totowa, N.J., 1980), 9–14.

reach them — while Washington rejected charges it was interfering in China's internal affairs.

In November 1945, Patrick J. Hurley, American ambassador to China, resigned in frustration over his inability to mediate successfully between Chiang's government and the rebellious Communist forces of Mao Zedong. Hurley publicly spread blame for his failure among imperialists, Communists, and foreign service officers. For domestic political reasons, Truman's aides deemed it essential that the president respond. The nature of the response was shaped by their interest in determining the Soviet role in China. There had been ambiguous indications of Soviet assistance to Chinese Communist forces in Manchuria and there was some fear that the Soviet presence in Manchuria might extend beyond the spheres agreed to at Yalta, to which Chiang had acceded in exchange for Soviet professions of support in the Sino-Japanese Treaty of August 1945. On the other hand, the looting of Manchuria by Soviet forces suggested they were on their way home. Truman decided to send America's most prestigious military man, General George C. Marshall, architect of victory in the war against Germany and Japan, to China to try to avert civil war there and, more important, to determine Soviet intentions.[2]

When Stalin learned of Marshall's assignment, he expressed pleasure. Soviet interests in China had been served by the Yalta agreements and the treaty with China. Stalin and Chiang had worked together before and understood although they did not trust each other. Stalin urged caution on the Chinese Communists. Their presence in China gave him valuable leverage in dealing with Chiang. A civil war, which they were not likely to win, could complicate relations with the United States. There was no point to tension between the Soviet Union and the United States in a peripheral area, vital to the interests of neither. Moreover, Mao could be difficult, unresponsive to control from Moscow. From Stalin's perspective, a divided China, with the Chinese Communists dependent on Mos-

2 Herbert Feis, *The China Tangle* (Princeton, 1953), 406–24; Russell D. Buhite, *Patrick J. Hurley and American Foreign Policy* (Ithaca, 1973), 253–78; Steven I. Levine, "A New Look at American Mediation in the Chinese Civil War: The Marshall Mission and Manchuria," *Diplomatic History* 3 (1979): 349–75.

cow, was most desirable. A Communist China, led by an assertive Mao, might not be an asset. Stalin was probably sincere in hoping Marshall would succeed in averting civil war, thus keeping China from becoming an issue in Soviet-American relations. He demonstrated his goodwill by adjusting the scheduled withdrawal of his forces from Manchuria at Chiang's request to assist Chiang's effort to move his forces there before Communist-led troops could seize control.

There was no question but that the United States and the Soviet Union had emerged from the war as the world's two dominant powers. Sometimes unilaterally, sometimes together, they groped toward some means of creating order and providing for their security and that of their friends in an anarchic world. Peoples over whom neither had much if any control struggled in pursuit of their own interests all over the globe. In Washington and in Moscow, men with little comprehension of other people's cultures and history tried to make decisions for the world. The Soviet experience provided that nation with no basis for trust in the outside forces that had tried to isolate and destroy the regime throughout its history. American repugnance toward the terror Stalin had inflicted on his own people, toward the totalitarian dictatorship he had consolidated at home and now extended into Eastern Europe, hampered cooperation after Hitler's defeat. What was extraordinary was the effort of each side, however warily, to ease the apprehensions of the other, to overcome the legacy of mistrust, to combine forces to keep the Germans and the Japanese down, and to create a peace that would endure. And they kept at it to the end of 1945 and on into 1946, with Stalin recognizing the absurdity of a gratuitous affront to the overwhelming power of the United States and Truman still persuaded he and Stalin could resolve any differences that emerged. A poll taken in December 1945 showed that an overwhelming majority of Americans were pleased with Truman's handling of foreign relations.[3]

3 Hadley Cantril and Mildred Strunk, eds., *Public Opinion, 1935–1946* (Princeton, 1951), 889–901.

In 1945, Soviet leaders seemed more suspicious, more apprehensive of the United States than American leaders were of the Soviet Union. In 1946, however, attitudes in Washington shifted significantly. Soviet actions throughout 1946 forced Truman and his advisers to reevaluate Soviet intentions, to reconsider their assumptions about the possibility of Soviet-American cooperation. Some of these Soviet actions and the American perceptions of them were classic demonstrations of what political scientists call the "security dilemma," where an increase in one state's security will automatically and inadvertently decrease that of another. On the basis of their historic experience of Western hostility and confronted by superior American power, the benign use of which could not be assured, Soviet leaders took a series of actions designed to enhance their national security. But each step they took to add to their security was viewed by American leaders as detracting from the security of the United States. Eventually, the United States responded with policies to enhance its security – which the Soviets saw imperiling their own. Each nation defined its own policies as defensive but saw the other's as threatening.[4]

A number of American officials had begun thinking of the Soviet Union as the next enemy well before the end of the war. A poll in December 1945 indicated that although hardly more than a third of Americans expected another major war in the next quarter of a century, those that did were most likely to name the Soviet Union as the nation that would start it.[5] In February 1946, Stalin, speaking in the context of elections to the Supreme Soviet, stressed the need for ideological purity, a new five-year plan, and new sacrifices in a world in which communism struggled for survival while the contradictions among capitalists threatened the peace. Those Americans who feared the Soviet Union and the ideology for which it stood deemed Stalin's speech hostile, a declaration of war.

Most Americans, however, and their president, were still not ready to surrender hope of Soviet-American cooperation. In March,

4 See Melvyn P. Leffler, *A Preponderance of Power: National Security, the Truman Administration, and the Cold War* (Stanford, 1992), for a similar and more detailed presentation of the "security dilemma" argument in this context.
5 Cantril and Strunk, *Public Opinion*, 783–4.

Churchill, now out of office, visited the United States and, in Fulton, Missouri, with Truman at his side, denounced the "Iron Curtain" he alleged the Soviets had drawn across Europe, separating the areas they controlled from the rest of the continent. His clarion call, warning America against the Soviet threat, resonated with those already of his persuasion but attracted few converts. Cynics suspected a connection between the dangers he evoked and the British loan bill, which was endangered in Congress. Many journalists and some congressmen feared Churchill was stirring fears in the United States designed to stimulate Americans to save the British Empire yet again. Cautiously, Truman disassociated himself from the speech. Although there was growing unhappiness with Truman's management of foreign affairs and increasing irritation with Soviet behavior, as late as September 1946 only 8 percent of Americans polled were willing to give up on accommodation with Moscow and 74 percent thought both countries were responsible for the misunderstandings that seemed to have developed between the United States and the Soviet Union.[6]

The serious differences developing between Moscow and Washington were inescapable. American behavior in Germany troubled, perhaps even frightened, the Soviets. In January 1946, Christian Democrats, unfriendly to the Soviet Union, unhappy with Soviet compensation of Polish losses with German territory, won elections in the American zone of Germany — and subsequently in the British and French zones. A few months later, the American proconsul in Germany, Lucius Clay, decided to withhold further reparations from the American zone. In July, the Americans began a program of amnesty for ex-Nazis. Soviet informants had long been aware that American agents were protecting Nazi civilians and military personnel who were considered to be scientific or intelligence assets. In September, James Byrnes, the American secretary of state, announced in Stuttgart a new, more lenient American policy toward Germany, which suggested that Washington was more concerned about the well-being of its erstwhile German enemies than about

6 Deborah Welch Larson, *Origins of Containment* (Princeton, 1985), 263–7, 288; Cantril and Strunk, *Public Opinion,* 964.

Soviet needs. Finally, in December, the Americans and their British friends merged their occupation zones, with offers to the French and Soviets to join them. In due course the French did. The Soviets could hardly be expected to surrender that fragment of Germany they could still exploit, any more than they could consider as serious Byrnes's April offer to demilitarize Germany. Twice in Stalin's lifetime the Germans had wrought enormous suffering on Mother Russia. Preventing a resurgence of German power was the highest priority of Soviet policy. American moves to rebuild Germany, to exonerate fascists, to encourage German revanchism were not to be taken lightly.

Truman and his advisers seemed oblivious to Soviet concerns and worried instead about Stalin's intentions in the Middle East – in Iran, Turkey, and Greece. In none of these countries could American leaders conceive of a threat to Soviet security, of any justifiable reason for Soviet behavior. The United States, Great Britain, and the Soviet Union had joined in a preemptive occupation of Iran, to deny its oil to the Germans and to preserve a route for lend-lease aid from the Americans to their Soviet allies. They had agreed to withdraw their forces after the war. The Americans and the British had withdrawn. The Soviets had stayed and were clearly scheming to separate an oil-rich province from the rest of Iran and to join it and its residents to their ethnic compatriots in the Soviet Socialist Republic of Azerbaijan. When the Security Council of the United Nations met in its inaugural session in January 1946, the United States denounced the continued Soviet presence in Iran. When Soviet tanks menaced Tehran in March, the United States sent a sharp warning – and the Soviets pulled back.

At war's end Moscow began to press Turkey for minor territorial adjustments and for a share in the control of the Dardanelles, the Soviets' only access to the Mediterranean. Truman, initially sympathetic to a Soviet role in the administration of the straits, reversed course as disagreeable Soviet behavior elsewhere raised doubts in his mind about Soviet intentions. When Soviet pressure came to a head in August 1946, Truman ordered the U.S.S. *Franklin D. Roosevelt,* the world's mightiest warship, to the eastern Mediterranean to strengthen Turkish resolve. Again Stalin backed off.

In Greece, a country Stalin had conceded to Britain's sphere of interest, a nasty civil war was under way between a corrupt, repressive regime, members of which had collaborated with the Germans, and Communist-led guerrillas, many of whom had been active in the resistance. The British were supporting the Greek government. Communist regimes in Yugoslavia, Bulgaria, and Albania were aiding the rebels. There was scant evidence of Soviet involvement, but Soviet press attacks on the British left no doubt where Stalin's sympathies lay. His influence with, if not control of, the Balkan Communists was assumed.

No American leader accepted the idea of a major role in the Middle East for the Soviet Union. The region was considered a British sphere. If the British faltered, historic Russian ambitions there would have to be thwarted by someone else. To a Soviet sphere of interest in Eastern Europe, to Soviet dominance in Eastern Europe, Roosevelt, Truman, and most of their principal advisers were prepared to accede, but not in Iran, or Greece, or Turkey, not in the Middle East. Even as they contemplated projecting American power more than five thousand miles from their shores, substituting it for declining British power in the proximity of Soviet borders, they perceived Soviet behavior in the area as threatening, American actions as defensive.

The matter of international control of atomic energy, of nuclear weapons, also served to undermine the ability of the two nations to cooperate. Truman and his aides knew that the Soviet Union would eventually develop nuclear power. Some thought it wisest to share the secret of the bomb as a demonstration of goodwill, to win Soviet confidence in American intentions. Others, less inclined to the grand gesture, nonetheless thought international control of weapons, international oversight of the uses of nuclear power, was feasible and could be managed without risk to the security of the United States. A number of proposals surfaced within the administration, most notably one with the imprimatur of Dean Acheson of the U.S. Department of State and David Lilienthal, chairman of the Tennessee Valley Authority, who worked with a group of scientific consultants, led by J. Robert Oppenheimer, who had directed the effort to build the bomb. The Acheson-Lilienthal report provided for the destruction of existing nuclear weapons once UN control had been established. UN control, and the inspection that entailed, would preclude research on weapon development, conceivably leaving the United States as the only nation with that capability. Before the United Nations had an opportunity to consider the plan, it was modified by presidential adviser Bernard Baruch to include sanctions *not subject to the veto,* leaving the security of the Soviet Union at the mercy of a United Nations easily dominated by the United States and its friends. Not surprisingly, the Soviets rejected the "Baruch Plan" when it was introduced in June 1946.

George Kennan, the foreign service officer who emerged as the leading American specialist on the Soviet Union, found his government depressingly slow to understand Soviet objectives and the need to be firm in resisting Stalin. In February 1946, from Moscow, he sent a long reflective cable, which made the rounds of Washington. He described the Soviet leaders as driven by the needs of the political system they had created and their own insecurities to expand their influence and power as far as other nations would permit. He warned that Stalin and his associates would interpret generosity and bluster as weakness and responded only to firmness, to clear signs that their actions would not be tolerated. The United States had to draw the line, stand firmly and patiently behind it, and wait until the Soviet system collapsed of its own weight and its inability to expand. His "long telegram" was welcomed by a number of American leaders who were in the process of formulating similar analyses of Soviet behavior and the appropriate American response. In March they persuaded Truman to obtain a one-year extension of the draft, to delay completion of the demobilization of American armed forces.[7]

Secretary of State Byrnes resisted the Kennan-Harriman analysis, but his confidence in his own negotiating skills wore thin before the year was over. In the spring the Soviets rejected American terms for

---

7 See Kennan's "long telegram" and comparable cables sent by the British and Soviet ambassadors to the United States to their respective governments at approximately the same time in Kenneth M. Jensen, ed., *Origins of the Cold War: The Novikov, Kennan, and Roberts 'Long Telegrams' of 1946* (Washington, D.C., 1991), and a symposium focused on the Novikov cable in *Diplomatic History* 15 (1991): 523–63.

a loan they were not likely to get and dismissed the opportunity to join the International Monetary Fund (IMF) or the World Bank. In August, the Soviet diplomat Andrei Vishinsky denounced American "dollar diplomacy" and Byrnes was enraged to observe Czech diplomats applauding. It was time for adjustments in American foreign economic policy. Perhaps a liberal international economic order was less important than rewarding friends and punishing antagonists. In April the Soviets rejected his proposals regarding Germany; in September Byrnes announced what he would do with or without them. Similarly, Acheson, who had not allowed his contempt for communism to cloud his vision, who had persistently been able to understand how the Soviets might view things from their presumably warped perspective, who had been willing always to concede Soviet security requirements, concluded that Soviet demands in the Middle East were unreasonable – and they would have to be resisted.[8]

The last major American figure to hold out hope of continued cooperation with the Soviets was Henry Wallace, onetime vice-president, serving as Truman's secretary of commerce. In September, with Truman's acquiescence, casually granted, Wallace publicly criticized the direction in which he believed American policy to be drifting and insisted the United States was needlessly alienating the Soviets. Before the month was out, Truman felt constrained to fire Wallace, lest the Soviets – and the American people – receive the wrong message. And a few weeks later, Marshal Georgii Zhukov, the great Soviet war hero, viewed in some quarters as friendly to the United States, was replaced as commander in chief of Soviet armed forces.

Few of the year's events augured well for the Soviet-American relationship, but Truman had other problems, which seemed hardly less pressing. He did not need and did not want an adversarial relationship with the Soviets. Mostly, he wanted them to behave civilly, carry out their obligations, defer to American plans for a peaceful and prosperous world, and leave him alone to cope with labor unrest, inflation, and the threatened resurgence of the Republican par-

8 Robert L. Messer, *The End of an Alliance* (Chapel Hill, 1982), 181–94; Larson, *Origins of Containment*, 256–7, 283–8.

ty – for all of which he was being held responsible by various sectors of American society. And the election results of November 1946, sweeping the Republicans back into control of Congress for the first time since 1930, suggested he was losing control of that small part of the world that had been his. It promised to be a lousy Christmas.

The Republicans returned to Washington determined to savage Roosevelt's legacy and Truman's efforts to maintain New Deal programs. Some of them were determined to carry out a rectification campaign, to purge the society, beginning with the federal government, of ideas about government responsibility for the welfare of the people, those "cryptocommunist" ideas of the New Dealers. They would stop the use of tax policy for social purposes, for the redistribution of wealth. They would end the government's protection of labor unions and the radicals who threatened the free-enterprise system. They would prevent the government from wasting American money subsidizing the British Empire. Hating "creeping socialism" at home, they would force Truman to stand up to Soviet Communists, to reverse Roosevelt's "treason" at Yalta. If Truman had any leadership ability, the Eightieth Congress would give him a chance to demonstrate it.

When they could obtain the president's attention, his foreign affairs advisers hammered home two grave and immediate concerns: first, the unexpected difficulty Western Europe was having with postwar recovery, the enormous suffering that had resulted, and the threat to civil society that now existed there; second, the collapse of European power, especially British power, around the world, and the importance of the United States acting promptly and convincingly to fill the vacuum. The 1946 loan to the British had proved inadequate, in part because of inflated U.S. prices for the goods they needed. The British were rationing bread at home, giving up India and Burma, unable to maintain their support to the government of Greece, reeling under the attacks of Zionist terrorists in Palestine.[9]

9 Joyce Kolko and Gabriel Kolko, *The Limits of Power* (New York, 1972), 365–7; Anton W. dePorte, *Europe Between the Superpowers* 2d ed. (New Haven, 1986), 131–2; Walter Isaacson and Evan Thomas, *The Wise Men* (New York, 1986), 386–9; Leffler, *Preponderance of Power,* 188–92.

In France, Charles de Gaulle, the imperious leader of the Free
French during the war, had resigned as president in the face of
strong opposition from both Communists and Socialists in January
1946. In the November elections, the Communists won a plurality
of seats in the French parliament. As the Republican-led conserva
tive coalition seized power on Capitol Hill in Washington in January
1947, the Communists seemed on the verge of winning control of
the government in France. In Italy, too, a weak government was
perceived in Washington as threatened by a strong Communist minority. Perhaps worst of all was the uncertainty about the direction
in which the Germans would move, whether they might ultimately
choose to align themselves with the Soviet Union.

None of Truman's advisers imagined a Soviet attack on the United
States *or* Western Europe. Kennan, despite rhetorical flourishes that
obscured his intent, was arguing for the existence of a political
threat. Most of the others were contemptuous of existing Soviet
power, secure in America's nuclear monopoly. But all of them recognized the importance of Western Europe to the United States. Western Europe was the heart of the civilization with which Americans
identified. Its participation was critical to the liberal economic order
Americans believed essential to the world's peace and prosperity.
American leaders considered friendly control of Western Europe
vital to the security of the United States. Any student of geopolitics
knew that control of the Eurasian landmass by one state would give
that state the power to dominate the world. Conceivably, the Soviet
Union could achieve that control – not with the bayonets of the Red
Army but by the collapse of existing Western European societies
unable to recover from war damage unaided, and subverted by the
activities of local Communists. The danger was not "clear and present," as Justice Oliver Wendell Holmes would have demanded, but
no country with a choice could risk inaction.[10]

If one assumed Truman understood the danger and was willing to
act, the scale of aid required by the Europeans was enormous, the
range of activities required of the United States beyond anything it
had ever attempted in peacetime. And the cost would be astronomi-
cal. How could a Congress, hostile to the administration, commit-

10 Leffler, *Preponderance of Power,* 162–3.

ted to cutting its budget, be persuaded to appropriate great sums of money to reconstruct the economies of America's competitors in order to oppose an imperceptible threat? How could a people who had been promised that the United Nations would spare them further concern with world affairs be persuaded to make the sacrifices necessary for the United States to exercise leadership in once remote corners of the globe?

An otherwise Herculean task was brought to manageable proportions as a result of an exceptionally wise appointment by Truman. In January 1947, George Marshall, denied the opportunity to retire after a frustrating year in China, replaced Byrnes as secretary of state. Marshall brought Kennan back from Moscow to head a newly created policy planning staff. He had Acheson in the first months and then Robert Lovett as undersecretary. It was, arguably, the strongest leadership the department had ever had and it used its resources well. Quickly, it fashioned a coherent set of policies, persuaded first the president, then the Congress, and finally the public to support those policies. As implemented, the policies developed by the Truman administration from 1947 to 1949 were hardly without flaws, but they constituted a sound, measured, manageable set of steps toward preserving the interests of the United States and those who shared its economic and political values. They provided the foundation for an extraordinary level of material prosperity for all who accepted American hegemony for the next two decades. These policies were unquestionably designed first and foremost to serve American interests, but they were designed by men and women who understood that those interests would not be well served by efforts to maximize economic or political advantage. Initially, it was America's friends abroad who were the greatest beneficiaries.[11]

Almost immediately, Marshall, Acheson, and Kennan accepted the notion that the United States had to assume Britain's historic role of

---

11 Isaacson and Thomas, *Wise Men*, 386–418; Charles S. Maier, "Politics of Productivity: Foundations of American International Economic Policy," in Peter Katzenstein, ed., *Between Power and Plenty* (Madison, 1978), 23–49; Robert O. Keohane and Joseph S. Nye, *Power and Interdependence* (Boston, 1977), 135–6; Michael J. Hogan, *The Marshall Plan* (Cambridge, 1990), 443.

containing the expansion of Russian power and influence in the eastern Mediterranean. Kennan had been eager to contain the Soviets everywhere in Europe and Acheson had been particularly troubled by Soviet pressures on Turkey. A crisis in Greece, which the British had lost the will and lacked the resources to manage, provided the opportunity to apply and explain what came to be known as the "containment" policy. The techniques devised to win support for the policy were successful, but created unexpected and ultimately uncontrollable problems.

Marshall, Acheson, and Kennan knew that the Greek government they intended to support was unworthy: corrupt, repressive, inept. They knew also that there was little indication of direct Soviet involvement in the Greek civil war, although they assumed the Soviets would benefit from and Stalin would be pleased by a Communist victory in Greece. Their ultimate concern was not Greece, but rather the assertion of American power in the Middle East. The region was of enormous strategic importance in the event of war with the Soviet Union and its oil reserves could not be allowed to fall into unfriendly hands. They intended to signal the succession of the United States to Britain's role as the dominant power in the area.[12]

Stalin found himself in an awkward situation. He had been willing to concede Greece to the West, as he had indicated to Churchill. Turkey and Iran interested him more, as evidenced by direct Soviet pressures on those countries. He did not want to provoke a confrontation with the United States over Greece. But Tito, the Yugoslav Communist leader, was eagerly supporting the Greek Communists. Stalin suggested restraint, but the Yugoslav dictator was not dependent on Soviet bayonets to maintain his power. He had seized control of Yugoslavia in the course of leading the resistance against the Germans. He would determine his country's goals and policies with minimal deference to Moscow. Stalin was caught between his fear of provoking the United States and his unwillingness to alienate an

12 Joseph M. Jones, *The Fifteen Weeks* (New York, 1955), 73; Kolko and Kolko, *Limits of Power*, 232–42; Larson, *Origins of Containment*, 302–23; Leffler, *Preponderance of Power*, 237–46, 286–91.

independent ally. Not until the Americans acted was Tito persuaded to lessen his role in Greece. [13]

In February 1947, when the British officially informed the United States that they could no longer support the Greek government, Marshall's team was ready, as was Truman. Congressional leaders were called to the White House where Marshall explained the situation in Greece and Turkey, the inability of the British to play their historic role, and asked for appropriation of the funds necessary for the United States to take over. The administration's worst fears were immediately realized. The leaders of the Eightieth Congress were unwilling to spend taxpayers' dollars to feed hungry Greeks or to solve Great Britain's problems. A more generous, Democratic party—controlled Congress had barely agreed to the British loan of 1946. This Congress had already rejected requests for increases in foreign aid and defense spending. It was not interested in rescuing British interests at American expense.

Acheson, however, knew which chords to sound. These congressmen were outspoken opponents of Soviet expansion, of communism. He warned them that the Soviets were on the march; they were engaged in a bold maneuver to gain access to three continents. If Greece fell into their hands, Turkey and Iran, Asia Minor, would follow. Nothing would stand in the way of the Russians moving on into Africa through Egypt, penetrating Europe through Italy and France. The stakes were high, the danger was imminent, and, with the collapse of British power, only the United States could stop the Soviets. Senator Arthur Vandenberg (R.-Mich.), who spoke for his party on foreign policy matters, assured Truman that if he addressed Congress as Acheson had, the Congress would respond favorably.

Truman's message to Congress, in March 1947, requesting $400 million in aid for Greece and Turkey, included the statements that became known as the Truman Doctrine:

> We shall not achieve our objectives [of freedom and independence for all members of the United Nations] unless we are willing to help free peoples

13 Milovan Djilas, *Conversations with Stalin* (New York, 1962), 81–2; William O. McCagg, Jr., *Stalin Embattled, 1943–1948* (Detroit, 1978), 242, 297, 300; William Taubman, *Stalin's American Policy* (New York, 1982), 150–1.

to maintain their free institutions and their national integrity against aggressive movements that seek to impose upon them totalitarian regimes. . . . I believe that it must be the policy of the United States to support free peoples who are resisting attempted subjugation by armed minorities or by outside pressures.

Grudgingly, Congress appropriated the funds.

At the time and for many years afterward, critics questioned the wisdom of describing the Soviet threat in such apocalyptic terms. As the historian Melvyn Leffler subsequently argued, Soviet actions "hardly justified the inflammatory rhetoric Acheson and Truman used."[14] Clearly, American leaders did not consider a Soviet attack anywhere to be imminent. American forces were not being readied for war. On the other hand, Marshall, Acheson, and Kennan were convinced that the Soviet Union was expansionist, that it would extend its influence beyond its security needs into any unguarded area in the world, and that both the Middle East (via Greece) and Western Europe were in imminent danger of being subverted by indigenous Communist forces. Only the United States had the power to stop them: Did it also have the will?

The overblown rhetoric Kennan used in his dispatches and his famous "X" article in *Foreign Affairs* (July 1947) was designed to gain attention, to shock readers into recognition of the existence of a serious problem. Acheson and others of Truman's aides shared a similar belief in the need to shock Congress and the American public into recognition of an external threat worthy of their attention and their money. In the American political system, presidential mastery over Congress is often limited, especially when it is controlled by the opposition. Congressmen have their own agendas and are generally more responsive, certainly in peacetime, to the demands of domestic special interest groups than to the foreign affairs concerns of the executive. In wartime it is relatively easy to focus congressional attention on foreign policy, relatively easy for the executive to get what it wants. The tactics applied by the Truman administration in

14 Melvyn P. Leffler, "The American Conception of National Security and the Beginnings of the Cold War, 1945–1948," *American Historical Review* 89 (1984): 368.

1947 were designed to create an atmosphere, in Washington at
least, in the country as a whole if necessary, that would enable the
executive to dominate the legislative agenda much as it would in
time of war. If misleading Congress and the people about the nature
and immediacy of the Soviet threat to American interests was necessary to gain congressional and public support, it seemed a small
price to pay. Conceivably, there was no alternative means of obtaining funds from the Eightieth Congress.[15]

Kennan quickly perceived that the approach taken with the Truman Doctrine posed serious problems. So did Walter Lippmann.
Although Truman's words were designed primarily for domestic
consumption, they could be read by everyone in Moscow. The
words, the contemplated military aid mission to Turkey, could be
viewed by Stalin as provocation, as a threat to the Soviet Union.
Moreover, Truman's words implied the United States was prepared
to aid any country anywhere in the world that was threatened by
Communist subversion, without calculation of American interests in
the area. He had implied a universal crusade, which the United
States could not afford and which, in any event, made little sense.
Acheson had little patience with such subtleties. His was an exercise
in politics, designed for minds more responsive to blunt instruments.

Kennan and Lippmann proved to be right in ways Acheson had
not anticipated. What about China, asked Congressman Walter
Judd (R.-Minn.) and other friends of Chiang Kai-shek? China, all of
George Marshall's efforts notwithstanding, had embarked upon a
civil war in which Communist forces linked to the Soviet Union
threatened to overthrow Chiang's regime. Certainly China was at
least as worthy of being rescued as Greece. Weakly, Acheson insisted

15 Kolko and Kolko, *Limits of Power*, 329–58, 374–6. See Dean Acheson, *Present
    at the Creation* (New York, 1970), 489, for his explanation of the need (in the
    context of NSC 68) to mislead the American people: "If we made our points
    clearer than truth, we did not differ from most other educators." See also
    Stephen O. Krasner, "United States Commercial and Monetary Policy: Unrav-
    elling the Paradox of External Strength and Internal Weakness," in Katzen-
    stein, *Between Power and Plenty*, 51–87, for a persuasive argument on the weak-
    ness of the American political system.

that the Truman Doctrine did not apply everywhere, that each situation would be judged on its merits, and that China was different. Yet more insidious was the question of why the Truman administration was so eager to stop communism abroad when it was doing so little to check its advance at home. Unwittingly, Acheson and his colleagues had armed those elements in the society determined to roll back the New Deal, to equate democracy with capitalism, the welfare state with communism, as well as Chiang's supporters. But for the moment he was successful. The funds had been appropriated, Greece and Turkey would be "saved."

The more critical problem was Western Europe. The economic situation in Britain, France, Italy, and Germany was desperate. Productivity had barely reached prewar levels, dollars to purchase essential goods from the United States were in short supply, inflation was dangerously high, internal distribution systems had collapsed, and there was mounting unrest. Accounts of terrible suffering filled the press and cables to the Department of State. These reports evoked humanitarian concerns in Washington, but the decision to act was driven by self-interest, by fear of chaos and subversion. It was essential to keep Western Europe out of Stalin's orbit, partly because of the area's enormous importance to America's trade and defense, but also because it was the repository of the shared values of Western civilization. It was essential to keep Western Europe free for twentieth-century Americans to feel free, to have any sense of security. European leaders, well aware of American anxieties, played upon them, exaggerated the Communist threat in hope of obtaining urgently needed aid. [16]

With help from Lippmann, Acheson, Kennan, and their colleagues devised a brilliant approach for providing economic aid to Europe. The United States would invite European governments to take the lead in developing an integrated plan for the recovery of Europe. American leaders had recognized the importance of the German economy to the economic well-being of Europe and were groping for a politically acceptable way to rebuild Germany. The integration of western Germany into a revitalized European econ-

16 Jones, *The Fifteen Weeks*, 239–54; Hogan, *Marshall Plan*, 445–7.

omy might be less threatening to France and tolerable to Congress and the American people. As the historian Wolfram Hanrieder has argued, American policy was one of "double-containment," serving to contain Germany as well as the Soviet Union.[17] But of greater importance was the central idea of allowing Europeans to design their recovery program rather than imposing one made in Washington.

To be sure, the Americans who worked on what Truman called the "Marshall Plan" developed a clear conception of what they wanted to see emerge. Again, they were intent on creating the liberal international economic order envisaged at Bretton Woods, stressing free trade and currency convertibility, exporting the social ideals of Roosevelt's New Deal program, emphasizing increased production, more for everyone, rather than class conflict and the redistribution of wealth. Postwar chaos had delayed implementation of the Bretton Woods system. The Marshall Plan would provide the funds to realize it. The system would serve the economic needs of the United States. It would be good for Europe. It would be good for the world. The European planners had ideas of their own, some less generous toward the working class, some less responsive to American economic needs, and they shaped the plan to suit themselves. The result was a tribute to farsighted men and women on both sides of the Atlantic.[18]

Although American officials and businessmen primarily worried about the economy were gratified by the promise of the Marshall Plan, the impetus for a European recovery plan was political as well. Truman and Marshall saw the plan as a means of defending American interests in Europe against Soviet encroachment, shoring up Western European economies so that the region would not be susceptible to Moscow-directed subversion. Their advisers, however, argued against presenting the program to the world as anti-Soviet. Indeed, they insisted that the Europeans be free to invite Soviet and Eastern European participation. They assumed no Communist coun-

17 Wolfram F. Hanrieder, *Germany, America, Europe: Forty Years of German Foreign Policy* (New Haven, 1989).
18 Hogan, *Marshall Plan*, 427–45.

try would accept such an invitation and were unnerved when the Soviet Union and the Polish regime chose to attend the first planning meeting in Paris. But the Soviets quickly withdrew, dragging after them the reluctant Poles and Czechs. Stalin was not interested in integrating his economy or that of any country he controlled in an American-dominated economic order. As Kennan anticipated, the Soviets took upon themselves the onus for dividing Europe into those who accepted Marshall Plan aid and those who did not.

Had the Soviet Union chosen to participate one might imagine a new world order in which the Soviet Union and its satellites opened their borders and their books to Marshall Plan auditors, surrendered communism and its command economy for a chance to compete in world markets, and allowed all the tension building between Moscow and Washington to drain away. On the other hand, given the resistance the Truman administration had encountered obtaining $400 million for aid to Greece and Turkey, it is difficult to conceive of the Eightieth Congress appropriating billions of dollars for foreign aid without some sense of the need to head off impending doom. In fact, even after the Soviets withdrew and denounced the plan, Congress appeared recalcitrant. Conservatives like Senator Robert Taft (R.-Ohio), hostile to the New Deal at home, were not eager to subsidize efforts to extend it abroad. Others had never liked the commitment to tariff reduction implicit in this new economic order. Still others, liberals as well as conservatives, were reluctant to send American tax dollars overseas. Liberals could find needy Americans; conservatives preferred to spend the money on defense – or to deny the government the tax revenues. Funding of the Marshall Plan was in doubt until February 1948, when Stalin inadvertently gave the Truman administration a little help.

Throughout the fall of 1947, on into the winter, into 1948, the Communist parties of Western Europe, under orders from Moscow, fought hard to prevent implementation of the Marshall Plan. The local economies were shaken, as were the governments the Communists attempted to bring down with general strikes. There were many indications that Stalin's strategy had changed, and there was less ambiguity in Soviet actions. Moscow created the Cominform, an organization designed to coordinate Communist activities around the world, an attempt to give substance to the myth of a monolithic international Communist movement. Soviet control over Eastern Europe increased. Stalin had not seemed markedly disturbed by earlier evidence of American displeasure. His most interesting reaction to the Truman Doctrine, which some scholars have seen as a declaration of cold war against the Soviet Union, was to assure Marshall only a few days later that all differences could still be compromised. But the Marshall Plan, especially the indications of American intent to rebuild Germany and incorporate it into an anti-Soviet bloc, set off alarms in Moscow. It was another classic illustration of the security dilemma at work. The Americans and their Western European friends were preparing what they perceived as defensive action to preserve their security against a potential threat from the Soviet Union. That action diminished what little sense of security the Soviets enjoyed. The Soviets responded quickly to the threat from the West, tightening their grip on what they had, but every step they took was perceived by the United States as threatening its security and that of its friends. As the United States and the Soviet Union moved along the spectrum from allies to adversaries, each lessened the security of the other by seeking to enhance its own.

On February 25, 1948, the Czech Communists, already dominant, staged a coup, punctuated by the unexplained death of the pro-Western foreign minister, Jan Masaryk, on March 10, assuring the Soviets of complete control over the country. In Washington, American leaders wondered if a major Soviet move was in the offing, if war might be imminent. The recently formed Central Intelligence Agency would only assure the president that war would not come in the next sixty days. The American military deliberately heightened anxieties in an effort to extort an increase in congressional appropriations. At the request of the Pentagon, General Clay reported from Germany that war could come with "dramatic suddenness." Ignoring Marshall's advice to the contrary, on March 17, Truman shrewdly used the war scare to ask Congress to fund the Marshall Plan. In the same message he asked for restoration of the draft, additional funds for defense spending, and for universal military training, stressing the threat posed by Soviet ruthlessness in Czechoslovakia. Congress gave him much of what he wanted. Stalin's "defensive" actions had facilitated passage of the program he dreaded. American economic power would unite the West against him – and this time the West included most of Germany.[19]

Tension increased significantly in June 1948. The Russians were unquestionably troubled by conditions in Germany – unification of the western zones, the end of denazification, and the decisions to rebuild German industrial power, create a strong West German state, and integrate it with Western Europe. Although the Soviets had provoked some of these developments, they had every reason to fear them and to attempt to reverse the process whereby a powerful Germany might rise to threaten them again. Stalin moved cautiously, harassing traffic between the western occupation zones and Berlin, part of which, although in the Soviet zone, was nonetheless under British, French, and American jurisdiction. On June 24, however, the Soviets stopped all traffic to West Berlin. General Clay called for action to force the blockade, for an ultimatum and an armed convoy to call the Soviet bluff. War seemed possible.

In Washington, Truman and his advisers, including the Joint Chiefs of Staff, rejected Clay's recommendation. They did not want to start a war. The military was not ready to fight one. But they could not acquiesce in the Soviet effort to deny them access to Berlin, to cut off the millions of Berliners from the West. Politically, the president could not appear weak. Public opinion polls already indicated that the American people thought his policies toward the Soviet Union "soft," and 1948 was an election year. Equally important was the need to demonstrate American resolve to the Soviets and the people of Western Europe. Eventually, the United States responded with an airlift, carrying food and coal in extraordinary quantities to the people of Berlin. Day after day, week after week, month after month, another huge cargo plane landed every few minutes. The operation was a costly but impressive success. Soviet planes occasionally harried the transport planes, but never threatened. Stalin was no more ready for war than Truman.

In May 1949, the Soviets admitted defeat and the blockade was

19 Daniel Yergin, *Shattered Peace* (Boston, 1978), 343–53; Jean Edward Smith, *Lucius D. Clay* (New York, 1990), 466–8.

lifted. With relative caution, Stalin had tried to prevent the creation of a potentially powerful and threatening German state – the most threatening step the United States had taken since the end of the war. He failed, but the confrontation over Berlin changed the nature of the relationship between the United States and the Soviet Union. American reproaches over Eastern European, especially Polish, affairs, had been irritating, but Stalin had brushed the Americans aside, thrown them an occasional bone, surrendered nothing of substance. Truman's prattle over Greece was also bothersome. Control of Greece would have been welcome, but the Soviet Union had long since conceded Greece to the West. It was Tito, not Stalin, who was engaged there. Unfriendly American gestures regarding Soviet interests in Iran and Turkey rankled more, but in due course, as Soviet power relative to the United States increased, there would be opportunity to bring about more satisfactory results. The rebuilding of Germany, however, the integrating of a German state in an American-led coalition against the Soviet Union, was frightening. The Germans had defeated Russia in World War I. They had wreaked enormous havoc on the Soviet nation, coming within a hair of defeating it in World War II. With the Americans behind them, vengeful Germans could erase all of Stalin's gains since 1945 and once again bring misery to the Soviet people. American actions had to be perceived as hostile and the Soviet Union responded accordingly, using all means short of war to persuade the Americans to back off – and failed. Unable to contest American power, the Soviet Union was forced to accept the division of Germany and of Europe on American terms.

The perception from Washington was quite different. The United States had no hostile intent toward the Soviet Union. It had indicated its willingness to recognize the requirements of Soviet security, to accept a Soviet sphere of influence in Eastern Europe and in northeastern China (Manchuria). It had offered the Soviets a role in the international economic order planned at Bretton Woods. The Soviets had behaved abusively, at times brutally, in Eastern Europe and rejected the Bretton Woods agreements. They had threatened Iran, Turkey, and Greece. Moscow was using Communist parties in Western Europe to disrupt efforts toward reconstruction and recovery. It had destroyed all semblance of independence in once democratic Czechoslovakia. Finally, it had challenged Western rights in Berlin. Truman's advisers suspected the Soviet Union of seeking to dominate the Eurasian landmass. Some thought that Stalin, like Hitler, sought to conquer the world. The Soviet Union threatened America's friends and America's interests abroad. Unless it was stopped, it would soon threaten the security of the United States. Years later, Andrei Kozryev, a senior Soviet diplomat, blamed Stalinism for the tensions that developed between his country and its wartime allies, arguing that there could be no trust in a "dictatorial, anti-popular regime" which "all but inevitably" spread violence beyond its borders. "Our partners [were] frightened by Stalinism [because] it is difficult to have confidence in a society which is mired in all-out suspicion, it is hard to trust a regime that has no faith in its own people."[20]

By the end of 1948, the United States and the Soviet Union were obviously no longer allies or friends. Certainly they were adversaries, but perhaps they were not quite enemies. Lippmann's term, "Cold War," seemed apt. Both nations had ended their processes of demobilization and had begun military preparedness programs, including planning for war against each other. Yet even the Berlin blockade, unsettling as it was, had been handled cautiously by both nations. They left each other room to retreat and they managed the crisis without bloodshed. The division of Germany, which both Moscow and Washington considered essential, had been achieved. There were no remaining issues. The world reflected an uneasy balance, superficially bipolar, in which preponderant American power, including sole possession of nuclear weapons, assured the security of the United States and its friends. The United States might have used its power to roll back Soviet gains; it might have been able to topple the Communist regime in Moscow. Clearly it was unwilling to pay the price and there is little to indicate that Stalin apprehended an American attack. With Europe divided tolerably, without any vital interests in conflict, the two greatest powers might have fo-

20 Quoted in Bruce Russett, *Controlling the Sword: The Democratic Governance of National Security* (Cambridge, Mass., 1990), 144.

cused their energies on their considerable internal problems. They did not.

The successful airlift to Berlin saved Harry Truman's political career. Given an opportunity to demonstrate that he could wield America's might, force a feared adversary to bend to his will, Truman won another chance to lead his people. In one of the great upsets in American electoral history, he defeated the highly favored Republican candidate, Thomas E. Dewey of New York — despite losing votes on the left to Henry Wallace running as a Progressive and to Strom Thurmond on the right, running as a Dixiecrat, drawing away the votes of Southern Democrats who thought Truman too sympathetic to black Americans. A seriously ailing George Marshall was allowed to retire. Dean Acheson was elevated to secretary of state and most of the rest of Truman's team stayed with him.

The next step was the creation of the North Atlantic Treaty Organization, derived from European initiatives early in 1948. The recipients of Marshall Plan aid were delighted by American generosity but feared economic assistance would not be enough to contain what they perceived as a political threat from the Soviet Union and the Cominform. Far across the Atlantic, thousands of miles from the nearest Soviet tank, hardly aware of their infinitesimally tiny, pathetically powerless Communist party, Americans in Washington might feel secure. Europeans did not. In March 1948, Great Britain, France, Belgium, the Netherlands, and Luxembourg joined forces in the Brussels Pact, aimed at protecting themselves from the Soviets and, if necessary, from a resurgent Germany as well. They hoped the United States would join their alliance, knowing full well that American power was essential to their security.

A peacetime military alliance with European states was unprecedented and not very appealing to American leaders (although they had signed a mutual defense pact with Latin American countries in 1947). Obviously, they were displeased by Soviet behavior on the Soviet periphery, irritated by Soviet-style diplomacy, disappointed by the lack of Soviet deference toward the world's greatest power, but through 1947, on into early 1948, they perceived no military threat from the Soviet Union, little likelihood of war in Europe or elsewhere. They saw no problems that economic assistance, American dollars, could not alleviate; nothing that required so radical a step as a peacetime alliance – a step that might outrage many members of the Eightieth Congress.

The coup in Czechoslovakia, followed by fears of a similar coup in Italy and Norwegian complaints of Soviet pressures, carried the day for those Americans who advocated a mutual security arrangement with European friends. Reluctantly, the U.S. military, ever fearful of overcommitment, of having to share supplies and secrets with Europeans, allowed itself to be dragged along. The Berlin blockade provided another needed stimulus, although the U.S. government held out for provisions that would reshape the ultimate organization more to its liking. Washington insisted, for example, on membership for Denmark, Iceland, Italy, Norway, and Portugal, diluting the influence of the original signatories. The politics of the 1948 American election campaign precluded consummation of an agreement before 1949. The treaty establishing NATO was finally signed in Washington in April 1949. At least on paper, Western European leaders had the assurance they desired of American political and military support.[21]

The diminished sense of urgency in Washington in the closing months of 1948 and early 1949, during the NATO negotiations, is striking. The American campaign to block a Communist victory in the April 1948 Italian elections had succeeded. The airlift had succeeded. The Norwegians were less apprehensive. Tito had split with Stalin and survived. If there had been a Soviet offensive, it appeared to have subsided. Moscow was clearly on the defensive. Stalin and his diplomatists were telling everyone who would listen of their urgent desire for peace. Conceivably, NATO would prove to be unnecessary, a response to a danger that had evaporated. Confronted with evidence of American resolve, comfortable with what they had already gained in Eastern and Central Europe, unwilling to pay the price of further expansion, the Soviets were ready to accept the status quo and exist in peaceful competition with the West, ending the tension before it brought the world any closer to the brink of war.

Of course, even peaceful competition meant the Soviet Union

21 Lawrence Kaplan, *NATO and the United States* (Boston, 1988), 16–30.

would strive for equality with the United States. Whether under Stalin's leadership or that of any subsequent, less villainous leader, the Soviet Union would demand respect as a superpower and exert every effort to develop the economic, political, and military power that required. Given ideological differences, Soviet leaders would likely remain mistrustful of their Western counterparts. They would not assume that every expansion of American influence was benign; they would not concede control of the periphery, of newly independent nations to the United States.

Again in 1949, as in 1946, the structure of the international system dictated Soviet-American competition. But in 1949, the United States and the Soviet Union had gained four years of experience in coping with each other, had managed their differences without bloodshed. Stalin clearly recognized the preponderance of American power, had a sense of its utility, and apprehended the circumstances in which it was likely to be used. Truman and his aides had drawn the line and forced Stalin to toe it. Again, there was a promise of respite, of time for each state to serve its people. But Soviet efforts to compete, and the decline in America's relative power, proved unacceptable to American leaders. They were appalled by evidence that areas on the periphery were slipping out of control. They continued to prepare for the worst.

The election of 1948 did not relieve the tensions in American society. Truman's surprise victory meant that at least four more years, a total of twenty years, would pass without a Republican in the White House – and he brought a Democratic majority in the Congress back to Washington with him. Rank-and-file Republican politicians were angered by the absence of power and patronage for which American political parties exist. They pressed their leaders for radical changes in strategy, for an end to bipartisanship in foreign policy, for an end to what they considered "me-tooism." They demanded and orchestrated a savage attack on the policies of the Truman administration. Criticism of Truman for being "soft on communism" was difficult to substantiate in face of the Truman Doctrine, the Marshall Plan, the Berlin airlift, and the NATO alliance, but the collapse of Chiang Kai-shek's regime in China provided an opportunity antiadministration forces did not waste.

Despite Marshall's mediation efforts in 1946, civil war broke out in China. Chiang dissipated the material assistance with which the United States provided him, the enormous manpower and firepower advantages with which he had begun the war, and was on the verge of total defeat at the hands of the Chinese Communists as Acheson took office as secretary of state in January 1949. Desperately, Chiang and his American friends begged the United States to redress the balance in China, to rescue Chiang's regime. Had Marshall or Acheson been able to conceive of a way to prevent the Communist victory in China, they doubtless would have done so, but their advisers warned that the task was impossible, the cost in men and treasure more than the United States could bear. American strategists had a low regard for China's importance relative to Europe, the Middle East, and Japan. Marshall, the architect of America's Europe-first strategy in World War II, and Acheson, the consummate Atlanticist, saw no reason to question their advisers. The fall of China to the Chinese Communists was undesirable and unfortunate, but it was not catastrophic. China was a weak country, likely to remain so for the foreseeable future, and more likely a burden than an asset to the Soviet Union. In due course the Chinese Communists, like Tito and Yugoslavia, would assert their independence of Moscow. The United States would do what it could to hasten that process.[22]

Neither Marshall nor Acheson, despite previous experience with lobbyists and congressmen supportive of Chiang, had anticipated the domestic political uses to which Chiang's defeat would be put. The Democratic administrations of Roosevelt and Truman were accused of betraying their loyal Chinese ally to the Soviets, of denying Chiang the material assistance with which he could have won. Government officials who had been critical of Chiang's corrupt, repressive, and inefficient regime were accused of being Communist agents. The Democrats were charged with responsibility for the "loss" of China, harassed mercilessly by their political opponents, many of whom in fact cared little about China's fate. One prominent

22 Dorothy Borg and Waldo Heinrichs, *Uncertain Years: Chinese-American Relations, 1947–1950* (New York, 1980), is the standard work on the subject.

antiadministration journalist, George Sokolsky, wrote signed columns attacking the administration for its failure to aid Chiang and unsigned editorials attacking the administration for wasting the taxpayers' money aiding Chiang. All that mattered was to pillory the Democrats in quest of political advantage.[23]

The attack on the Truman administration was also ideological, however, transcending party politics. Anti–New Deal forces had won an important victory over organized labor in 1947 with passage of the Taft-Hartley Act, significantly weakening unions, over Truman's veto. The Senate consistently blocked Truman's modest efforts to prevent discrimination against blacks in the job market. Self-styled conservatives identified the New Deal – one of those occasional efforts in American history to provide a minimal level of decency for less fortunate citizens, to protect them from the miseries that accompany the business cycle in a market economy – with communism. Support for workers, for minorities, for health insurance, even for social security, was labeled Communist agitation. In the 1930s, capitalism had been a dirty word in the United States, as Americans held capitalists responsible for the Great Depression. Now some of those elements in the society who had lost status in the 1930s were on the offensive. Tension with the Soviet Union, the widespread perception of communism as an alien and hostile force served their purposes well.

The Alger Hiss case, which created a sensation in 1948 and 1949, provided the perfect link for those who wanted to identify pro–New Deal Democrats with communism and treason. Hiss was a Harvard Law School graduate, a protégé of Felix Frankfurter, law clerk to Oliver Wendell Holmes, who had served in Roosevelt's Agricultural Adjustment Administration and Solicitor General's Office and held several midlevel positions in the Department of State, before accepting appointment as president of the Carnegie Endowment for International Peace. He could be associated with the New Deal social and economic reforms and the liberal internationalism that was also

23 Nancy Bernkopf Tucker, *Patterns in the Dust* (New York, 1983); Warren I. Cohen, *The Chinese Connection: Roger S. Greene, Thomas W. Lamont, George E. Sokolsky and American–East Asian Relations* (New York, 1982), 260–72.

anathema to conservatives. He seemed typical of the eastern establishment WASPs whose rule was so bitterly resented in much of the country. In 1948, Hiss was accused of having passed classified information to the Soviet Union in the late 1930s and indicted for perjury (for having denied espionage charges under oath). After a first trial ended with a hung jury in July 1949, he was convicted in January 1950, in part due to the successful efforts of Congressman Richard Nixon (R.-Calif.) to turn up evidence against him. Here was proof – or so it was alleged – that New Deal Democrats had betrayed the country. Their programs at home and abroad had violated the principles for which America stood and would have to be reversed. Acheson, sometime law partner of Hiss's brother, played into the hands of the administration's enemies by declaring that he would not turn his back on Alger Hiss.

Acheson and Truman, contemptuous of their tormenters, convinced they were on the right course, held steady. Chiang's China would be abandoned, the modest reforms of Roosevelt's welfare state preserved, and the nation's public servants protected against vilification by the House Un-American Activities Committee and other bastions of the men Acheson dismissed as the "primitives." But they yielded a little here and there to lubricate the political process, to appease their more reasonable critics, to arm their defenders in the Congress and the press. They refrained from recognizing the Communist regime in China and continued their ties to Chiang's government, the remnants of which had fled to Taiwan, waiting for the Communists to apply the coup de grace. Truman instituted a loyalty program to search for Communists in the government. The administration had to combat congressional obstruction, but the restraints were not severe.

Perhaps the major foreign policy issue the second Truman administration had to resolve in its first year was defense spending, the military posture the United States would take in its confrontation with the Soviet Union. Truman had resisted strenuously efforts by the military to obtain significant budget increases. He was satisfied that American economic assistance to its friends abroad, backed by a nuclear arsenal that had been increased substantially, would suffice to protect the security and interests of the United States. Truman

had presided over a reorganization of the American military establishment, now headed by a secretary of defense, and, in 1949,
appointed to that post Louis Johnson, a man committed to holding
down military spending. Acheson was less certain. Some of his
advisers were troubled by the size of Soviet conventional forces,
troubled by what they argued was the ability of the Soviets to march
through Western Europe at will. Acheson believed in operating
from a position of strength. He had little patience with men like
Kennan who argued that the Soviets had no intention of marching
through Europe. He doubted whether anyone could determine the
intent of the closed, secretive Stalinist state. The United States had
to respond to the capabilities of the Soviet military. It had to prepare
for the worst, to be able to overwhelm the Soviets at every point of
interest. But an extensive program of military preparedness was
unlikely, given the opposition of the president, the secretary of
defense, the Congress, and the American people.[24]

The Soviets eased the burden of those who argued for an American
military buildup by exploding a nuclear device in August 1949.
Scientists had warned Roosevelt in 1944 that the Soviets likely
would develop their own bomb in five years, but when the day
came, Truman was shaken and there was evidence of enormous
anxiety among the American people. Now Americans, too, would
have to live in the shadow of Hiroshima and Nagasaki. Now the
American nuclear arsenal might not suffice to deter Stalin from war.
The United States had to build a bigger and better bomb. The
United States had to reconsider the size and deployment of its
conventional forces. In January 1950, Truman approved development of the hydrogen bomb and authorized a reappraisal of American security policy.

The Communist conquest of China, the Alger Hiss case, the
Soviet nuclear explosion fed disparate but overlapping forces in the
United States.[25] Men and women displeased with the Truman ad-
ministration for political and ideological reasons or because of genu-

24 Leffler, *Preponderance of Power,* 304–11.
25 Eric F. Goldman, *The Crucial Decade – and After, 1945–1960* (New York,
1960), captures the mood in America in 1949.

ine concerns about the adequacy of the American strategic posture, pressed for changes, all of which might be satisfied with a more aggressive anti-Soviet policy. The Soviet Union had done little to create the climate. It had contributed little to Mao's victory in China, a fact of which the Chinese would remind Soviet leaders often. Spying was a nasty business, in which both sides unquestionably were engaged in 1949, but Hiss was charged with acts of treachery in the late 1930s. And surely the Soviets had not been expected to allow the United States the luxury of a nuclear monopoly forever. In short, the Soviets had provoked without being provocative, almost by existing. Truman and Acheson took steps designed to maintain American military superiority, but in the same month, January 1950, they rejected demands from prominent Republican leaders that they intervene in the Chinese civil war. In an important speech, Acheson declared that the Asian mainland and the island of Taiwan lay outside the defensive perimeter of the United States.

In March, the new study of security policy was ready, labeled NSC-68. It was intended to justify, in no uncertain terms, a major expansion of American military forces, sufficient to ensure the continued ability of the United States to meet any threat with overwhelming force. An aggressively expansionist Soviet Union was postulated, its capabilities exaggerated, the danger estimated on a "worst case" basis: If every variable was evaluated as being as favorable as possible to the Soviet Union, what would the United States need to counter the threat? The answer was a tripling of the military budget. Again, the "security dilemma" was obvious. The Soviets had no choice but to acquire nuclear weapons. They might reasonably perceive a threat in the Marshall Plan and the creation of NATO and arm against it. But any increment to Soviet power, any effort by the Soviets to enhance their security was perceived by Washington to be a threat to the security of the United States. And yet Acheson was preparing to stimulate the next cycle, projecting a major "defensive" buildup by the United States, unable to imagine how his adversary might perceive such action as threatening. Perhaps fortunately, although Truman shared his premises, he was unable to persuade the president to commit the required resources. The program languished, the Cold War stabilized, Stalin called for peace – and, in the early months of 1950, there seemed a chance he might get it.

The structure of the international system that emerged after the defeat of Germany and Japan contained two major powers, the United States and the Soviet Union, each with the opportunity to expand its influence. Historically, when such opportunities have existed, nations have seized them. The United States and the Soviet Union acted predictably. Equally predictable was the likelihood of friction between them as they competed for dominance over some of the areas between them. Soviet determination to control Eastern Europe had been apparent throughout the war. The reemergence of the traditional Russian goal of dominating northeast Asia, Iran, and Turkey should not have been surprising. That the United States, long abstaining from influence in the Eastern Hemisphere, content to dominate much of the Western Hemisphere, should assert itself not only in East Asia but in the Middle East, Western and Central Europe as well, would probably have surprised Roosevelt as much as it apparently did Stalin. In the ensuing struggle for influence, wealth, and power, the economic and technological strength of the United States provided it with a huge advantage, if it did not overreach itself.

The competition that began after World War II would have existed no matter which two countries had emerged triumphant. The nature of the competition that occurred, the hostility, the "Cold War," derived from the fact that one of the competing states was a brutal dictatorship that brought intolerable misery to the peoples who came under its control, a totalitarian state whose methods engendered fear everywhere, a closed society whose secretiveness allowed no means for verifying agreements. Moreover, the Soviet state had rejected customary diplomatic practice in the two decades following the Russian revolutions and had had little time to develop new habits on the eve of World War II. Communication between Moscow and Washington was always difficult, suspicion quick to bubble up from beneath the surface, mutual understanding and trust perhaps decades away.

The attributes of the American political system exacerbated the problem. The political scientist Stephen Krasner has referred to the "paradox of external strength and internal weakness."[26] The leaders of the world's most powerful nation were constantly constrained by domestic interest groups and the reins given to Congress by the Constitution. Roosevelt and Truman evaded those constraints in pursuit of their conceptions of the national interest. Truman and his advisers concluded that overcoming public and congressional lassitude required magnification of the Soviet threat, the Soviet role in undesirable outcomes. That exaggerated view of the Soviet threat took root, to the advantage of anti-Communist ideologues who ultimately dominated American political discourse after 1950.

The United States perceived itself – and was perceived by much of the world – as the great liberator. Its leaders were prepared to be generous, but they expected deference, acceptance of American principles for the reorganization of the world. They were angered by Soviet mistrust of the United States, by Soviet unwillingness to accept a subordinate role in the Pax Americana. They had little respect for the Soviet Union, were appalled by its political culture and the ruthlessness with which it was extended to other peoples. Having learned from Hitler of the unspeakable atrocities of which totalitarian dictators were capable, they expected comparable horrors from Stalin. They equated the two men and the systems by which they ruled. But, arguably, the most important point was that despite Stalin's malevolence, despite American arrogance, despite the systemic rivalry, the United States and the Soviet Union had not gone to war. Glower at each other they did indeed, bristle with weapons they would when they could, but neither side had incentive to fight. In time they might learn how to talk to each other.

26 Krasner, "United States Commercial and Monetary Policy: Unravelling the Paradox of External Strength and Internal Weakness," in Katzenstein, *Between Power and Plenty*, 51–87.

3. The Korean War and Its Consequences

The principal focus of Soviet-American tensions was Europe. The Soviets considered control of Eastern Europe vital to their security. The Americans considered a non-Communist Western Europe vital to theirs. Neither was ready to risk a united Germany that might align itself with the other. The only serious crisis of the postwar era had come when the United States, Britain, and France confronted the Soviet Union with their plans to create a strong German state out of their occupation zones and to integrate that state politically and economically with the West. Stalin had responded with the blockade of Berlin.

Both the United States and the Soviet Union had important interests in Asia. Indeed, the Soviet Union dominated the northern part of the Asian landscape, shared borders with Korea, China, Mongolia, and Afghanistan. The United States had long vied for and had finally achieved dominance in the Pacific. Asia had not been excluded from great power rivalries in the past. It would not be excluded from the competition between the Soviet Union and the United States. But for both, Asia was less important than Europe.

And yet, East Asia was destined to be the region in which a war would be fought, a war that would alter the nature of the Soviet-American confrontation, change it from a systemic political competition into an ideologically driven, militarized contest that threatened the very survival of the globe. Local actors played an enormous role in shaping that conflict and others in Asia, as elsewhere in what came to be known as the Third World. Over time, and especially after Stalin's death, the Soviet Union developed a policy of assisting all movements hostile to imperialism, all movements with "socialist orientations." American leaders, once eager for the United States to be seen as the leading opponent of imperialism, quickly concluded that all leftist movements were either instruments of Moscow or likely to become adjuncts of Soviet power, that "wars of national liberation" were Communist plots that had to be crushed. Generally too cautious to risk direct confrontation, the superpowers shed the blood of their surrogates. But more than 100,000 American servicemen and -women lost their lives fighting communism in East Asia.

World War II had set the stage for decolonization, probably the most important series of events in the last half of the twentieth century. The great colonial powers, Britain, France, and the Netherlands, had been weakened seriously by the war. Throughout Asia, the Japanese had stirred nationalist sentiment, promising an Asia for Asians, and succeeding in driving the Westerners out of East Asia, out of French Indochina, out of British Malaya and Burma, out of the Dutch East Indies, out of the American Philippines. When the war ended, the peoples of those colonies did not welcome back their imperial masters, nor were the people of the Indian subcontinent, however less responsive to Japanese promises, content to remain British subjects. With the defeat of Japan, the peoples over whom they had held dominion, not least the Chinese and Koreans, sought to establish their freedom and independence from all would-be overlords. And, in time, they all did, a few with Soviet help, a few with American support, some with minimal suffering, some with terribly destructive wars. These wars were fought not only for independence but to determine who would rule whom after independence. It was a scene that would have been chaotic, even deadly, under any circumstances. The success of local leaders in drawing in the superpowers intensified and enlarged the dangers, with renewed world war a conceivable outcome.

Japan itself was shielded from much of the unrest that swept Asia. Devastated by the war, by merciless American bombing, including the firebombing of Tokyo and the atomic attacks on Hiroshima and Nagasaki, their armed forces decimated by fierce battles such as had occurred on Iwo Jima and Okinawa, the Japanese were relatively docile. They accepted the benign rule of the American proconsul, General Douglas MacArthur, manipulating him as best they could. The Soviets had obtained control of Sakhalin and a small group of islands to the north of the Japanese main islands, the so-called Northern Islands that troubled Japanese-Soviet relations for generations. They were otherwise excluded from any substantive role in the occupation of Japan.

The American occupiers proceeded to demilitarize and democratize Japan with considerable success, largely the result of Japanese receptivity. Great concentrations of industrial power, the *zaibatsu*, were broken up, land redistributed, and organized labor empowered. Visions of a New Deal for Japan emanated from MacArthur's civilian planners in Tokyo. In due course, however, American leaders in Washington, increasingly more fearful of the Soviet Union than of a resurgent Japan, "reversed course," choosing to rebuild Japanese economic power and integrate Japan with the emerging anti-Soviet bloc, much as they were doing with Germany. As in Germany, the United States had little trouble finding an anti-Soviet leadership among traditional Japanese elites. And as with the reconstruction of Germany, the reconstruction of Japan was at least as frightening to America's friends in the western Pacific as to its rivals. [1]

At the end of the war, Roosevelt's reflexive interest in eliminating French imperial rule over Indochina was forgotten, liberation of the territory left to the British and Chinese. The Chinese effort to impede the return of the French was not equal to the British effort to facilitate it. Vietnamese nationalists, the Communist-led Vietminh, were unable to attain independence peacefully and, by 1946, were engaged in a revolutionary war. Vietnamese appeals to the memory of Jefferson and Lincoln notwithstanding, the United States showed little interest in their cause and became increasingly unfriendly as Communists everywhere came to be viewed with suspicion. [2]

---

1 Michael Schaller, *The American Occupation of Japan* (New York, 1985). For a discussion of the issues and the literature, see Carol Gluck, "Entangling Illusions – Japanese and American Views of the Occupation," in Warren I. Cohen, ed., *New Frontiers in American–East Asian Relations* (New York, 1983), 169–236.

2 Bernard Fall, *Street Without Joy* (New York, 1972); Ellen J. Hammer, *The Struggle for Indochina, 1940–1955* (Stanford, 1956); Gary Hess, *The United States' Emergence as a Southeast Asian Power, 1940–1950* (New York, 1987), 159–214, 311–32.

In contrast, the United States gradually became more supportive of the men and women fighting for their freedom against the Dutch in the Indies, providing the pressure that ultimately assured Indonesian independence. In this instance, however, the Americans intervened largely because of fears that a non-Communist independence movement would succumb to the Communists if it could not rid the islands of the Dutch. As in Indochina, the long-standing American commitment to the principle of self-determination, historic American opposition to imperialism, was subordinated first to the determination not to undermine an important European friend – and then to anticommunism.[3]

The pattern could be seen with situational variations in two countries with which the United States was more deeply involved: the Philippines and China. In 1946 the United States, demonstrating its antiimperialism in the most substantial way, granted independence to its own subjects, the Filipinos. The imperial power did not leave cleanly, however. The United States retained control of major bases in the islands and continued to manipulate local politics so that traditional elites, often men who had collaborated with the Japanese as they had with the Americans before and after the war, retained control. The disintegration of the islands' economy, suddenly bereft of colonial connections, troubled few in Washington until a leftist-led peasant revolution, the Hukbalahap, gathered force. Thereafter, the United States government was quick to provide the advice and assistance necessary to suppress it.[4]

China was a more complicated and much more important case. At war's end, Washington was unsympathetic to Chiang's regime, which had proved to be a difficult ally. But wartime comradery with Mao's Communist rebels quickly gave way to concern for their connection to Moscow. As everywhere else, Americans would have liked to recreate China in their own image, serving their sense of mission by creating a coalition of Guomindang and Communist "moder-

3 Robert J. McMahon, *Colonialism and the Cold War: The United States and the Struggle for Indonesian Independence, 1945–1949* (Ithaca, 1981).
4 James C. Thomson, Jr., Peter W. Stanley, and John Curtis Perry, *Sentimental Imperialist* (New York, 1981), 268–75; Hess, *US as Southeast Asian Power*, 217–50.

ates" – a New Deal for China. Clearly, the United States anticipated a patron–client relationship with China, not easily achieved in dealing with obstreperous patriots like Chiang and Mao. When Marshall failed, in 1946, to prevent civil war, American leaders surrendered their hope of a China that would advance American ends. A victory for Chiang became their clear preference and they continued to provide his forces with aid, not as much as he would have liked, but more than they thought his regime was worth. His collapse in 1948 and the subsequent establishment by the Communists of the People's Republic of China was perceived by men like Marshall, Acheson, and Kennan as unfortunate, contrary to American interests, but not a disaster. They knew Mao would be more responsive to Moscow than to Washington, but they also knew that he and those closest to him were intensely nationalistic. They assumed, as they devised policy toward China in November 1948, that Communist China could be prevented from becoming an "adjunct of Soviet power."[5]

In the course of 1949, Acheson determined to abandon Chiang, who had fled to Taiwan, and to seek accommodation with the People's Republic. The domestic political context hampered his efforts, and the activities and pronouncements of the Chinese Communists did little to facilitate his task. Most of his advisers in the Department of State, the secretary of defense and his aides, and key congressmen of both parties opposed and sometimes obstructed his policies. Acheson held course, supported by a wavering president. Time, he assumed was on his side. In due course the Communists would eliminate Chiang and Americans would learn to live with the reality of a Communist China. Mao's trip to Moscow in December 1949 and the resultant Sino-Soviet alliance were a clear setback, but Acheson persisted in believing that China and the Soviet Union were not natural allies. Chinese nationalism would prevent the Soviets from controlling China and the day would come when the issues between the two countries would divide them. In January 1950,

5 Warren I. Cohen, "Acheson, His Advisers, and China, 1949–1950," in Dorothy Borg and Waldo Heinrichs, eds., *Uncertain Years: Chinese-American Relations, 1947–1950* (New York, 1980), 13–52.

Acheson had spoken publicly of an American defensive perimeter that excluded Taiwan and had hinted that the United States would recognize Mao's Peking government when the dust of the civil war had settled. His aides were struggling desperately to come up with a plan to save Taiwan as spring passed and summer came to Washington. And then war broke out in Korea.[6]

That a civil war in Korea would provide the critical turning point in the postwar Soviet-American relationship, and raise the possibility of world war, seems, in retrospect, nothing short of bizarre. Quite likely, an explosion elsewhere would have done as well, sooner or later, but perhaps not. In the tense days of 1949 and 1950, American analysts waiting for the Soviets to strike looked toward Europe. Yugoslavia was the most plausible target. The Soviet Red Army did not move, however, even to punish a deviant Communist leader who had challenged Stalin's claim to speak for all Communists. But on June 25, troops and tanks of the Soviet-trained and -equipped forces of the Democratic People's Republic of Korea launched a major offensive across the thirty-eighth parallel, against the American-trained and -equipped forces of the Republic of Korea to the south.

American missionaries, businessmen, and naval officers had established contacts with Korea in the nineteenth century, but the United States had little contact with that country after the Japanese established their hegemony there in 1905, at the conclusion of the Russo-Japanese War. In the closing days of World War II, the United States and its Soviet allies agreed to liberate Korea jointly, dividing the areas of their responsibilities at the thirty-eighth parallel, the very point at which Japan and tsarist Russia had once divided their spheres of influence. Soviet forces reached Korea first, drove past the thirty-eighth parallel, but unhesitatingly moved north of it when American forces arrived, several weeks after the war was over. Neither the Soviets nor the Americans knew a great deal about Korea, but the Americans, thousands of miles away, doubtless knew less

6 Cohen, "Acheson and His Advisers," and Nancy B. Tucker, *Patterns in the Dust* (New York, 1983). For views contrary to the "Cohen-Tucker thesis," see Robert Blum, *Drawing the Line* (New York, 1982), and William W. Stueck, Jr., *The Road to Confrontation* (Chapel Hill, 1981).

than the Russians, who shared a tiny border with the Koreans and had a historic interest in controlling the country.

Korea was liberated. The Koreans demanded their independence. Neither the Americans nor the Soviets were quite sure what to do with them beyond the vague idea of establishing some kind of trusteeship until unspecified conditions for independence were met. Koreans, regardless of their politics, were outraged by the concept of trusteeship, intent upon achieving freedom immediately. As the liberating forces set about the temporary business of administering their respective sectors, the Soviets turned to local Communists and Koreans who had fought alongside Soviet forces against the Japanese. The Americans were attracted to those most familiar with the vocabulary of liberal democracy, many of whom had collaborated with the Japanese. When Soviet-American tensions developed, the thirty-eighth parallel ceased to be a temporary line dividing the operational theaters of two allied forces and hardened into something more akin to an international border in the eyes of Russians and Americans, if not Koreans. Each side trained and armed Koreans under its jurisdiction. Several years passed without agreement on reunification. Separate governments were established in 1948. Koreans on both sides refused to accept the division of their country, fought constant skirmishes at the border, and did what they could to infiltrate territory controlled by the other. Politics in the American sector were incomprehensible and unpleasant, with Syngman Rhee, a ruthless Princeton-educated autocrat, anti-Communist to be sure, but unamenable to American advice, emerging as the dominant figure. The American military wanted to go home.[7]

By 1949, the Joint Chiefs were able to persuade the National Security Council to order the withdrawal of American troops from Korea. The Department of State was opposed, leery of what intelligence estimates indicated were superior Korean Communist forces, of estimates that indicated that perhaps as many as one-third of Rhee's citizenry was sympathetic to the Communists and probably many more simply hostile to Rhee. Without the presence of Ameri-

---

7 Bruce Cumings, *Origins of the Korean War,* 2 vols. (Princeton, 1981, 1990); Burton I. Kaufman, *The Korean War* (New York, 1986), 7–22.

can forces, southern Korea likely would be overrun by the Communists and a united Communist Korea would result. The threat caused minimal concern in Washington in 1949. The president and the secretary of defense were committed to limiting the defense budget. Korea was low on nearly everyone's list of priorities. The Asian mainland was determined to lie beyond the defensive perimeter of the United States. Troops in Korea would be useless in a war with the Soviet Union. They were needed elsewhere. Economic assistance, military advice, and supplies would have to suffice to keep the Rhee regime afloat. In Acheson's speech in January 1950, in statements by other military and political leaders that spring, and most obviously by the earlier withdrawal of American troops, the United States had signaled its low estimate of Korea's strategic importance in a global confrontation with the Soviets.[8]

We do not know much about thinking in Moscow at this time. Stalin clearly did not want war with the United States. He was fully aware of American strategic superiority. He still needed several years before his forces would have credible nuclear weapons. He probably assumed the United States would not hesitate to use its growing nuclear arsenal if he were to unleash the Red Army against Western Europe. To everyone who would listen – and to many who would not – he and his agents, covert as well as overt, spoke of the need for peace, of their belief that communists and capitalists could coexist on this planet. His peace offensive was doubtless tactical, designed to buy time until the Soviet Union could match or surpass American power. He was not ready in 1950; a united Communist Korea was not worth the risk.[9]

On the other hand, his Korean protégés, like Rhee's regime to the south, were determined to fight, to unite Korea by force. For some long time, Stalin's policy had mirrored American policy. He tried to keep Korean Communist forces on a tight rein and supplied primarily with defensive weapons. But when American troops left the Korean peninsula, Stalin and his advisers might have concluded, quite

---

8 Kaufman, *The Korean War,* 22–5; James I. Matray, *The Reluctant Crusade* (Honolulu, 1985), 175–225.

9 Marshall D. Shulman, *Stalin's Foreign Policy Reappraised* (New York, 1966), 80–138.

reasonably, that the United States was indifferent to the outcome of the Korean civil war. Stalin had urged prudence on the Chinese Communists, apprehensive of American intervention in the Chinese civil war. The Chinese had ignored him — and his fears had not been realized. Korea was far less important to the Americans and the threat of intervention had all but vanished. Stalin decided to provide the Korean Communists with the equipment they needed to carry out an offensive. The operation promised to be brief and carried little risk. Stalin's successor, Nikita Khrushchev, subsequently contended that "no real Communist would have tried to dissuade Kim Il-sung [the North Korean Communist leader] from his compelling desire to liberate South Korea from Syngman Rhee and from reactionary American influence."[10]

Stalin and his advisers, little understanding the United States, misjudged the American response. Arming the North Koreans and acquiescing in their invasion of the South proved to be Stalin's most disastrous Cold War gamble. It postponed détente with the United States for twenty years. It intensified a confrontation that continued for forty years at enormous cost to the major antagonists and to much of the rest of the world. The war shifted the balance of forces within the United States to the advantage of the most militant opponents of social justice, racist politicians like Eugene Talmadge of Georgia and John Rankin of Mississippi, opponents of organized labor like the journalist George Sokolsky, the National Association of Manufacturers, and the R. J. Reynolds Tobacco Company, opportunists like Joe McCarthy and Richard Nixon, and powerful bureaucrats like J. Edgar Hoover of the FBI, allowing them to divert the attention and energies of the American people from needed reform to the hunt for Communists at home and abroad. It allowed men and organizations like these, working with the aviation industry in particular, to create a military-industrial complex that consumed the productive power of the American economy and fueled conflict all over the world. These elements existed in American society indepen-

10 Okonogi Masao, "The Domestic Roots of the Korean War," in Akira Iriye and Nagai Yonosuke, eds., *The Origins of the Cold War in Asia* (New York, 1977), 299–320; Edward Crankshaw and Strobe Talbott, *Khrushchev Remembers* (Boston, 1970), 368.

dently of any Soviet threat. They might well have dominated the society in any event. They might have succeeded in conjuring up a threat from Mars. But it was Stalin's opportunism in Korea that opened the door for them.

The initial response of American leaders to news of the outbreak of war in Korea was relief that Rhee had not started it. Given the opportunity he no doubt would have – but he had not. The Communists had invaded the South and Truman would have to decide whether to respond and, if so, how. If Korea was outside the defensive perimeter of the United States, if the National Security Council had reached consensus on its relative lack of importance, why respond at all? Surprisingly, all of Truman's advisers reversed themselves and argued that the invasion had to be repelled, that the United States could not stand by and allow what was perceived as an act of aggression to go unchallenged. Some contended that the credibility of the United Nations was at stake if aggressors were allowed to go unpunished; some feared the credibility of the United States as guardian of the non-Communist world was at risk. All of Truman's advisers saw the events in Korea as a test of American will to resist Soviet attempts to expand their power, and their system. If Stalin was allowed to succeed in Korea, he would probe somewhere else – and keep probing until he had either conquered the Eurasian landmass or started World War III. Now was the time to stop him.[11]

Unspoken was another grave concern – for the political future of Harry Truman, for his ability to govern for the remainder of his term as president. His administration had been accused of betraying China, of allowing the Soviet Union to expand its influence into Asia. Acheson's relative indifference to Asia was notorious and troubled many of his most loyal aides, several of whom had been work-

11 Glen D. Paige, *The Korean Decision, June 24–30, 1950* (New York, 1968); Dean Acheson, *Present at the Creation* (New York, 1969), 524–37; Warren I. Cohen, *Dean Rusk* (Totowa, N.J., 1980), 51–2. See also the fascinating analysis of the policy reversal in Jack Snyder, *Myths of Empire* (Ithaca, 1991), 289–96.

ing on elaborate plans to provide at least the appearance of administration action in East Asia. Failure to respond in Korea could be politically catastrophic. Successful action could silence the administration's critics and perhaps even provide a third term in the White House for Truman.

The combination of reasons for action — stopping an aggressor, containing Soviet expansion, demonstrating American resolve to Stalin, to America's European allies, and to nervous Asians, preserving the credibility of the United Nations, protecting Truman at home — was overwhelming. To Stalin's dismay, the United States intervened in the Korean civil war. Mobilizing the United Nations, which it still dominated, assisted by units as disparate as British, Turk, and Ethiopian, the United States sent its military forces to fight alongside those of Syngman Rhee. He was an unworthy ally, but the United States could not risk the consequences of inaction.

Initially, UN forces under the command of an American general, Douglas MacArthur, fared poorly. Rhee's troops were not as well equipped as their northern counterparts, the American troops included few with combat experience, and they were chewed up by the invading forces. American airpower functioned ineffectively. Eventually, however, MacArthur's men held a line outside of the southeastern port city of Pusan from which they counterattacked simultaneously with a brilliantly conceived and extraordinarily risky landing he ordered at Inchon on the northwest coast of southern Korea. By late September, they had trapped the troops from northern Korea in a classic pincer movement and had routed them. In less than three months, UN forces under American leadership had defeated the aggressor, were on the verge of liberating the south, and had demonstrated both the viability of the United Nations and the resolve of the United States to the entire world.

Unfortunately, in its moment of triumph, the Truman administration succumbed to one of the most treacherous temptations confronting any victor, the temptation to expand war aims. Repelling aggression, liberating southern Korea would not be enough. Truman and his advisers concluded that Stalin would not come to the aid of his Korean surrogates, that they could send UN forces across the thirty-eighth parallel dividing non-Communist South from Communist North, purge the North of Communists, and unite all of Korea, presumably under a government more democratic than that of Rhee. There were risks to be sure – and the Chinese were threatening to intervene if UN forces crossed the thirty-eighth parallel – but Acheson, no less than MacArthur, was contemptuous of the Chinese, inclined to discount their threats as bluff, confident that they would not dare risk confrontation with overwhelming American firepower. And, judging by American experience with Chinese troops during World War II, American leaders assumed that if the Chinese dared to intervene, they would be disposed of quickly. The Communists were in retreat, the United States resurgent.[12]

There were voices in Washington favoring a halt in the vicinity of the thirty-eighth parallel. George Kennan argued that there was an opportunity to divide the Chinese from the Soviet Communists, that they had responded differently to an Indian proposal for a cease-fire agreement that would have included seating the Chinese Communists in the United Nations. Paul Nitze, architect of NSC-68, the plan for the massive military buildup to contain the growing Soviet threat, argued that the time was not propitious for risking a larger war, that until his plan was implemented, military advantage in what would likely become World War III rested with the Soviets. Military men who saw the Soviets as the enemy were disinclined to commit their forces in a peripheral area. And there were some who thought the Chinese might well intervene, forcing a larger war.

The opportunity to roll back the Communists in Korea, the vision of creating a united Korea as a showcase for democracy and an answer to critics who claimed Truman was soft on communism, proved irresistible. MacArthur sent his men racing up the coastal plains on both sides of the Korean peninsula, on both sides of the mountain spine that ran up the center. The only restraint placed on him was to send Korean troops ahead into those provinces bordering on China

---

12 Kaufman, *Korean War,* 84–7; James I. Matray, "Truman's Plan for Victory: National Self-Determination and the Thirty-eighth Parallel Decision in Korea," *Journal of American History* 66 (1979): 314–33; Rosemary Foot, *The Wrong War* (Ithaca, 1985), 66–74.

and the Soviet Union and to halt his advance if he ran into significant Chinese or Soviet forces. Truman, uneasy about the Chinese, flew to Wake Island in the Pacific to meet his field commander. An exuberant MacArthur assured the president of a quick victory even if the Chinese were so foolish as to intervene.

In Beijing, Mao and his advisers were terribly apprehensive about American intentions. Communications between China and the United States had broken down early in 1950 after the Chinese had seized U.S. government property in Beijing despite a warning that seizure would result in the recall of all American diplomats. The alliance Mao and Stalin signed in February 1950 forced Acheson to surrender hope of a rift between the two Communist states in the immediate future. Ever the realist, Acheson still looked toward eventual recognition of the People's Republic of China, but he was in no hurry to reward the friend of his enemy. Mao, on the other hand, was convinced that the United States was implacably hostile, that sooner or later it would attack the People's Republic of China and try to reverse his victory. American actions following the outbreak of the war in Korea intensified his anxiety. The United States ordered warships to the Taiwan Straits to prevent Mao's forces from invading Taiwan and mopping up the remnants of Chiang's army there. Mac-Arthur flew to Taibei and stood shoulder to shoulder with Chiang, indicating his support for Chiang and his view of Taiwan as an unsinkable aircraft carrier that could not be allowed to fall to the Communists. Once again, the Americans were interfering in the Chinese civil war, supporting Chiang against the Communists.

Mao was troubled deeply by the dispatch of American troops to Korea and then by their success at Inchon. Relying on the *New York Times* for their information about the United States, his advisers reported growing sentiment in favor of uniting Korea and then continuing on into China to throw the Communists out.[13] China was weak. It desperately needed time and all of its resources to reconstruct and then modernize the country, parts of which had been

13 Warren I. Cohen, "Conversations with Chinese Friends: Zhou Enlai's Associates Reflect on Chinese-American Relations in the 1940s and the Korean War," *Diplomatic History* 11 (1987): 283–9; see also Zhang Shuguang, *Deterrence and Strategic Culture* (Ithaca, 1993).

at war since 1931. It could hardly expect to win a war against the most powerful nation the world had ever known. The Chinese leaders did not want to fight, but Mao, convinced the Americans would leave him no choice, chose to fight on Korean rather than Chinese soil. In October, as UN forces crossed the thirty-eighth parallel and marched toward the Yalu River that separated Korea from China, Mao ordered Chinese troops into Korea. Again and again, the Chinese sent warnings that they would attack if UN troops continued to march north. Arrogantly, the Americans and their allies charged on, confident of a quick victory.[14]

Acheson tried to assure the Chinese that the United States did not intend to attack China, but American assurances lacked credibility in Beijing. The Americans had said Korea was beyond their defensive perimeter, but they sent their forces to defend it nonetheless. They said they wanted to repel aggression and drive the North Koreans back across the thirty-eighth parallel – and now they were headed for the Yalu. If unopposed, would they stop there? Acheson said they had no hostile designs on China, but various congressmen were calling for restoring Chiang's government on the mainland. MacArthur and Chiang were conspiring. American planes were bombing Chinese airfields. Mao was not reassured. Given the absence of trust, of understanding, of unambiguous American signals, prudence required China to intervene in Korea.

In mid-October Chinese forces struck at American troops, bloodied them, and withdrew to observe the American response. MacArthur was undeterred. Two weeks later, UN forces were attacked by 200,000 "volunteers" from the Chinese People's Liberation Army. The Chinese shattered discipline among the UN troops, who

14 Chinese scholars have contributed mightily to our understanding of the Chinese decision to intervene. See especially Hao Yufan and Zhai Zhihai, "China's Decision to Enter the Korean War: History Revisited," *China Quarterly* 121 (1990): 94–115; Zhang Shuguang, "Preparedness Eliminates Mishaps: The CCP's Security Concerns in 1949–1950 and the Origins of Sino-American Confrontation," and Chen Jian, "China's Changing Aims During the Korean War," both in *Journal of American-East Asian Relations* 1 (1992): 42–72, 8–41. See also the classic by Allen S. Whiting, *China Crosses the Yalu* (Stanford, 1960).

fled in disarray back across the thirty-eighth parallel, suffering severe casualties along the way. By the end of November, the American military was preparing to flee Korea, to accept defeat. Truman's opportunism had proved very costly.

In Washington, George Marshall had returned to take charge of the Department of Defense, and he, Kennan, and Dean Rusk, Acheson's assistant secretary for Far Eastern affairs, rallied the U.S. government. They rejected MacArthur's defeatism and vowed to go down fighting. American forces held again, north of the Pusan perimeter. Truman and his advisers, military and civilian, fearful of provoking Soviet intervention, rejected MacArthur's demand for permission to attack China. American forces were expanding rapidly, but they were not yet ready for World War III. Fierce aerial assaults against overextended Chinese lines began to take an enormous toll and gradually the Chinese were driven back across the thirty-eighth parallel. Efforts to end the war largely on the basis of prewar conditions began in earnest in the spring of 1951. Instead of the popular victory Truman might have claimed in September 1950, the administration had continued fighting to the point where the war was intensely unpopular with the American people and enormously costly in blood and treasure. It had brought upon itself a war it could not win without risking a world war for which the American military was not ready. MacArthur, vacillating between manic euphoria and depression, at odds with both military and civilian leaders in Washington, had to be fired, a bitter end for a great American hero. Unfortunately, his firing brought added opprobrium on the administration.

It took two more years to end the war and by then Harry Truman and his aides had returned to private life. The scale of military spending Nitze had imagined in NSC-68 had begun. American military power, especially nuclear power, increased dramatically. An arms race, in which the Soviet Union could not easily compete, was under way. By the end of 1952, according to the historian Marc Trachtenberg, American military leaders thought they were ready to take on the Soviets.[15] Having perceived the outbreak of war in

15 Marc Trachtenberg, *History and Strategy* (Princeton, 1991), 100–52.

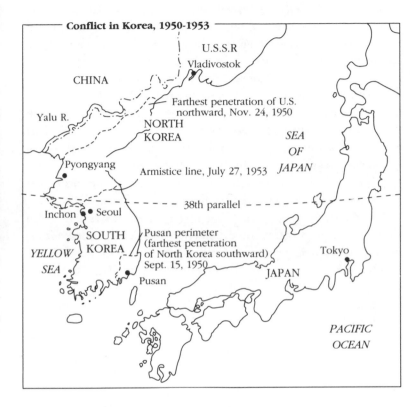

Korea and Chinese intervention as evidence that the Soviet Union did not fear the United States, American leaders interpreted Soviet willingness to allow their Korean and Chinese surrogates to be slaughtered as evidence that the balance had shifted in favor of the United States. Once again, America could act aggressively in support of its interests.

Throughout the Korean War, the Soviet Union gave diplomatic support to its Korean and Chinese allies, but reneged on the air cover Stalin had led Mao to expect.[16] The Soviets did provide the

16 Chen Jian, "The Sino-Soviet Alliance and China's Entry into the Korean War," paper presented to workshop on Chinese Foreign Policy at Michigan State University (cosponsored by the Cold War History Project of the Woodrow Wilson International Center for Scholars, Smithsonian Institution), November 1, 1991.

Chinese with military equipment, but at a cost the Chinese found outrageous. A few Soviet pilots flew missions in the North, but at no time did the Soviet Union ever threaten military action in Korea. At no time did it create a crisis in Europe, which might have distracted UN forces in Korea. At no time did it threaten to open up a "second front" in Europe. Moscow cheered on East Asian Communists confronting American military power, but it took no risks itself. However advantageous American analysts imagined the situation to be for the Soviets, Stalin would not countenance escalation. Caution was again the watchword in the Kremlin where Stalin had long proclaimed that interests of international communism were best served when Soviet interests and security were assured.

The Korean War ended in 1953, shortly after the death of Stalin. In the Kremlin the great succession crisis was being played out and Soviet leaders were preoccupied with the power struggle at home, uninterested for the moment in foreign adventure. The Chinese had suffered huge casualties, including the loss of Mao's son. They had contained the American imperialists, preserved their regime, and won great prestige for it. They had preserved the North Korean Communist regime as a buffer between their border and the unfriendly forces to the south with minimal assistance from the Soviet Union. It was time to return to the task of building socialism at home.

The mood in the United States was ugly. The nation had been rent by wartime hysteria, stimulated by demagogues, some seeking personal power, some partisan advantage, some a return to the time when oppression of the poor, the blacks, the Jews, and anyone else outside the mainstream of mid-American culture, was condoned. There had long been a streak of nativism in American society that became explosive when combined with fear of radicalism. The Haymarket affair in 1886, the Red Scare of 1919–20, the Sacco-Vanzetti case in the 1920s were earlier indications of how the nation might respond. In the years immediately following the war, as conservatives attempted to roll back the New Deal, especially labor gains, they appealed to fear of radicalism, labeled everything they disliked communism, everyone who opposed them a Communist, and blurred the lines between democratic socialism and communism, even between liberalism and communism. Their cause was strengthened tremendously by the tensions that emerged between the United States and the Soviet Union.

One reason the Red Scare had evaporated so quickly in 1920 was the absurdity of suggesting that Soviet Russia posed a threat to the United States. In the late 1940s, that notion was no longer absurd. For reasons of its own, to gain popular acceptance of America's new hegemonic role and its costs, the Truman administration had exaggerated the Soviet threat. Stalin unquestionably attempted to use Communists and Communist sympathizers all over the world to serve the ends of Soviet policy. Though inconsequential in number and potential for damage, Communists serving as Soviet agents unquestionably existed in the United States. The Hiss case underscored the danger. As early as 1947, Truman had created a loyalty board to purify the bureaucracy and he indulged in Red-baiting to get himself elected in 1948. The House Un-American Activities Committee cast its net wide, and allegations spread alarmingly.

In February 1950, the obscure junior senator from Wisconsin, Joseph R. McCarthy, bid for recognition with a speech claiming that he had a list of 205 card-carrying members of the Communist party who were employed by the Department of State to shape American foreign policy. The technique came to be known as the "big lie." McCarthy had a handful of names of men who had been accused several times in the 1940s, generally of being friendly to the Chinese Communists. Several proved guilty of indiscretion. None was a Communist; none was guilty of espionage; most were no longer in the government. But if a U.S. senator claimed there were 205 Communists in the State Department, surely there were some – maybe only 200, 100, 50 – but *some*. McCarthy had no evidence of any. His charges were investigated and rejected by a bipartisan committee headed by the conservative anti–New Dealer, Senator Millard Tydings (D.-Md.). McCarthy was undaunted. Moreover, he was encouraged by other Republican senators, eager to portray Democrats as the "party of treason," with an eye to achieving gains in the election of 1950 and regaining the White House at last in the election of 1952.

In coping with what he called the "attack of the primitives,"

Acheson's arrogance initially shielded him and American foreign policy. Disdainful of public opinion generally, and congressmen in particular, he ignored the charges of McCarthy and others like him, and continued to do as he thought best. On occasion, he yielded to political expediency as directed by Truman, but only on matters he considered tactical. McCarthy and his colleagues were being fed information by the friends of Chiang Kai-shek, and Acheson was amenable to pressures to delay recognition of Mao's government until Chiang was eliminated. He would not countenance reversing his policy of seeking accommodation with Mao – until anti-Communist hysteria generated during the Korean War left him no choice.

The rantings of men like McCarthy seem to be a recurring thread in the fabric of a society that prides itself on free speech. The great American historian Richard Hofstadter wrote of the "paranoid style in American politics."[17] Occasionally, these men or women gain a small devoted following, flame incandescently for a moment, and are gone. A fraction of the American people believe in them and await their next prophet. Painful as their activities are for their victims, the impact of such demagogues on the larger society is usually minimal. McCarthy and other would-be leaders of the anti-Communist crusade would likely have disappeared from sight, an ephemeral blemish on the record of the American past, had it not been for the Korean War.

Once Americans were dying at the hands of Communists in Korea, the anxieties that had been generated by knowledge that the Soviets had the atom bomb, by the Hiss case, and by awareness that there were in fact Communist agents operating in the United States were channeled into an anti-Communist frenzy. Anyone who had ever been associated with a leftist organization, anyone committed to social justice for all Americans, anyone associated with unpopular views – such as support for labor or civil rights in the South – anyone critical of Chiang Kai-shek or thought to be apologizing for Soviet behavior, anyone who had ever angered a neighbor, might be

17 Richard Hofstadter, *The Paranoid Style in American Politics* (New York, 1967), 3–40.

accused of being a Communist. The accusation, the investigation, often sufficed to destroy careers. Evidence was not necessary. Blacklists were created in the entertainment industry to keep suspect actors from getting parts in motion pictures or on television, to prevent suspect writers from having their work produced for the public. A great composer like Aaron Copland could be harassed and ultimately spared only because George Sokolsky, at the heart of McCarthy's journalistic claque, was especially fond of his music. Many innocent government officials, university and public school teachers, civil rights leaders, and labor organizers were less fortunate, as they lost their jobs and sometimes the opportunity to find comparable work.

If the Korean War created a climate in which McCarthyism could flourish, the margin of difference between a minor footnote and a major disaster for the American people, McCarthyism created a climate in which reducing Soviet-American tensions became extraordinarily difficult. Most unfortunately, the success of McCarthy's supporters in exciting anti-Communist passions in the United States left little room for a nuanced foreign policy based on recognition of contradictions among Communist countries, on understanding of the difference between Third World radical nationalists who thought of themselves as socialists and Communists subject to the Kremlin's discipline. Red-baiting at home was unquestionably disagreeable. As the basis of a foreign policy, it resulted in the wasting of millions of lives and countless billions of dollars. The intersection of McCarthyism and the Korean War, of American paranoia and Soviet opportunism, brought recurring misery for the next four decades.

The first major victim of McCarthy and Korea was Acheson's policy toward China. Mao's Red hordes had killed thousands of Americans and maimed many more. Gone were the images of weak, docile Chinese, grateful for American largesse and hungering for Christianity, democracy, and the free-enterprise system. Now hundreds of millions of Chinese were perceived as being instruments of the international Communist conspiracy, attacking Americans at Stalin's orders. A Gallup poll indicated that only 5 percent of the American people believed the Chinese had intervened in Korea on their own initiative. Accusations that Truman and Acheson, advised by Communist sympathizers, had betrayed their loyal ally Chiang Kai-shek and "lost" China to the Communists took root, the best evidence of what McCarthy called "twenty years of treason" by the Democratic administrations of Roosevelt and Truman. Mao's China became America's most feared and hated enemy, the return of the yellow peril. Recognition of the Beijing regime was impossible, as was American acquiescence in seating it in the United Nations. Chiang's critics were purged from the Department of State or assigned to obscure posts and those who tended to equate his interests with those of the United States came to dominate the Office of Chinese Affairs. In 1951, assistant secretary Dean Rusk signaled the shift in policy by denouncing Mao's China as a gigantic "Slavic Manchukuo," not to be recognized because it was a Soviet puppet rather than an independent Chinese state. That fiction poisoned Chinese-American relations for decades — even after China and the Soviet Union were at each other's throats. [18]

Direct confrontation led to intense hostility between the United States and China, but American leaders did not forget that their principal adversary was the Soviet Union. If, as General Omar Bradley, chairman of the Joint Chiefs of Staff, argued, in response to calls to attack China, it would be the wrong war in the wrong place at the wrong time, the right war would be against the Soviet Union when the American military buildup was completed. By the end of 1952, the American military was ready, eager to launch a preemptive strike against the Soviets. [19]

To meet the Soviet threat, European leaders wanted a stronger NATO. Consequently fearful that American dalliance on the Asian periphery would result in neglect of Europe, British, French, and German leaders anxiously sought a larger, permanent U.S. military force on the continent. The Soviet effort to create a united Communist Korea presaged an attempt to unite the two German states under the red banner. The American government shared some of Europe's apprehensions but wanted Europeans to contribute more to

18 George H. Gallup, *The Gallup Poll: Public Opinion, 1935–1971* (New York, 1972), 2:955; Cohen, *Dean Rusk*, 62–7.
19 Trachtenberg, *History and Strategy*, 100–52.

their own defense. Increasingly, the men in Washington thought in terms of the need to rearm Germany, of a German army that would provide critical manpower for NATO forces in Central Europe. In December 1950, formal discussions on a German contribution to the defense of Western Europe began. On the same day, as a symbol of American commitment, Dwight D. Eisenhower was named supreme commander of Allied Forces in Europe, with four additional American divisions to follow. There was considerable hesitation along the way, but the path to German remilitarization had been taken.

Perhaps the greatest beneficiaries of the Korean War were the Japanese. When the U.S. Navy had trouble clearing mines from Korean harbors, remnants of the former Imperial Japanese Navy were activated to do the job. Most of the goods and services required by American forces in Korea were procured in Japan, providing the economy with a $4 billion stimulus. And in San Francisco in September 1951, forty-eight nations, led by the United States, signed a peace treaty with Japan, leading to the end of the occupation in May 1952. On the same day the treaty was signed, Japan and the United States signed a mutual security treaty to provide a demilitarized Japan with protection in an uncertain world. The Americans, who retained bases in Japan, had simultaneously restored Japanese sovereignty and further integrated the country into the anti-Communist alliance.[20]

The Korean War was a momentous turning point in the Cold War. An almost inevitable civil war among a people, Communist and non-Communist, determined to unite their country, became an international war and a catalyst for a terrifying arms race. Whatever Stalin's responsibility, whatever his intentions, the results could hardly have been more disastrous for the Soviet Union or unfortunate for the rest of the world. His peace offensive was compromised,

20 James E. Auer, *The Postwar Rearmament of Japanese Maritime Forces, 1945–1971* (New York, 1973); T. E. Vadney, *The World Since 1945* (New York, 1987), 363; Michael Yoshitsu, *Japan and the San Francisco Peace Settlement* (New York, 1983).

American wealth rapidly extended American military superiority, especially nuclear, perceived as well as actual, over Soviet forces. The process of rearming Germany began. Turkey and Greece were brought into NATO. Japan and the Philippines, Australia and New Zealand signed security treaties with the United States. American aid to the French in Indochina increased. What little reluctance to replace British influence in the Middle East remained in Washington was overcome. For the people of the Soviet Union, the Korean War produced a nightmare, mitigated only by the coincidence of Stalin's death before it was over. In addition to Japan, the winners were the likes of Syngman Rhee, Chiang Kai-shek, and all the other merciless dictators who, professing anticommunism, could count on American support. In the United States the winners were the advocates of rollback, of rolling back the Communists abroad and programs of social justice at home.

4. New Leaders and New Arenas in the Cold War

Stalin died. Slowly the terror eased within the Soviet Union, especially after those competing for primacy within the leadership rid themselves of Lavrenti Beria, dreaded head of the secret police. Georgii Malenkov, who, in 1953, seemed to be Stalin's likely successor, sought to reduce international tensions as well. He called for peaceful coexistence with the capitalist world, held out his hand to Tito in Yugoslavia, and offered assurances of Soviet goodwill to Turkey, Iran, and Greece. Israel, India, and Japan similarly received indications that Stalin's death might mean improved relations with the Soviet Union. But Malenkov's hold on power was tenuous and those who vied with him were critical of his efforts to redirect foreign policy. It was not until after he was shunted aside, and Nikita Khrushchev continued his initiatives while providing a few of his own, that the main outlines of post-Stalinist policy were manifest. [1]

The new Soviet leadership inherited a world in which the dominant power, the United States, had just undertaken a rapid military buildup and had demonstrated its ability to project its power many thousands of miles from its shores. Only weeks before Stalin's death, a new administration had arrived in Washington, led by men who called for a more aggressive anti-Soviet policy, for the liberation of Eastern Europe, and for the "unleashing" of Chiang Kai-shek. These were people who would deny the Soviet Union the fruits of victory in World War II, deny the Soviets the influence and respect to which the world's second most powerful nation was entitled. In addition, Stalin's death had prompted the Chinese government to become more independent, a workers' revolt exploded in East Germany in June 1953, and unrest mounted elsewhere in Stalin's new empire.

1 Adam Ulam, *Expansion and Coexistence* (New York, 1974), 544–7.

The outside world would not allow the men in the Kremlin the luxury of concentrating on the internal struggle for power.

The legacy of Stalinism handicapped the new Soviet leadership. Other than Molotov, the longtime foreign minister, its members had little experience with foreign affairs and knew little more of Soviet policies than Stalin had chosen to tell them. The study of international relations, or of the social sciences generally, hardly existed in the years of Stalin's rule. There were few academic specialists to come forward with fresh ideas, to scrape away the layers of ideological propaganda that passed for scholarship while Stalin lived. The analysis of the United States and its friends upon which Stalin had relied bore little relation to reality. Stalin had been confident that the capitalist world would be devastated by depression soon after the world war ended, that the capitalist countries would soon be at each other's throats. The leading scholar in the Institute of World Economy and World Politics, E. S. Varga, argued that the capitalist countries were likely to prosper after the war. Stalin was enraged, Varga lost favor, his institute was disbanded, and the mere fact of his survival astonished his contemporaries. Varga's argument was not repeated in Stalin's lifetime as the dictator waited impatiently for catastrophe to strike the West.[2]

Similarly, Stalin had been traumatized by his experience of supporting Chiang Kai-shek's "bourgeois nationalist" revolution in the 1920s. Chiang had outmaneuvered him, massacred the Chinese Communists, and thrown out his Soviet advisers. Stalin was not going to repeat his mistake by supporting "bourgeois nationalist" leaders like Nehru of India, Sukarno of Indonesia, or Nasser of Egypt. The world, as Stalin saw it in the late 1940s, was divided into two camps, socialist and imperialist. Nehru, Sukarno, Nasser, and others of their ilk merely did the bidding of their former colonial masters, were still part of the imperialist camp. Stalin was contemptuous of the newly independent states and they found few defenders among Soviet scholars during his lifetime.[3]

2 William Zimmerman, *Soviet Perspectives on International Relations, 1956–1967* (Princeton, 1969), 26–32.
3 Bruce D. Porter, *The USSR in Third World Conflicts* (Cambridge, 1984), 14–16.

Efforts to transcend Stalinist dogmatism began with the resurrection of the social sciences and the legitimate study of international relations. In 1956 an Institute of World Economics and International Relations was formed at the Soviet Academy of Sciences. Western sources of information became available. Cautiously at first and with increasing boldness after the Twentieth Party Congress in 1956, Soviet analysts discovered and described the achievements of the Marshall Plan, the successful integration of the American, Western European, and Japanese economies, and the absence of conflict among the capitalist countries relative to what dogmatic Marxists had predicted. They reported the rapid recovery of European economies and the impressive rates of growth they demonstrated. Neither war nor depression was imminent in the capitalist world. At the same time, they reevaluated the role played in world affairs by newly independent states and saw some of them as potential allies in the struggle against American imperialism. They recognized the need to study these countries more closely, to develop area specialists in the academy. In general, by the mid-1950s they were beginning to provide their leaders in the Kremlin with information and advice more closely related to reality, less circumscribed by ideology, than had been possible while Stalin lived.[4]

In February 1956, at the Twentieth Party Congress, Khrushchev roused the delegates with a stirring denunciation of Stalin and his crimes against his people. News of the speech quickly reached the West. But Stalin's successors had long since signaled their determination to change course. Their actions left no reason to doubt them. At home, Stalin's paranoid delusions, like the alleged "Doctors' Plot," with its anti-Semitic implications and threat to all around him, were denounced. Men and women wrongly imprisoned or exiled, including Foreign Minister Molotov's wife and Politburo member Anastas Mikoyan's sons, returned to their families. Laws decreed in accordance with Stalin's whims were erased. In the satellite states of Eastern Europe, Soviet economic pressures were relieved and, after the volatile summer of 1953, local regimes were allowed greater authority over the allocation of resources. In East Asia,

4 Zimmerman, *Soviet Perspectives*, 32–62.

Malenkov and his colleagues quickly indicated their willingness to bring the war in Korea to an end. A year later they surrendered to their Chinese comrades the imperial privileges Stalin had demanded at Yalta and obtained from China in 1945.

Further evidence of the relatively benign intentions of the new Soviet regime was apparent when Moscow dropped its territorial claims against Turkey and returned to Finland a naval base extorted by Stalin. Diplomatic relations were restored with Greece and Israel. The Red Army withdrew from eastern Austria, allowing the re-unification and freedom of the Austrian people. The new Soviet leadership offered recognition to the West German state and accepted its rearmament with astonishing equanimity. It reached out to the United States in search of an agreement to limit the arms race. And, shortly after the Twentieth Congress, in April 1956, the Soviet Union formally abolished the Cominform, the instrument through which Stalin had attempted to control the international Communist movement.

Stalin was gone. First under Malenkov's leadership, then Khrushchev's, the apparatus of terror was being dismantled. The Soviet Union remained a Communist state. It continued to hold against their will most of the peoples of Eastern Europe. It had allies capable of menacing the interests and friends of the United States in East Asia. It had five million men and women under arms and, in August 1953, it exploded a thermonuclear ("hydrogen") bomb. The Soviets would be dangerous rivals in the continuing competition for power and influence. But the post-Stalinist Soviet Union was a different country, led by relatively reasonable and responsible men, with whom agreement upon norms for peaceful competition might be attainable. Khrushchev quickly understood that the Leninist view that war between imperialism and socialism was inevitable was obsolete, that a major war had to be avoided in the nuclear age when radiation and fallout respected no ideology. He remained ebulliently confident that socialism would prevail but without the cataclysm Lenin and Stalin foresaw. The superpowers would deter each other from using nuclear weapons, from a major confrontation, and the revolution would trickle in from the periphery, where the competition for wealth and power would continue. Soviet state interests would be protected and ideology adapted to reality. In Khrushchev, the United States encountered a bold and innovative leader, eager for good relations with the United States, yet unwilling to surrender the messianic vision of an ultimately socialist world. Much would depend on the response from Washington.

In Dwight David Eisenhower and John Foster Dulles, the Republican party and the American people had selected two men extraordinarily well qualified to manage world affairs. Dulles, grandson of one secretary of state, nephew of another, had been active in international politics since the Paris peace conference of 1919. He had been a prominent Republican spokesman on foreign policy issues throughout the years Roosevelt and Truman sat in the White House. Had Thomas Dewey been elected president in 1948, Dulles would have been his secretary of state. Seeking to stave off Republican attacks on policy toward East Asia, Truman had appointed Dulles to a post in the Department of State in 1950 and allowed him primary responsibility for negotiating the peace treaty with Japan. Dulles was intelligent, knowledgeable, experienced, and highly respected at home and abroad.

Eisenhower had been the prominent commander of the allied assault on Europe and the defeat of Hitler's legions. He subsequently served as Supreme Allied Commander, Europe, after the creation of a NATO military force. In both capacities, he had had extensive contact with European leaders and with the Soviets. A stint as president of Columbia University did little to diminish his stature, except among the faculty and students. He was a highly popular, avuncular figure, sought after as a candidate by both major parties. Affecting a posture of being above politics, he seemed the ideal man to put an end to McCarthyism, to calm the anxieties of the American people and reunite the country for the grave domestic and international tasks it confronted in 1953.

Both men, however, were viewed with suspicion by the right wing of their party. Their experience in world affairs, their service under Truman, their popularity with the eastern "internationalist" wing of the Republican party left them suspect. Would the "twenty years of treason" the Right attributed to the Roosevelt and Truman administrations become twenty-one under Eisenhower?

Throughout the campaign of 1952, Eisenhower and Dulles tailored their activities to appease the Right. Eisenhower accepted Richard M. Nixon, a young senator with a reputation for Red-baiting, as his running mate, and assigned Nixon the dirty work of discrediting the Democrats. Eisenhower allowed McCarthy to campaign for him, and stood by silently as McCarthy impugned the loyalty of George Marshall, to whom Eisenhower's career owed so much. Dulles condemned the containment policy of Truman and Acheson as immoral and promised the "liberation of captive nations," the rollback of Soviet influence in Eastern Europe and East Asia. Aware of how anti-Communist hysteria had impaired the Truman administration's ability to govern, Eisenhower and Dulles hoped to deflect the Right with their rhetoric and by appointing a number of the darlings of the Right to nominally important posts. For Eisenhower and Dulles, the dogmatism of the Right created shoals only marginally easier to navigate than those Stalinist dogma left for Khrushchev. The censure of McCarthy by the Senate in 1954 probably provided the administration with less additional leeway than Khrushchev and his allies gained by denouncing Stalin in 1956.

The massive military buildup the United States carried out between 1951 and 1953 had eased fears in the American military and intelligence community of a Soviet nuclear attack in the mid-1950s. American superiority became so obvious that even the normally cautious military leaders, heeding administration bluster, eager to strike at the heart of Communist power, contemplated a preemptive attack against the Soviets. It took Dulles two years to bury the idea. But the enormous increase in military spending worried Eisenhower for other reasons. As an experienced military planner, he considered military budgets to be excessive, far higher than necessary to permit the armed services to perform their missions. As an economic thinker, Eisenhower ranked with Truman – pre-Keynesian, determined to balance the budget, fearful that deficits caused by the arms race would weaken the United States dangerously, resulting in an economic collapse that would leave it vulnerable. As the only postwar president whose views on military budgets were unimpeachable, Eisenhower was uniquely suited to depress the appetite of the Pentagon.[5]

To cut military expenses, Eisenhower revised American Cold War strategy. Whereas the Truman administration, when implementing NSC-68, was attempting to expand both conventional and nuclear forces to meet any Soviet action with overwhelming force of the same kind, Eisenhower's "New Look" stressed air and nuclear power. The historian John Lewis Gaddis has argued that Truman intended a "symmetrical" response, a policy of meeting Soviet probes with comparable force. Eisenhower's strategy implied the possibility of a nuclear response even if the offending Soviet act was carried out by conventional means, of responding in an area other than that chosen by the Soviets – an "asymmetrical" response, designed to seize the initiative for the United States.[6] But at the time, with Gaddis unavailable, Eisenhower relied on Dulles to explain his strategy. Dulles put forward the doctrine of "massive retaliation," the notion that the United States might respond with overwhelming force to the slightest provocation. Others, aware of the president's fiscal conservatism, referred to the "New Look" as "more bang for the buck."

Eisenhower and Dulles were not insensitive to the changes taking place in the Soviet Union but responded cautiously. They were constrained by the intensity of anticommunism in the United States and persuaded that even after Stalin, the Soviet Union would be a dangerous adversary. Nonetheless, they were confident of American power, confident that the Soviets would not challenge NATO. Despite their rhetoric, they had no intention of mounting a military challenge to the Soviet sphere of influence in Eastern Europe. By the mid-1950s, with West Germany in NATO, and Austria free, with impressive economic growth in those countries linked to the Marshall Plan, Eisenhower and Dulles perceived little reason for fear in Europe. With each superpower capable of launching a devastating

5 Marc Trachtenberg, *History and Strategy* (Princeton, 1991), 100–52; Seyom Brown, *Faces of Power* (New York, 1968), 65–75.
6 John L. Gaddis, *Strategies of Containment* (New York, 1982), 147–8.

nuclear strike against the other, they had achieved a stalemate in the central arena of their competition. And the United States still enjoyed an enormous advantage in ability to project power abroad.

The Soviet Union and the United States were preparing to arm themselves with thermonuclear weapons, capable of inflicting incredible damage on each other. With such weapons in place, the illusion of a winnable war faded. The cost of conflict became unacceptably high. Aware of the dangers, leaders in both countries began to develop proposals for arms limitation. They were hampered by mistrust of each other, by internal dissent as to the wisdom of specific proposals or agreement in general, or, on the American side, doubt about the wisdom of even negotiating. Dulles and others feared that sitting down with the Soviets, in addition to arousing the wrath of the domestic Right, might alleviate fear of the Soviet Union and thus weaken the resolve of the American people and their allies. The United States was further handicapped by the inability to find a negotiating position satisfactory to its major allies and, not least, by Eisenhower's apparent ambivalence. And neither Soviets nor Americans seemed able to resist the temptation to seek propaganda advantages.

Despite too frequent suggestions that he viewed nuclear weapons like any others, devices to be used when appropriate – and the implications of his New Look emphasis on such weapons – Eisenhower was eager to find a way both to reduce the danger of nuclear war and to seize the opportunity to respond favorably to the overtures of the new Soviet leaders. After a speech he gave in March 1953 fell flat at home and abroad, he tried again with his "Atoms for Peace" plan, offered to the United Nations in December 1953. Eisenhower called for the nuclear powers to contribute fissionable material to an international agency that would oversee its use for peaceful purposes. Ultimately, his proposal led to creation of the International Atomic Energy Agency, but it had no impact on the arms race. The Soviets perceived the speech as a propaganda ploy, which they countered by repeating their call for a joint declaration banning the atom bomb. The United States did not follow up with any proposal to stop producing weapons or a diplomatic campaign to engage the Soviets in serious discussion of the issues. Eisenhower characteristically seemed satisfied with the applause his speech won, and Dulles had been dubious about the venture from the outset.[7]

A year and a half later, as Eisenhower prepared for his first meeting with the new Soviet leaders, one of his aides came forward with what came to be known as the "Open Skies" proposal. It gained support from men uninterested in arms control who saw an opportunity to gain an intelligence advantage or a propaganda victory over the Soviets. At the summit meeting in July 1955, Eisenhower proposed that each participant give the other a blueprint of its military establishments and permit aerial surveillance adequate to assure that no surprise attack was in preparation. Khrushchev, suspicious of American intentions, perhaps fearful that the United States would learn too much about relative Soviet weakness if granted broad access to Soviet airspace, was not interested. Two years later, however, when the Soviets agreed to a partial version of the aerial inspection proposal, the United States reversed itself. The best Eisenhower and Khrushchev could accomplish was a moratorium on nuclear testing, gingerly reached and unenforceable, but at least an indication that both men recognized the dangers of radioactive fallout and that the two nations, slowly and ineptly, were learning to work together.[8]

The major Soviet goal of the years immediately following the Korean War was a security agreement in Europe, preferably one that gained American recognition of the Soviet sphere of influence in Eastern Europe and protected the Soviet Union against a resurgent Germany. For a neutralized, unarmed Germany, committed to its existing boundaries, Moscow was prepared to offer important concessions, including reunification of both Germany and Austria. Harboring no ambitions in Western Europe, the new Soviet leadership was willing to reduce its armed forces and withdraw its troops from Central Europe, conceivably even much or all of Eastern Europe —

7 Herbert S. Parmet, *Eisenhower and the American Crusades* (New York, 1972), 385–90; McGeorge Bundy, *Danger and Survival* (New York, 1990), 287–95.
8 Gregg Herken, *Counsels of War* (New York, 1987), 108–10, 122; McGeorge Bundy, *Danger and Survival*, 295–305, 328–33.

provided American forces withdrew as well, presumably across the Atlantic.

American strategic thinking was moving in the opposite direction, however. American leaders were convinced that a rearmed Germany, integrated into the Western alliance, was essential to European and ultimately American security. The creation of a European Defense Community (EDC) had been proposed during the Truman administration and the idea was pursued vigorously by Dulles. When the French balked, at least as fearful of potential German power as they were of Soviet, unwilling to have their forces submerged in a multinational force, Dulles threatened an "agonizing reappraisal" of the American role in Europe. Failure of France to ratify the EDC agreement did not deter the United States. In October 1954 the British brokered a new agreement, which narrowly won French approval. Critical among its provisions was a British commitment to send troops to the continent, an American pledge to retain forces in Europe, and German agreement not to challenge post—World War II boundaries or to acquire missiles or nuclear, biological, or chemical weapons without NATO approval. The occupation of the Federal Republic of Germany ended and Germany was invited to join NATO, which it did in May 1955.[9]

The Soviet response to the rearming of Germany and its membership in NATO was astonishingly benign. Initially, Moscow tried to purchase German neutrality with the promise of reunification and demonstrated its bona fides by withdrawing its forces from Austria and allowing a united, free nation to emerge. When that effort failed, the Soviets created an alliance designed to mirror NATO, the Warsaw Pact, to which the Democratic Republic of Germany (East Germany) adhered. Most striking was the Soviet invitation to the West German leader, Konrad Adenauer, to Moscow where he won formal recognition for his country. The Soviet leadership had concluded that a rearmed Germany was tolerable and that accommodation with Adenauer's regime was its wisest course.

In July 1955, the United States, responding to pressures from its

9 Lawrence Kaplan, *NATO and the United States* (Boston, 1988), 62–6; Frank Ninkovich, *Germany and the United States* (Boston, 1988), 90–106.

European allies and to the markedly less threatening Soviet posture, attended a summit meeting in Geneva, where Eisenhower met Khrushchev for the first time and recognized his power (although it was Premier Nikolai Bulganin who was the nominal head of the Soviet delegation). Little of substance was accomplished at the meeting, but the symbolic importance was enormous. Soviet and American leaders were talking for the first time since Potsdam in 1945 and attempting to persuade rather than bludgeon each other. The "spirit of Geneva," the reemergence of the idea that problems might be solved by diplomacy rather than force, was a source of hope to men and women of goodwill everywhere. Once again it was clear that the existing division of Europe was acceptable to both sides. War was unnecessary as well as unthinkable.

Despite the failure of a foreign ministers' conference that followed the summit, the year after the Eisenhower-Khrushchev encounter was marked by further indications that the Cold War might be winding down. In February 1956, Khrushchev delivered his famous speech to the Twentieth Party Congress, denouncing Stalin and endorsing peaceful coexistence. In April, Mikoyan announced dissolution of the Cominform, relinquishing Moscow's claim to control of all foreign Communist parties. In May, the Soviets reported major troop reductions, from 4 million to 2.8 million. Stalinist Russia was slowly being dismantled and the Soviets were changing both their approach to world affairs and the nature of the regime. As fear drained out of Europe and the anti-Communist crusaders in the United States perceived a shrinking target, Dulles and other advisers to the president worried about the loss of American resolve. [10]

Events in Eastern Europe soon tested the limits of Soviet tolerance and rescued those Americans determined not to drop their guard. In Poland and in Hungary demands for an end to Soviet domination erupted in riots in the summer of 1956. The Poles won the right to a Communist leader of their own choosing, but the Hungarians, encouraged by Voice of America and Radio Free Europe broadcasts,

---

10 Walter LaFeber, *America, Russia, and the Cold War, 1945–1984*, 5th ed. (New York, 1985), 182–3; Paul Y. Hammond, *Cold War and Détente* (New York, 1975), 97.

pushed harder, tried to withdraw from the Warsaw Pact, and were crushed by Soviet tanks. Much of the world was appalled by the uneven struggle of young Hungarians defending their government with rocks and broomsticks against tanks and machine guns, but no one came to their rescue. For all its prattle about "Captive Nations" and "liberation," the Eisenhower administration would not risk World War III by intervening in the Soviet sphere of influence, where Soviet interests were vital and the Soviets were certain to fight.

Soviet actions in Hungary, like Stalin's in Berlin and Korea, were a boon to those determined to maintain a high level of readiness to fight the Soviet Union. They were able to discount Soviet willingness to compromise in Poland and Soviet willingness to accept a considerable degree of diversity among Communist states. They were able to brush aside "de-Stalinization" and argue that all the perceived changes were cosmetic or tactical, that the United States still confronted a brutal, ruthless, totalitarian enemy, unyielding in its determination to dominate the world. And when the Soviets succeeded in winning the space race, sending Sputnik, the first space capsule, into orbit in 1957, Eisenhower was dismayed to find himself under attack for disregarding the security of the United States, for putting a price limit on American defense.

The Eisenhower-Dulles campaign promise to be more assertive in East Asia had pleased the American Right, especially the friends of Chiang Kai-shek. Visions of rolling back the Communists and restoring their idol to power on the Chinese mainland danced in their minds. But Eisenhower was eager to disengage American forces from the Asian mainland, determined to terminate the war in Korea, and contain communism in the region with threatening gestures from offshore. Neither he nor Dulles trusted Chiang and they were apprehensive of his schemes to return from his refuge on Taiwan to the mainland. They recognized his eagerness to use American troops to accomplish what his own could not and had no intention of indulging him. Had the domestic political climate been less inhibiting, Eisenhower would have sought accommodation with the People's Republic of China. He argued publicly against the trade embargo and ultimately forced the Washington bureaucracy and Congress to accept a relaxation of trade restrictions on Japanese and European trade with China. Qing Simei, a Chinese historian, has discovered that the Eisenhower administration secretly permitted American firms to trade with China through their Canadian subsidiaries.[11]

American policy toward East Asia in the Eisenhower administration was remarkably similar to that devised by the Truman administration, both in assumptions and goals. Both the president and his secretary of state considered East Asia less important than Europe. They were unwilling, nonetheless, to acquiesce in the expansion of communism, which they equated with Soviet influence, and prepared to use American power and influence, short of a major troop involvement, to halt the Red tide. They were trapped moreover by their rhetoric, by their promises to be more aggressive than their predecessors.

In East Asia, the principal threat perceived by Washington emanated from Beijing. Eisenhower and Dulles knew China was not a Soviet puppet and were very much interested in the possibility of fomenting friction between the two Communist giants. After Chinese intervention in Korea, the intensity of public hostility to the Chinese Communists, whipped up by Chiang's supporters in Congress and the media, the so-called China Lobby, prevented the administration from attempting to woo the Chinese away from the Soviets by friendly gestures. Convinced that he had little choice but to exude belligerence toward Mao and his followers, Dulles worked out an elaborate justification for intensifying the pressure on the Chinese. He hoped that their demands on the Soviets might be so great as to anger the Soviets whose failure to respond adequately would alienate the Chinese. Increased pressure rather than American generosity would shatter the Sino-Soviet alliance. But when the

11 Nancy B. Tucker, "John Foster Dulles and the Taiwan Roots of the Two Chinas Policy," in Richard H. Immerman, ed., *John Foster Dulles and the Diplomacy of the Cold War* (Princeton, 1990), 236–62; Qing Simei, "The Eisenhower Administration and Changes in Western Embargo Policy Against China," in Warren I. Cohen and Akira Iriye, eds., *The Great Powers in East Asia, 1953–1960* (New York, 1990), 121–42.

Chinese, eager to lessen their dependence on the Soviets, reached out to the United States, Dulles was unwilling or unable to respond, revealing the sterility of his policy. [12]

The first post-Korean crisis in the region came in Indochina, where the Vietnamese were fighting for their independence from the French empire. American anticommunism proved stronger than American antiimperialism. Eager for French support for the rearming of Germany and European integration against the Soviets generally, the United States had become, by 1953, an active supporter of France against the Vietnamese Communist–led revolutionaries. Proponents of American assistance to the French effort in Indochina also argued that the region's strategic resources had to be kept out of Communist hands, that its markets were essential to the viability of the Japanese economy. Aid to the French, begun before the Korean War, accelerated after it. American consciences were assuaged by giving much of the material support directly to Vietnamese who were collaborating with the French, an effort to distance the United States from French imperialism. But American money and equipment did not suffice. By March 1954, the French faced certain defeat and ultimate expulsion, unless American military forces came to their rescue.

As the French prepared to make their last stand at Dienbienphu, Eisenhower and Dulles contemplated intervention. General Nathan Twining, Air Force chief of staff, was persuaded that a few small nuclear bombs dropped on Vietnamese forces in the hills overlooking the French camp would turn the tide of battle. Admiral Arthur Radford, chairman of the Joint Chiefs of Staff, naval aviator, thought a carrier task force would be ideal for the assignment. General Matthew Ridgway, Army chief of staff, the man who had cleaned up after MacArthur in Korea, argued that air power would not suffice,

---

12 David Mayers, "Eisenhower and Communism: Later Findings," in Richard A. Melanson and David Mayers, eds., *Reevaluating Eisenhower* (Urbana, Ill., 1987), 88–120; John Lewis Gaddis, "The American 'Wedge' Strategy, 1949–55," in Harry Harding and Yuan Ming, eds., *Sino-American Relations, 1945–1955* (Wilmington, Del., 1989), 157–83.

that a half-million American troops would probably be necessary, and that it would be a mistake to put them on the Asian mainland. Eisenhower was not eager to send troops, but he was unwilling to abandon Indochina to the Communists. Conceding that Indochina was itself of marginal importance to the United States, he outlined what came to be known as his "domino theory": If Indochina fell, the remaining states of Southeast Asia would fall one after another, like a row of dominoes. Wisely, however, the president insisted on prior congressional approval, a British agreement to join forces with the United States, and a French commitment to grant independence to Vietnam as preconditions for American intervention, none of which was forthcoming. The United States did not intervene militarily and the French were defeated at Dienbienphu in May, on the eve of great power talks on Indochina at a conference in Geneva. [13]

Ho Chi Minh's forces had won a great victory in their long struggle for freedom from French imperialism, but the accords that emerged from the Geneva Conference in February did not reflect the triumph adequately. A truce was arranged between Vietnamese and French forces. Vietnam was partitioned *temporarily* to enable the combatants to disengage on either side of the seventeenth parallel. The temporary partition, to be followed by a nationwide election in 1956, was forced on Ho by his erstwhile Soviet and Chinese supporters, the former hoping to curry favor with France and the latter fearful that Vietnamese recalcitrance might bring American intervention and jeopardize their interests in the region. But Ho could count on an easy victory in the election and accepted the delay in the creation of a united, independent Vietnam.

The United States participated in the Geneva Conference but did not sign the accords, promising only that it would not upset them by force. Immediately, however, the American government set about subverting the agreement, substituting American influence for French and attempting to convert the truce line into a permanent

13 Melanie Billings-Yun, *Decision Against War* (New York, 1988); George C. Herring and Richard H. Immerman, "Eisenhower, Dulles, and Dienbienphu: 'The Day We Didn't Go to War,' Revisited," *Journal of American History* 71 (1984): 343–63; Marilyn Young, *The Vietnam Wars, 1945–1990* (New York, 1991), 33–4.

boundary. The United States tried to create a separate Vietnamese state in the south, intended to be part of the anti-Communist bloc. There would be no election to unify Vietnam in 1956. Communism would be contained at the seventeenth parallel, with a southern Vietnamese regime, Cambodia, and Laos becoming American protectorates. None of these nations was of particular importance to the United States, but through use of the domino analogy, the idea that the fall of any one of them would result in the "loss" of all of Southeast Asia, Eisenhower had invested each tiny state with the importance of the entire region. Declining to intervene militarily but refusing to accept Communist domination of Indochina, the Eisenhower administration directed the United States deeper into the quagmire.[14]

A few weeks after the Geneva Conference, in September 1954, the United States staged a fateful meeting in Manila. There, under Dulles's supervision, the Southeast Asian Treaty Organization (SEATO) was created to provide for the region's security. The United States joined Great Britain, France, Australia, New Zealand, Thailand, the Philippines, and Pakistan in an attempt to deter the further expansion of Communist influence in the area, with specific reference to southern Vietnam, Cambodia, and Laos. India and Indonesia, the most important states of South and Southeast Asia, rejected membership, as did Burma. Obviously, SEATO was but a shadow analogue of NATO, but Washington now claimed a legal basis for intervention. Ho and Mao were forewarned.

One issue that plagued Eisenhower and Dulles was the shape of the security relationship with the Republic of China, Chiang's rump regime on Taiwan. Chiang's friends, including Walter Robertson, assistant secretary of state for Far Eastern affairs, had long urged including Taiwan in some kind of mutual defense pact. Most of the other SEATO participants were adamantly opposed to so obvious a provocation to Beijing. A bilateral pact seemed to be the only option and Robertson pressed the idea on a reluctant Dulles. As the histo-

14 Richard H. Immerman, "Between the Unattainable and the Unacceptable: Eisenhower and Dienbienphu," in Melanson and Mayers, *Reevaluating Eisenhower,* 120–54; George McT. Kahin, *Intervention* (New York, 1986), 66–92.

rian Nancy Bernkopf Tucker has demonstrated, Dulles mistrusted Chiang profoundly.[15] He was convinced the Chinese Nationalist leader was searching for a way to entangle the United States in a war with the Chinese Communists, a war in which Americans would fight and die to facilitate Chiang's triumphant return to the mainland. Chiang was frustrated and angered by his failure to obtain the desired treaty. But a miscalculation by Mao forced Dulles into Chiang's embrace.

Uneasy about the creation of SEATO, fearful of an alliance between Chiang's government and the United States, Mao chose to precipitate a crisis in the Taiwan Straits, beginning with the bombardment of Nationalist-held islands a few miles from the mainland of China. The Chinese scholar He Di has argued that Mao and his colleagues were unaware of tensions between Taibei and Washington.[16] They perceived an American plot to separate Taiwan from the mainland permanently. Chinese leaders thought they could forestall the alliance by demonstrating its potential danger to the Americans: the danger of becoming embroiled in a war over tiny islands within reach of mainland batteries. Eisenhower and Dulles understood the message and took the necessary precautions when negotiating the alliance with Chiang, but they refused to be intimidated. Mao's display of power proved to be counterproductive.

Chiang won his treaty but at a very high price. He had to surrender the right to attack the mainland without the consent of the United States and he could not commit the United States to the defense of any of the offshore islands still manned by his troops. Before the crisis ended, he was forced to evacuate the Dachen Islands. Jinmen and Mazu (Quemoy and Matsu) remained under Nationalist control, but the Americans would defend them only if Washington perceived a threat to Taiwan itself. Chiang was further angered in March 1955 when Dulles told him to stop telling his people that their return to the mainland was imminent. The mutual defense treaty to which the Americans agreed was designed not only

15 Tucker, "John Foster Dulles and the Taiwan Roots of the Two Chinas Policy."
16 He Di, "The Evolution of the People's Republic of China's Policy Toward the Offshore Islands," in Cohen and Iriye, *Great Powers in East Asia*, 222–45.

to deter a Communist attack against Taiwan but also as a means of insuring Washington's control over Chiang.

Eisenhower and Dulles remained apprehensive of war with China, uncertain of Mao's intentions. An effort to obtain a UN-supervised cease-fire in the straits was rejected by Chinese on both sides. America's allies and much of the rest of the world appeared horrified by Dulles's willingness to risk war over Jinmen and Mazu. The administration had no illusions about the importance of the islands, but Eisenhower feared that if the Nationalists were forced to withdraw from them, their morale would drop precipitously and American credibility would suffer throughout Asia. Once again, Eisenhower, in a variation on his domino theory, invested territory of little strategic import with enormous weight: If the United States let the Chinese Communists seize Jinmen and Mazu, the Taiwan regime might collapse, much of Asia might turn to the Communists, the Cold War might be lost. "For want of a nail . . . " The solution Eisenhower and Dulles hit upon was atomic blackmail, indirect warnings to the Chinese that they would use nuclear weapons to defend the islands.

The Chinese, however, had already pushed as far as they had intended and were not prepared to invade Jinmen and Mazu. Their effort to prevent the mutual defense treaty between the United States and the Republic of China had failed, but they had succeeded in alarming many of America's allies, especially Europeans unwilling to participate in a third world war precipitated by a confrontation over the islands. Having gained Washington's attention, the Chinese offered to negotiate existing differences with the United States, including the release of Americans held in China and Chinese stranded in the United States when the two countries became enemies in 1950. When the United States agreed to ambassadorial level talks in the summer of 1955, the crisis passed.

After a quick agreement on the exchange of each other's nationals, the talks degenerated into a stalemate on the Taiwan issue. The United States demanded that China renounce the right to use force to seize the island and China refused. To Mao and his comrades in Beijing, the Taiwan issue was a domestic issue, unfinished business in a civil war. They hinted broadly that force would not be used, stressed the likelihood of peaceful liberation of the island, but would not give the explicit assurances the United States required. Hemmed in by Chiang's supporters in the United States, accepting as reality his own rationalization for a policy of maintaining pressure on the People's Republic, Dulles evidenced no flexibility. In the summer of 1957, despite Chinese efforts to continue the dialogue, the United States broke off the talks.

In Beijing the initiative passed to those Chinese leaders, Mao among them, who preferred a more aggressive approach. Buoyed by Soviet successes in the space race, Mao contended that the time had come for a bold Communist offensive against imperialism. He found Khrushchev unresponsive. Khrushchev, too, was confident that the tide was running his way, but he had no illusions about American power or Soviet vulnerability. He did not want a confrontation, certainly not one of China's choosing. Contemptuous of Khrushchev's prudence, Mao chose his own moment. In late August 1958, China initiated a campaign to seize Jinmen and Mazu, precipitating a second crisis in the Taiwan Straits.[17]

Chiang had used the intervening years to reinforce his garrisons on the offshore islands, deliberately raising the stakes to compel the United States to protect the islands. Eisenhower and Dulles tried unsuccessfully to get Chiang to withdraw his troops – and then decided they would be forced to come to the rescue. Once again, the Americans threatened to use nuclear weapons against China, and sent over a hundred warships including seven carriers to the straits. Khrushchev warned Washington that the Soviet Union would retaliate if the United States launched a nuclear strike. Fortunately, Chiang's air force was able to achieve supremacy over the islands, staving off the attack without an American offensive against the Chinese mainland.

Having gained the attention of the United States, Mao backed off. Quickly, he demonstrated his capacity for self-delusion by discovering that retreat was an act of genius: To have succeeded in capturing the islands would have eliminated Taiwan's last links to the mainland and contributed to the permanent division of China.

17 He Di, "The Evolution of PRC Policy Toward the Offshore Islands."

By allowing Chiang to retain control of the islands, he had thwarted Washington's "two Chinas" plot. [18]

The Americans indicated their willingness to resume discussions. Responding to public outrage at home and abroad over the administration's willingness to risk world war over Jinmen and Mazu, Dulles openly criticized Chiang and began to explore the possibility of recognizing the Beijing government. Nothing substantial came of the renewed conversations between the two governments, but diplomacy had advantages over threats, especially if there was to be any hope of persuading China to abide by existing norms of international behavior. Dulles's policy of isolation and pressure increased the likelihood of China behaving irresponsibly and dangerously. Regularly scheduled ambassadorial conversations provided a mechanism for venting rage, providing and obtaining explanations, exploring and even inching toward resolution of differences.

Mao's tactics in the straits crises troubled Khrushchev perhaps as much as they did the Americans. Much like Eisenhower, the Soviet leader worried about his nation's credibility. He could not stand by idly while the United States pummeled his principal ally – not without sending the wrong message to uncommitted nations the Soviets were wooing. No Third World ruler could be expected to cast his lot with the Soviet Union if the Soviets could not be relied upon for protection. On the other hand, if the Soviet Union was to risk its own destruction in a nuclear confrontation with the United States, Khrushchev wanted to be sure that he was in control, that war would come over an issue he deemed worth fighting and dying for, and at a time and place of his choosing. But Mao – jealous of his prerogatives as leader of a great nation and capable of provoking war – was not amenable to Soviet advice. And perhaps worst of all, Soviet scientists and technicians were in China helping the Chinese to build an atom bomb!

Gradually the ties that bound the Communist giants began to fray. Soviet advice designed to moderate Chinese policy, to avoid provocation, irritated Mao. Soviet offers of military advisers and

18 He Di, "The Evolution of PRC Policy Toward the Offshore Islands"; Thomas E. Stolper, *China, Taiwan, and the Offshore Islands* (New York, 1985), 124–30.

requests for submarine basing rights and a radio station on Chinese soil to broadcast to Soviet submarines aroused Mao's suspicions. The terms of Soviet economic and technical assistance did not satisfy Mao. In the late 1950s Soviet foreign policy generally evoked Mao's contempt, and Soviet domestic policies, specifically de-Staliniization, did little to warm his heart. Khrushchev's suggestion that Beijing accept the two Chinas policy toward which the United States had moved struck at the core of Mao's intense nationalism, confirmed Mao's sense of Soviet indifference to China's interests, and may have precipitated the break. Angry exchanges, focused primarily on differences over ideological matters, led to Khrushchev's recall of Soviet technicians in 1959 and his effort to scuttle China's atom bomb project. [19]

The Eisenhower administration, however, could not devise a policy to capitalize on the long-desired Sino-Soviet split when it finally occurred. Anticommunism, the containment of communism, did not provide a useful framework for exploiting a situation in which the two major Communist powers were at each other's throats. With Dulles's death early in 1959 and Eisenhower weary of Asian affairs, there were no new initiatives coming out of Washington in 1959 or 1960. Only a growing involvement in Indochina and awareness of a falling domino in Laos marked Eisenhower's last days in office.

If Mao's assertiveness complicated life in the Kremlin, some American allies did what they could to prevent complacency in Washington. Foremost of these was Charles de Gaulle, the imperious French leader, who returned to power in 1958 and objected strenuously to what he perceived as Anglo-American control of NATO, and the relegation of France to an inferior role. He raised a question fundamental to the alliance in an era when the Soviets were preparing to deploy intercontinental ballistic missiles: Would the United States risk a nuclear attack on its own cities by responding to a Soviet attack on Western Europe? Unpersuaded by American assurances, he

19 Edward Crankshaw and Strobe Talbott, *Khrushchev Remembers* (Boston, 1970), 463–71; John Wilson Lewis and Xue Litai, *China Builds the Bomb* (Stanford, Calif., 1988), 60–72.

developed an independent nuclear force for France. Dissatisfied by American unwillingness to share responsibility for directing the alliance, he began to withdraw French forces from NATO control. France remained a loyal ally but very much on de Gaulle's terms.

Less dramatically, the Japanese, too, became more assertive in the 1950s. Freed of the forces of occupation in 1952, secured from external threat by alliance with the United States, Japan concentrated on rapid economic growth, aided by profits from supply and support services it provided during the Korean War. The Japanese wanted access to American and Chinese markets and persuaded Eisenhower to support them. The president perceived Japan's economic stability as essential to American security interests. He argued frequently against protectionism in the United States and against posing obstacles to Japan's trade with Beijing. The bureaucracy procrastinated, and Eisenhower did little to prod it, but he opened whatever doors were under presidential control.[20]

The Japanese were also eager to regain territories lost to the Soviet Union at the close of World War II and toward that end responded to a Soviet initiative and reestablished diplomatic relations with Moscow in 1956. Dulles was apprehensive and did what he could to obstruct a Soviet-Japanese rapprochement, but it was the inability of the Soviet and Japanese negotiators to reach an acceptable compromise on the territorial question that kept the two nations apart for many years to follow.

Nonetheless, Japanese assertiveness worried American intelligence analysts who warned that Japan might dissociate itself from the West unless the United States allowed for greater equality in bilateral relations. Japanese public anger over American nuclear testing in the Pacific was intense in the mid-1950s, especially after the crew of the Japanese fishing boat *Lucky Dragon* was irradiated by a thermonuclear test on Bikini atoll in March 1954. In 1960, anti-

---

20 Warren I. Cohen, "China in Japanese-American Relations," in Akira Iriye and Warren I. Cohen, eds., *The United States and Japan in the Postwar World* (Lexington, Ky., 1989), 36–60; Qing, "The Eisenhower Administration and Changes in Western Embargo Policy Against China, 1954–1958," and Burton I. Kaufman, "Eisenhower's Foreign Economic Policy with Respect to East Asia," both in Cohen and Iriye, *Great Powers in East Asia,* 121–42, 104–20.

American riots in Japan, organized by opponents of the renewal of the Japanese-American security treaty, reflected pacifist and neutralist tendencies. There was cause for alarm in Washington.[21]

Much of the world, of course, went about its business with minimal regard for the antics of the United States, the Soviet Union, and their respective allies. The ethnic and religious strife, the class struggles and instability that have always been the stuff of human existence persisted, quite apart from the Cold War, quite apart from great power politics. But as the United States and the Soviet Union acquired the ability to project their power all over the globe and as they achieved an uneasy balance in the areas of vital concern, such as Europe, the superpowers began to intervene in local struggles in Latin America, the Middle East, and Africa, as well as Asia. Some of the American and Soviet activity could be justified strategically, especially if one accepted variations on the domino theme or fretted about credibility. Some of it involved vital economic interests, such as American concern for the oil of the Middle East. Some of it was merely mechanical: The power to intervene existed; use it, demonstrate it, experiment with it.

Eisenhower was relatively relaxed about the struggle for control of the Third World. Concerned primarily with European affairs, he did not believe America's future rested upon the outcome of the struggle for dominance over distant, undeveloped, tribal societies. But there were those dominoes and the need to contain communism. Sometimes, Third World countries were important sources of raw materials, most obviously oil, or potential trading partners for the United States or Japan or Western Europe. Brandishing nuclear weapons might protect American interests when the Soviets or Chinese were involved and demonstrations of power might suffice in other situations. And there was another, rather less well-defined tool at hand: covert operations, a less familiar device whose potential intrigued him.

21 Cohen, "China in Japanese-American Relations," 47; Roger Dingman, "Alliance in Crisis: The Lucky Dragon Incident and Japanese-American Relations," in Cohen and Iriye, *Great Powers in East Asia*, 187–214; George R. Packard, III, *Protest in Tokyo* (Princeton, 1966).

One of the administration's first major Third World interventions occurred in Guatemala, a Caribbean state assumed to be within the American sphere of influence, off limits to any other great power. Latin America was the lowest priority for American military leaders because Soviet intervention in the region was deemed highly unlikely. And, indeed, there was no evidence of Soviet involvement in Guatemala. There was, however, a nationalist, reformist government that had come to power by constitutional means, and had dared to expropriate holdings of the United Fruit Company an American-based firm that was a major force in Guatemalan politics as well as in the economy. The government unquestionably had the support of the handful of Communists in the country, but it was neither Communist-controlled nor -led.[22]

The Guatemalan president, Colonel Jacobo Arbenz Guzman, rejected State Department demands for compensation deemed adequate by United Fruit and was generally unresponsive to American pressure. Prodded by United Fruit executives, the American government determined that Arbenz's recalcitrance and labor unrest in United Fruit operations elsewhere in Central America were Communist-inspired. The cancer of communism had appeared in the American sphere, and it would have to be excised quickly. The Central Intelligence Agency (CIA) developed plans to remedy the situation.

As American pressure mounted and Arbenz learned of a scheme for an exile invasion of Guatemala, he searched desperately for arms, ultimately risking all by turning to the Soviet Union. The Soviets responded favorably to what was probably perceived as a low-cost, low-risk opportunity to worry the United States. In due course the CIA discovered that a shipment of Czech arms was en route to Guatemala, a public relations coup for those who saw international communism behind Guatemalan reforms. A CIA-organized raid (150 men and a handful of planes) followed, and the Arbenz government collapsed. An American-supported regime seized power in Guatemala and soon turned the country into one of the most repres-

22 My discussion of Guatemala derives largely from Richard Immerman's *The CIA in Guatemala* (Austin, Tex., 1982). See also Stephen Rabe, "Dulles, Latin America, and Cold War Anticommunism," in Immerman, *Dulles and Diplomacy of the Cold War*, 159–87.

sive in the world. From Washington's perspective, it had won an important victory over communism, an important victory in the Cold War, at minimal cost and almost without showing its hand. The Guatemalan operation was impressive evidence of what could be accomplished by covert operations.

Judaism, Christianity, and Islam all had their roots in the Middle East. For centuries Christians and Muslims fought for control of the Holy Land. For centuries Jews in the diaspora called for a return to Jerusalem as part of their Passover celebration. Secular Jewish nationalism, Zionism, emerged in Europe late in the nineteenth century and a few thousand Jews trickled into Palestine in the years that followed. The British, who took control of Palestine from the Ottoman Empire during World War I, made conflicting promises to the Arab Muslims who lived there and to the European Jews who sought a homeland there. After the Holocaust, the German murder of 6 million Jews during World War II, American and British leaders saw Palestine as a convenient refuge for the Jewish survivors of the Nazi death camps. Palestinian Arabs and the Arabs of neighboring states forcibly opposed the UN decision to partition Palestine in order to create a Jewish homeland there. In April 1948, the Jews declared the existence of the state of Israel on that part of Palestine allotted to them by the United Nations. A major war followed, in which the Jews, thanks in part to arms provided by Soviet-dominated Czechoslovakia, prevailed over vastly larger Arab armies and created a state even larger than the United Nations had intended. The state of Israel had won the first round in an Arab-Israeli conflict that was to plague the region for decades to come.

Some American leaders, such as Harry Truman, seem to have been genuinely sympathetic to the living skeletons that emerged from Auschwitz and Buchenwald. They were responsive to the pleas of Zionists who argued that the Jewish people required their own state, to protect them from the persecution, the pogroms, and the massacres that had befallen them too often in Europe. They were also conscious of the fact that in the aftermath of the Holocaust, there was enormous public support among American Christians as well as Jews for the creation of a Jewish homeland. Politicians were not unaware that there were votes to be gained from supporting creation of the state of Israel, from being quick to recognize it. And, in the election campaign of 1948, despite an effort to keep the issue out of partisan politics, Truman moved hastily to recognize Israel, undermining efforts by the American UN delegation to find a peaceful solution to the partition question.

Other American leaders, urging the president to put sentiment aside, argued that the national interest required the United States to align itself with the Arabs. The Middle East, loosely defined as Arab North Africa, the Arabian peninsula, and Southwest Asia, contained an enormous percentage of the world's estimated oil reserves. The area was almost entirely Muslim, largely Arab, and broadly hostile to the encroachment of Europeans. Support for a handful of Jews would alienate many millions of Muslims who controlled the strategic crossroads connecting three continents – and those vast quantities of oil. Kennan, who had shown himself strikingly insensitive to Jewish suffering, proved much more sensitive to the arguments of Arabists within the Department of State. Robert Lovett, undersecretary of state in 1948, worried about Soviet sympathizers among the Jewish refugees and ineptly warned Truman against "buying a pig in a poke" by accepting a Jewish state.

In brief, the Middle East, in the half-century following World War II, was an extraordinarily important repository of oil upon which the United States increasingly, and its European and Japanese friends to a much greater extent, were dependent. It was the site of the Arab-Israeli clash that rapidly became one of history's most intractable conflicts. And, with part of it constituting the rimland of the Soviet empire, it was, inevitably, a critical arena for the Soviet-American confrontation.

The Truman administration had responded sharply to Soviet pressures on Iran and Turkey and formulated the Truman Doctrine to prevent Communist guerrillas from overthrowing the Greek government. It had demonstrated the intent of the United States to succeed to the British role in the region and to deny the legitimacy of Soviet aspirations there. Stalin's blatant imperialism, his attempts to appropriate territory belonging to Iran and Turkey, were obviously objectionable, and relatively easy to counter. His meddling in the Arab-Israeli war of 1948, apparently intended to aggravate Britain's problems as regional hegemon, was more difficult to counter, more worrisome. It was Soviet economic and military support for Middle Eastern states that posed the threat to American interests in the area after Stalin's death.

The quest for freedom from the European imperialists who had dominated the region since the late nineteenth century united politically mobile Arabs. Iranians, Muslims but not Arabs, were equally restive. By 1947, Great Britain was drawing back; the French were more tenacious, but the process of decolonization ground on, slower in some places than others, but inexorably. The Soviets, forced to ease pressure on Turkey and Iran, displeased by the appeal to Soviet Jews of the Zionist state they had helped create, ignorant of and uninterested in the Arab world, were quiescent in the Middle East in the late 1940s and early 1950s. The United States, historically uninvolved, traditionally antiimperialist, perceived as nonthreatening by local nationalists, utilized its capabilities to project power by moving into the vacuum.

From the outset, the motives for American intervention in the Middle East were mixed, an extension of the nation's antiimperialist mission combined with determination to block Soviet expansion. American leaders were not willing to work toward the end of British and French imperialism to facilitate Soviet imperialism. Support for Israel was an irritating complication, driven by humanitarian and domestic political concerns – and a fervent prayer that somehow it could be reconciled with concrete interests. The men in Washington did what they thought they had to do for Israel and hoped for the best. The complexity of regional issues proved overwhelming, however. The Arab-Israeli conflict could not be isolated from the Soviet-American rivalry. Nor could a historic commitment to antiimperialism inoculate Americans against the virus of imperialism when the opportunity appeared.

American policy toward Iran in the early 1950s is highly illustrative of the corrupting influence of imperial responsibilities. The Soviet threat to Iran's territorial integrity and independence had been countered successfully in 1946. The British had withdrawn their forces from Iran almost immediately after the war. But British interest in Iranian oil remained intense and the British continued to control Iran's oil long after the troops were gone. When tensions arose between an Iranian nationalist regime determined to command its own resources and the British, the United States tried to mediate. Efforts by the Truman administration to broker an Anglo-Iranian compromise failed and the Iranian government continued to assert itself in a number of disturbing directions.

Washington came to fear that Communist influence was growing in Tehran, that Mohammed Mossadegh, the Iranian prime minister, might allow his country to slip under Soviet control. It was an unlikely scenario, but the Eisenhower administration was unwilling to allow Iran to alienate itself from the West. Like any nineteenth-century imperial power exercising suzerainty over a client state, the United States decided to replace the Iranian leadership. Covertly, with the assistance of British operatives, the American Central Intelligence Agency facilitated a military coup in August 1953, resulting in the arrest of Mossadegh and the shift of power in Iran to the Shah. For many years afterward, the Shah responded to American needs with appropriate gratitude, including a 40 percent share for American companies in a new international consortium to manage Iranian oil production. His own people fared less well.[23]

As Eisenhower, Dulles, and their advisers surveyed the world, they noted that the Middle East constituted a gap in the network of alliances with which they were determined to encircle the Communist bloc. Between Turkey and Pakistan sat the Arab world, Iran, and two-thirds of the oil reserves accessible to the West – all terribly vulnerable to a Soviet thrust. The Truman administration had recognized the danger but failed in its effort to enroll Egypt in a Middle East defense command. Egypt remained uninterested and opposed to any Arab nation aligning itself with the West. Nonetheless, it was time to complete the circle. Turkey was eager to strengthen its eastern flank against the Soviets. Iraq saw an opportunity to protect

23 Barry Rubin, *Paved with Good Intentions* (New York, 1980), 54–90; George
   Lenczowski, *American Presidents and the Middle East* (Durham, N.C., 1990), 32–
   40.

itself against possible Soviet pressures while simultaneously alleviating its dependence on the British. Pakistan perceived an opportunity to obtain military aid more likely to be needed against India than the Soviet Union. As the Americans and British hovered in the background, desirous of proceeding, but still groping for a formula that would not enrage the Israelis and Egyptians, the Turks seized the initiative. In February 1956, Turkey and Iraq signed what came to be called the Baghdad Pact, to which the British, Pakistanis, and Iranians adhered in the course of the year. Unable to pacify Israelis or Egyptians, both resentful of Iraqi access to Western military aid, the United States never joined what became the Middle East Treaty Organization (METO), although it was the principal source of the group's support.[24]

With Turkey, Iran, and Iraq linked to each other and individually to the United States, the Soviet bloc was, nominally, ringed by hostile nations, all receiving military assistance from or protected by the Americans. But for most denizens of the Middle East, including Iraqis, the Soviet threat was imperceptible. Western, especially British, imperialism had blighted their lives for generations. They preferred to assert themselves against Western imperialism and Zionism, which they perceived as its most recent manifestation. Only the Turks and Iranians had experienced Soviet pressures, and many Iranians were at least as unhappy with the Americans who had deposed Mossadegh. There was little popular support for the containment of the Soviet Union. On the other hand, there was a vast quantity of combustible material waiting to be ignited by a leader who would strike out against Israel and reverse the decades of humiliation by the West.

The man most likely to lead the Arab world to renewed glory and respect was Gamal Abdul Nasser of Egypt. Nasser emerged as master of Egypt after a group of young officers, appalled by defeat in the 1948 war with Israel and evidence of government corruption and incompetence, overthrew a decadent king in 1952. Nasser and his colleagues were quick to demand elimination of European restrictions on Egyptian sovereignty, and the British had neither the will

24 John C. Campbell, *Defense of the Middle East* (New York, 1960), 49–62.

nor the resources to resist. The United States, sympathetic to Egyptian aspirations, impressed favorably by Nasser and eager to win his friendship, favored the initial British retreat. Nasser's satisfaction with the American position did not extend to the point of willingness to be enlisted in the containment of the Soviet Union; nor did he prove willing to moderate the anti-Israeli and antiimperialist rhetoric so popular in the Arab world. [25]

The Baghdad Pact angered the many Arabs who preached non-alignment in the Cold War, but Nasser especially. Iraq was undermining his vision of rejecting Western hegemony and uniting the Arab peoples under his leadership. The West was enhancing the power of his rival, maintaining Western influence in the region. Nasser was not unaware that the Soviet Union was equally unhappy about the pact and increasingly supportive of the Arabs against both Israel and the West in the United Nations and in its propaganda. When Israel launched a devastating and humiliating raid into Egyptian-controlled territory in February 1955, in retaliation for commando raids originating there, Nasser decided to turn to the Soviets for help.

Khrushchev, unlike Stalin, was definitely interested in competing with the United States for influence among the Arabs. Confident of the superiority of the Soviet system, unburdened by commitment to Israel, sharing Arab hostility to Western imperialism, Khrushchev and his colleagues accepted the challenge of the Baghdad Pact and the opportunity Nasser provided. The Soviets were prepared to supply economic and military assistance to nonaligned leaders who sought an alternative to dependence on the West or a more radical model for rapid development of their countries. In September 1955, arrangements were concluded for arms manufactured in Czechoslovakia to be shipped to Egypt. By inducing Iraq to join in the American-led effort to contain the Soviet Union, the United States had facilitated Soviet penetration of the region, giving the Soviets an opportunity to befriend Iraq's rival, Egypt.

As Nasser's relations with the Communist bloc warmed, the United States continued to court him. For Nasser and leaders of

25 Campbell, *Defense of the Middle East,* 63–72.

other nonaligned states who mastered the art, it was a delightful situation. The competing superpowers were manipulated with varying degrees of artistry. American and Soviet leaders sang the virtues of a wide range of African and Asian rulers and contributed generously of their treasure, their technology, and their guns. With Czech arms on the way, Nasser found the Americans (and the British) eager to build a dam for him, to help him subdue the Nile, and to use its power to irrigate and electrify the Nile Valley. He wanted the aid, but with Soviet assistance also available, he saw no need to trim his sails to comfort the Americans. The arms deal, perceived as a slap at the West, had enhanced Nasser's stature among the Arab masses. He promised them he would do something unpleasant to Israel. To demonstrate further his independence from the United States, he brushed aside American pleas to the contrary and recognized the People's Republic of China in May 1956.[26]

There were many in the U.S. Congress who did not like giving money to foreigners. There were Southern congressmen unwilling to subsidize cotton-growing nations such as Egypt. There was a substantial number of congressmen and women who did not like giving aid to countries that threatened Israel. And there was also a congressional bloc sympathetic to Chiang Kai-shek and utterly opposed to assisting any country that recognized the People's Republic of China. Giving foreign aid to countries that demonstrated no gratitude, that performed in a manner contrary to American wishes, was not politically popular or sensible. Eisenhower and Dulles, skeptical of Soviet willingness to commit the necessary funds, decided to back away from Nasser's dam project, did so publicly and in a manner designed to embarrass the Egyptian leader.[27]

Enraged, lacking assurance of Soviet funding for his dam, Nasser nationalized the Suez Canal, owned by a British-controlled corporation. Once again, he stuck his finger in the eye of the Western imperialists, to the delight of many Arabs. Perhaps he would be able

26 Campbell, *Defense of the Middle East,* 72–6; Kennett Love, *Suez* (New York, 1969), 297–327.
27 W. Roger Louis, "Dulles, Suez, and the British," in Immerman, *Dulles and Diplomacy of the Cold War,* 133–58, notes reporting by the British Embassy in Washington on lobbying activities against the Aswan loan.

to finance his dam project with the canal's revenues. Eisenhower and Dulles responded cautiously; British Prime Minister Anthony Eden did not. To the Americans, Suez was far away, a convenience rather than a vital interest. Who controlled the canal was less important than keeping the Arabs friendly, friendly enough to keep oil flowing to the West and Soviet influence out of the region. The use of force to keep the canal under European or international management was not an acceptable option. To Eden, however, the canal was a critical artery linking British and western European industry to Persian Gulf oil. Nasser had committed an act of wanton aggression. As he had opposed the appeasement of Hitler in the 1930s, Eden was determined not to appease Nasser. He was convinced that Nasser, like Hitler, could only be stopped with force.[28]

In deference to American insistence on a negotiated resolution of the canal issue, the British restrained themselves through the late summer and early autumn of 1956. They talked, they listened, and they prepared for the military action they believed necessary. In the French and the Israelis they found willing accomplices. The French shared British concerns about the canal and were angered by Nasser's support for Algerian efforts to achieve independence from French rule. The Israelis were profoundly troubled by the shipment of Soviet arms to Egypt and the refusal of the United States to provide Israel with either additional arms or assurances. Israeli leaders perceived the United States as having abandoned the Jews as the Arabs prepared to destroy them. They would not watch passively: After the Holocaust, never again! British and French assistance provided an opportunity that could not be wasted. American intelligence analysts underestimated the likelihood that Nasser's enemies would strike.

On October 29, 1956, while much of the world focused on the Soviet response to the Hungarian Revolution, Israeli tanks raced across the Sinai and, in a matter of hours, destroyed much of the Egyptian army. The following day, in a move coordinated with

28 Lenczowski, *American Presidents and the Middle East,* 40–52, is a succinct overview of the Suez Crisis. See also Love, *Suez,* for an account highly sympathetic to Nasser, and Herman Finer, *Dulles over Suez* (Chicago, 1964), for a diatribe against American policy during the crisis.

Israel, the British and French warned Israeli and Egyptian forces to stay away from the canal and, ostensibly to protect the canal, attacked nearby Egyptian forces. Before the military activity ended, British and French troops headed for Suez. America's allies had resorted to a classic nineteenth-century means of coping with unruly natives.

Eisenhower and Dulles were in an extraordinarily difficult situation. To support the British, French, and Israelis would mean alienating the Arab world and almost certainly much of the rest of the Third World. It would mean abandoning traditional opposition to imperialism and aggression, exposing the nation to charges of hypocrisy. It would mean allowing the Soviets to claim the high ground in the Middle East, allowing them to pose as the sole supporters of the Arabs against Western and Zionist imperialism. It would give Khrushchev, who was threatening the British and French with nuclear weapons, an enormous propaganda victory at a time when the world should have been railing against Soviet brutality in Hungary. The price was too high and the United States chose to lead the attack on the British and French in the United Nations. For once the United States and the Soviet Union were on the same side of an issue, denouncing imperialism as they vied for influence in the Arab world. The British, French, and ultimately the Israelis were forced by American pressure to withdraw, although the Israelis were able to exact from Eisenhower assurances of access to the Gulf of Aqaba. Relations with its NATO allies might never be the same, but the United States had preserved its influence in the Middle East. Unfortunately from Washington's perspective, so had the Soviet Union, and it seemed poised to improve its position in the region.

It was evident from Nasser's actions that he was competing with the United States and the Soviet Union for power and influence. Like a number of other Third World leaders, he was at least as shrewd as his American and Soviet counterparts in using them for his ends as they attempted to use him for theirs. Neither Washington nor Moscow could ever hope to control him or the Middle East. Throughout the 1950s and 1960s, however, he threatened American rather than Soviet interests. It was the United States and its allies who had a growing dependence on Middle Eastern oil and feared that Nasser's Pan-Arab movement would one day control the spigot, would one day interrupt the flow so essential to Western and Japanese industry. It was the United States that could not abandon Israel and dreaded the moment when Nasser or another Arab leader would attempt to reclaim Palestine for the Palestinians. And Khrushchev, unlike Stalin, was willing to aid Nasser, confident that a stronger Egypt would be an asset to the Soviet Union, that disruption of the flow of oil and conflict between Arabs and Israelis would weaken the United States.

In the aftermath of the Suez crisis, Eisenhower, signaling the gravity of American concern, asked for and received from Congress a resolution that declared the Middle East to be a vital national interest. It gave the president discretion to aid countries there, with American forces if necessary, when a country asked for help to repel "overt armed aggression from any nation controlled by international communism." The resolution was soon known as the Eisenhower Doctrine. Designed to check Nasser's influence as well as Soviet, it was applicable to no known situation in the region. The doctrine was used in 1957 when the king of Jordan, threatened by pro-Nasser forces within his country and without, appealed for help, claiming, not surprisingly, that the danger came from "international communism." The U.S. Sixth Fleet showed the flag in the eastern Mediterranean and the king received $10 million in American aid.

A more dangerous situation shocked Washington in the summer of 1958. The Christian president of Lebanon had been appealing for help against pro-Nasser forces to anyone with an available ear. There was no evidence that international communism was involved, although both Egypt and Syria, with links to the Soviets, were. Washington was unresponsive until a coup in Iraq substituted a pro-Nasser, pro-Soviet regime for the one that had signed the Baghdad Pact. Confronted with a situation in which Nasser's power seemed to have united the Arab world, eliminated the West's principal ally, and become an increment to Soviet influence in the area, the United States sent marines to Lebanon. Khrushchev, fearing American intervention in Iraq, threatened war. Quickly, the United States determined that the Soviets were not involved in the coup in Iraq; that the new Iraqi leadership was intensely nationalistic, anti-Western to be sure, but unlikely to submit to their country becoming a Soviet satellite. Recognition of the Baghdad regime by Washington defused the crisis. Nasser, undesirous of a permanent American military presence in the region, used his influence to calm his friends in Lebanon and Syria, facilitating the withdrawal of the marines. The United States made few friends among the Arabs, but no shots were fired in anger.[29]

The American position in the Middle East, as it developed in the 1950s, was that of a traditional great power. The United States was interested primarily in the resources of the area, in an uninterrupted flow of oil at a reasonable price. Toward this end it desired order and stability, exotic commodities in the Middle East, as in most of the developing world. The problems for American policymakers would have been similar and difficult had the Soviet Union not existed. Intra-Arab rivalries, especially those involving Egypt, Iraq, and Syria, states seeking to lead pan-Arab movements, but also between secular and religious nations, would have created turbulence. Similarly tensions within countries, religious, ethnic, and socio-economic, promised strife in the absence of established patterns for the peaceful resolution of differences, assuming such differences were resolvable. All of these issues bubbled in a cauldron to which the addition of Israel's presence guaranteed an explosive mixture. American ties to Israel constituted a further, inescapable vexation.

The Soviets played the classic role of the competing but weaker great power. Although it bordered the Middle East, the Soviet Union was unable to dislodge the United States from the region. It could, and in the 1950s did, stir the pot at times and in places of its own choosing, facilitating local resistance to American visions, raising the cost of the Pax Americana. To Arabs dissatisfied with their relations with the United States, for whatever reason, the Soviet Union provided an alternative. None of this had much to do with international communism, which had little appeal in the Arab world and gained a foothold nowhere within it during this period.

---

29 Lenczowski, *American Presidents and the Middle East*, 57–64; William Stivers, "Eisenhower and the Middle East," in Melanson and Mayers, *Reevaluating Eisenhower*, 206–9.

The American effort to contain the Soviet Union by enlisting the so-called northern tier states, Turkey, Iraq, and Iran, in the Baghdad Pact does not explain the Soviet role in the area. The Soviets did not jump in because they were provoked. The Baghdad Pact gave the Soviets an opportunity to establish ties with Egypt at a particular moment, but as the world's second greatest power, with a historic interest in the region, they could not have been kept out. After Stalin's death, the Soviet leadership actively pursued links in the Arab world. Sooner or later an Arab leader would have found it in his interest to accept their overtures.

Two other examples are perhaps more useful in illustrating Khrushchev's confidence that the Soviet Union could compete successfully on the periphery. Indonesia and the Congo were places where the Soviets had no historic concerns and were far removed from any vital interests. To establish footholds in Southeast Asia and Africa, but perhaps primarily to demonstrate that the Soviet Union was worthy of respect as a world power, Khrushchev committed Soviet resources at critical moments in the development of both countries.

Sukarno of Indonesia had hosted the Bandung Conference of non-aligned states in 1955 and developed the delusions of grandeur that so often accompany power. He perceived himself to be a world leader, sought to arrogate additional power to himself at home and to expand the territory under Indonesian rule. Dissatisfied with the extent and conditions of American aid, he flew to Moscow where Khrushchev offered a $100 million credit. Returning to Indonesia, he attempted to use the Soviet offer to encourage greater generosity in Washington. At the same time, with the support of the Indonesian Communist party, he changed the existing Indonesian parliamentary system into something he called "guided democracy." It was by no means a Leninist system that he had created, but he had increased his personal power and reduced the chances for genuine democratic government.

Washington found Sukarno's egomania distasteful, but it was much more troubled by his flirtation with the Soviets, by evidence that local Communists had lined up behind him, and by his claims to territory on New Guinea still held by America's Dutch allies. The United States increased its aid to Indonesia and Southeast Asia generally in 1957, trying to protect the region against a possible threat from Mao's China, but it was unwilling to provide the Indonesian Army with weapons it might use against the Dutch and unhappy about competing with the Soviets. Khrushchev, on the other hand, was delighted to have the opportunity to provide the Indonesian military with arms. The Soviet Union became its principal supplier in the late 1950s, a role the Soviets played for almost a decade.

Never very influential in Indonesia, having supported independence there primarily as a means of preempting Communist control of the country, the United States could view the breakup of the nation with notable ease. Eisenhower and Dulles had each indicated his preference for several smaller island states to a unified Indonesia aligned with the Communists. In 1958, the CIA, Eisenhower's weapon of choice, was instructed to support Sumatran secession. The Sumatran rebels received equipment and training from CIA agents and CIA-operated planes flew bombing missions in their support. The effort failed and was exposed when one of the bombers was shot down and its pilot captured. Washington's efforts to deny culpability were unsuccessful.[30]

Indonesia's resources and strategic location were beyond American control. Soviet aid sustained an unpredictable friend in Indonesia, and the United States continued its own modest aid program, fearful of driving Sukarno into dependence on the Soviets. Neither superpower gained much of substance from wooing Sukarno, but Khrushchev had more to be happy about.

In the Congo, Khrushchev's gambit was less successful and the Soviets were no match for the CIA. The Republic of the Congo was granted independence by Belgium in June 1960 and its first premier was Patrice Lumumba, a man American Africanists regarded highly. He was perceived as the only national leader in a country in which tribalism posed a serious threat to internal unity. Although the mineral resources of the area were valued, neither Eisenhower nor

30 Howard Palfrey Jones, *Indonesia: The Possible Dream* (New York, 1971), 129–46.

Dulles conceived of strategic interests in Central Africa. No one in the Eisenhower administration thought American economic interests in the Congo were endangered. Here was one part of the world that might be spared the taint of superpower rivalry.[31]

A few days after the Congo became independent, Lumumba had reason to suspect that the Belgians were not quite ready to leave their holdings in his hands. A mutiny in the Congolese Army was followed first by the rapid reinforcement of the forces the Belgians had retained in the Congo and then by the secession of Katanga province, the center of European investment. Belgian paratroopers prevented Lumumba from landing at Katanga's principal airport. Shaken by these events, Lumumba appealed successively to the United States, the United Nations, and the Soviet Union.

Initially, both the Americans and the Soviets deferred to the United Nations. A resolution calling for the withdrawal of Belgian troops and military assistance to Lumumba's government passed the Security Council. Several weeks passed without progress toward reunification. Lumumba appealed again to the Soviet Union. This time Khrushchev could not resist. Stretching the limits of Soviet airlift capabilities, he sent large quantities of equipment and a number of Soviet and Czech technicians to the Congo.

Soviet involvement changed the American perception of Lumumba and of the strategic importance of the Congo. Despite the fact that Lumumba had appealed first to the United States, the Eisenhower administration came to see him as an unstable and dangerous radical likely to facilitate Communist inroads into Central Africa. The Congo, once Soviet interest had been manifested, became the keystone of sub-Saharan Africa. If Communists seized control of the Congo, they would be in position to dominate black Africa. Once again, the value of a peripheral area was enhanced by imbuing it with the weight of a dozen or more countries in its vicinity. Its loss became tantamount to the loss of the region, perhaps of a continent. Ultimately the world balance of power was at

31 Stephan R. Weissman, *American Foreign Policy in the Congo, 1960–1964* (Ithaca, 1974), is my principal source on the Congo. See also Brian Urquhart, *A Life in Peace and War* (New York, 1987), 145–73.

stake. The Soviets had to be stopped. The United States had to intervene.

The Eisenhower administration hoped to thwart Soviet designs without a direct confrontation. It rested its hopes on the United Nations, supplemented by a CIA operation to assassinate Lumumba. In September 1960 the president of the Congo, acting upon the advice of the American ambassador and the UN representative in the Congo, dismissed Lumumba. Lumumba attempted to seize power, but UN forces closed the airports, preventing Soviet planes from moving pro-Lumumba forces to the capital. Lumumba was placed under house arrest, and Joseph Mobutu, supported by the CIA, emerged as the strong man in the new regime.

The activities of the UN force in the Congo in opposition to Lumumba infuriated Khrushchev. For the next few months the battlefield shifted to New York where the Soviet delegation, led by Khrushchev personally, attacked Secretary General Dag Hammarskjold. It was in the midst of this verbal abuse that Khrushchev performed his long-remembered shoe-pounding scene, expressing his displeasure at the remarks of another speaker. But the Soviets had been outmaneuvered in the Congo. They could not match American ability to project power into the region. The internal strife in the Congo continued for several years, through the Kennedy and Johnson administrations, through the end of Khrushchev's tenure, until Mobutu consolidated his power. Lumumba was murdered in 1961, the Soviets and several African states supported his political allies, but ultimately a regime satisfactory to the United States prevailed. In the 1960s, the Soviets were a distant second in the competition with the United States for establishing influence in Africa.

After Stalin's death, after the Korean War, the Soviets and the Americans again began to grope toward some means of regulating their rivalry, of confronting each other without threatening the survival of the world. Khrushchev and his colleagues began the dismantling of the Stalinist state. They were dedicated Communists and, in Khrushchev's case, more committed to a messianic vision than Stalin had been. But they wanted to spare their people the terror and brutality of Stalinism and they were willing to allow greater freedom to the peoples of nations within their sphere of influence. Haltingly, clumsily, they tried to create a more open, humane society in the Soviet Union. They tried to be less terrifying to their neighbors than Stalin had been. But the Soviet Union under Khrushchev's leadership became more of a threat to world peace. Stalin was malevolent, but a prudent man. Khrushchev was a decent man, but at times an impulsive, high stakes gambler. Khrushchev was convinced that communism would prevail and that the days of American hegemony were numbered. He craved respect for his country and worked assiduously to plant the Hammer and Sickle around the world. The desire to make the Soviet Union a world power, at least equal to the United States, drove him to invest Soviet resources in remote regions of dubious importance. He would not concede the periphery to the Americans.

Soviet activity in the Third World raised the stakes in American eyes. Wherever a Soviet threat was alleged, the American national security apparatus was eager to counter it and Congress was likely to provide the necessary funds. Because Soviet capabilities were limited in the 1950s, the American response was usually a CIA operation. Some were arguably successful, as in Iran, Guatemala, and the Congo; others, as in Indonesia, were not.

In the 1950s, Europe, the central arena for both the United States and the Soviet Union, was relatively stable, the great power contest stalemated. In Moscow, as in Washington, advisers to the leaders looked to the Third World for areas in which their nations might compete, might test the allure of their ideas and the skill of their operatives. The involvement of one superpower invariably changed a peripheral affair into an important one. Each had to demonstrate its resolve, lest its image as would-be hegemon be questioned, its ability to lead its bloc become suspect, as indeed occurred when Mao challenged Soviet leadership and de Gaulle refused to defer to the Americans.

5. Crisis Resolution

The tension of the years 1958–62 was without parallel in the four decades following World War II. Concerns over Berlin and Cuba led American forces to confront Soviet forces in situations in which a misstep, a rash action by an aggressive or nervous officer, might have led to war, might have led to the incineration and irradiation of much of the world. Nikita Khrushchev provoked each of these crises. The Soviet triumph in the space race, the launching of Sputnik in 1957, confirmed his faith in the ultimate triumph of communism, and he hoped to accelerate the process in the era of his leadership. He found American arrogance intolerable and was intensely eager to terminate it by reversing the strategic balance. Berlin he delighted in calling the "testicles" of the West: "Every time I give them a yank they holler."[1] Cuba, ninety miles from the coast of Florida, provided a convenient platform for placing the nuclear missiles that would teach Americans what it felt like to live under the shadow of the bomb, would put an end to the American penchant for nuclear blackmail.

Although provoked or precipitated by Soviet behavior, the crises of this era cannot be understood without recognizing the interactive quality of Soviet actions and statements, the extent to which they were responses to the policies of the United States and its allies. The Soviets had reacted with notable calm to West German integration into NATO, presumably recognizing that NATO contained the Germans as well as the Soviet bloc. Soviet apprehensions about a resurgent Germany did not disappear, however. Germany's economic revival probably worried all non-Germans, but it was fear that the

---

1 Quoted in Cyrus Sulzberger, *Last of the Giants* (New York, 1970), 860. Much of Khrushchev's personality and style is apparent in Edward Crankshaw and Strobe Talbott, *Khrushchev Remembers* (Boston, 1970).

West Germans would gain access to nuclear weapons that most troubled Khrushchev and his colleagues. The United States was stockpiling "tactical" nuclear weapons and ballistic missiles capable of reaching the Soviet Union on German soil. The Germans had demanded and had been given nuclear-capable artillery and fighter bombers. The Soviets were anxious to negotiate a settlement of European political issues that would recognize the status quo, including a divided Germany. They were equally interested in arms talks that would lead to a demilitarized or at least nuclear-free Central Europe. But Soviet overtures were unwelcome in Washington where domestic and alliance politics precluded serious consideration of any plan approximating the neutralization of Central Europe, even when it came from George Kennan in his "disengagement" lectures of 1957. Provoking a crisis was a crude and dangerous means of winning Eisenhower's attention, but Khrushchev was not known for his finesse – and there may well have been no other means.

Similarly, widespread evidence of intensive American efforts to overthrow the Castro regime in Cuba led Soviet and Cuban leaders to anticipate an American attack in 1962. CIA and U.S.-based émigré operations against Cuba were frequent, the development of contingency plans for an invasion of Cuba by American forces was known to Soviet and Cuban intelligence, and plans for major U.S. military exercises in the Caribbean in the fall were no secret. The desire to protect his newfound friend in Cuba may not have been Khrushchev's primary reason for installing nuclear missiles on the island, but it unquestionably entered into his thinking and was later used by the Soviets to justify their actions.

The point is a simple one: Each step by one of the superpowers was taken in accord with its assessment of the other's intentions. Soviet activity in Berlin and Cuba was prompted by Soviet perceptions of German and American aggressiveness. Perceiving themselves as defenders of the status quo in Europe and Cuba, and as victims of American intimidation, Soviet leaders sought to forestall change in both while simultaneously using missiles in Cuba to deter the American nuclear threat, to redress the strategic balance. American leaders who sent missiles to Germany out of fear of superior

Soviet conventional capabilities could not conceive of Khrushchev's pressure on Berlin as defensive. When they determined to destroy Castro, they were eager to prevent Cuba from becoming a Soviet bastion in the Western Hemisphere. They were defending vital American interests. As usual, each saw the other's actions as threatening, its own as defensive. Neither acted in a vacuum: Each responded to its sense of the adversary's machinations.

Khrushchev's foreign policy seemed to be driven by three emotions, ultimately constrained by a pragmatic concern for the well-being of the Soviet state. He wanted the Soviet Union to achieve a status of at least equality with the United States and be accorded the respect due a superpower. He wanted to see communism prevail in the competition with capitalism. And he feared German power. The Berlin crisis he created in 1958 provides a useful example of how he functioned.

The revival of German power in the late 1950s, and evidence of growing German influence within the Western alliance, worried Soviet analysts. The ability of the West German government to frustrate American demands that it enlarge its conventional forces, and to obtain nuclear-capable weapons instead, demonstrated the lengths to which Washington would go to court the Bonn regime. It was obvious that the West German army wanted at least tactical nuclear weapons and was interested in strategic missiles – and that the United States was leaning toward acquiescence. In February 1958, the American commander of NATO declared that "defensive atomic weapons are absolutely indispensable for the strengthening of the defensive power of the Bundeswehr."[2] A project to train a German air force unit for atomic attack and the installation of a storage facility near where it was stationed were completed late in 1958. These were not the kind of operations that could be hidden from Soviet and East German intelligence.

Similarly, Bonn's refusal to countenance the permanent division of Germany was troublesome. For the Soviet Union, a divided Ger-

2 Quoted in Catherine Kelleher, *Germany and the Politics of Nuclear Weapons* (New York, 1975), 94.

many was a relatively safe Germany. Unable to achieve an unarmed or neutral Germany in the mid-1950s, the Soviets were prepared to accept the status quo. They wanted to gain American assent to an independent East Germany and they wanted assurances that the West Germans would never obtain control of nuclear weapons. The United States remained committed to German reunification and increasingly looked to nuclear arms as essential to NATO forces outnumbered by the Red Army.

For the Eisenhower administration, always skeptical of Soviet intentions, unwilling to concede legitimacy to Soviet striving for strategic parity, negotiations with Moscow were not an easy option. To the Republican Right any arrangement with the Soviets short of Soviet capitulation was likely to evoke cries of appeasement, of "Munich" or "Yalta." Any concessions to the Soviets over Germany would be labeled a betrayal. Similarly, the Bonn government was apprehensive of any Soviet-American talks that might compromise its stated goal of a unified Germany or its sovereignty. The NATO allies were not of one mind about negotiations with the Soviets over Germany. Only the British were enthusiastic supporters of the idea. Rather than risk antagonizing Bonn and roiling the political waters at home, the Eisenhower administration ignored Soviet signals.

Late in 1957, after the launching of Sputnik, Khrushchev began to campaign for a summit meeting with Eisenhower. Mao, in Beijing, certainly thought the time had come for the international Communist movement to take the initiative, as did several of Khrushchev's more belligerent colleagues in the Kremlin. Auspicious as the moment may have been from the Soviet perspective, it was hardly an opportune time for the Americans, who were left sputtering like their fizzled Vanguard rockets. Khrushchev waited a year, until after the Taiwan Straits crisis had passed, until after the midterm congressional elections of 1958, and then announced that the Western powers had six months in which to negotiate the status of West Berlin with East German authorities. When the deadline passed, the Soviets would sign a separate peace treaty with the East Germans, leaving them responsible for Western access to Berlin. To Dulles's warning that the West would use force if necessary to ensure its access to Berlin, Khrushchev replied that World War III would follow. Later in the Berlin crisis Khrushchev told Averell Harriman, "If you send in tanks, they will burn and make no mistake about it. If you want war, you can have it, and remember it will be your war. Our rockets will fly automatically."[3]

Eisenhower was not stampeded by Khrushchev's rhetoric and refused to negotiate under ultimatum. He and Dulles, before the latter's death in 1959, both recognized the need to treat the Soviets with more civility, however – a relatively easy matter at the end of their days in office, when there was no political capital left to squander. Khrushchev was invited to the United States, spent a weekend at Camp David with Eisenhower, toured Hollywood, and went home unfulfilled when security precautions cheated him out of an opportunity to visit Disneyland. The deadline on Berlin was lifted, nonetheless. Khrushchev continued to raise the issue and apparently expected to resolve it at the summit meeting scheduled for May 1960. West German opposition, however, probably precluded any compromise over Berlin. By the spring of 1960, the American government knew unequivocally, from intelligence gathered by U-2 overflights of the Soviet Union, that Khrushchev's claims of missile superiority were unwarranted. Khrushchev knew, from the downing of a U-2 on the eve of the conference, that the Americans were aware that he was bluffing, were aware of the relative weakness of the Soviet Union. Khrushchev walked out of the summit, ostensibly over the U-2 issue; the Berlin issue smoldered, and flared dangerously again in June of 1961, to be confronted by the administration of John F. Kennedy.

Closer to home, the Eisenhower administration became intensely irritated with Fidel Castro, the Cuban leader who had been transmogrified from a Robin Hood–like figure, liberating his people from the evil ruler, Fulgencio Batista, into a possible Marxist-Leninist, an instrument of the international Communist movement suddenly rooted in America's sphere of influence. Batista had lost the confidence of Cuban elites and ultimately any hope of support

3 Quoted in David Holloway, *The Soviet Union and the Arms Race* (New Haven, 1983), 84.

from Washington, despite rumors of Communist influence in the revolutionary forces that sought to depose him. In due course he left for Miami, and early in January 1959, Castro led his men, the major fighting force of the revolution, into Havana and quickly organized a government.

The new Cuban government was passionately nationalistic and moderately leftist. In Latin American terms, that meant suspicion of the United States, long-time regional hegemon, and especially of American economic power. But initially, the regime in Havana was non-Communist, even anti-Communist, and included many men considered proponents of democratic capitalism, of programs no more radical than Roosevelt's New Deal. Quickly, however, moderate leaders gave way to radicals, the pace of reforms, including the expropriation of property owned by Americans, accelerated, the prospects for liberal democracy dimmed, and Castro gave a series of speeches critical of the United States. The Cuban Communist party was legalized and its members began to play a role, although relatively minor, in the implementation of Castro's programs. Indications of increased Communist influence worried Eisenhower, but the CIA detected no evidence of a Soviet role, no evidence that Castro might himself be a Communist. In February 1960, however, responding to Castro's overtures, Khrushchev sent his deputy premier, Anastas Mikoyan, to Cuba, ostensibly to visit a trade fair. A Cuban-Soviet trade agreement followed. That was enough to galvanize Eisenhower. An alternative to Castro, a Cuban government composed of the kind of democratic reformers who had worked with Castro to overthrow Batista, was clearly necessary. Eisenhower would not countenance sending in the marines, as Teddy Roosevelt or Woodrow Wilson might well have done. On the other hand, he hardly needed the marines: He had the CIA.[4]

Eisenhower's preference for dealing with unruly Third World leaders was to minimize overt American involvement. As with Iran and Guatemala, he wanted the CIA to find local forces more recep-

4 Richard E. Welch, Jr., *The Response to Revolution: The United States and the Cuban Revolution, 1959–1961* (Chapel Hill, 1985), 3–63.

tive to American political and economic values and to support such forces in a coup. Soon the CIA was training Cuban exiles for the invasion of their homeland, but the CIA could never pull together the Cuban "government-in-exile" that was the prerequisite for Eisenhower's order to send the men ashore. In the interim, the American government initiated a process of economic pressures, beginning with reduction of the quota of Cuban sugar the United States was committed to buy. Ultimately, the CIA developed a series of bizarre plots to assassinate Castro, including subcontracting the assignment to the Mafia in the early 1960s.[5]

American hostility served Castro well, both in rallying the Cuban people behind his increasingly radical domestic program and in gaining the support of a wary Khrushchev. In May 1960, diplomatic relations were established between Cuba and the Soviet Union and Khrushchev once again rattled his rockets, warning the United States not to attack Cuba. Soviet leaders were still skeptical about Castro's intentions and uneasy about challenging the United States in its sphere of interest, but the opportunity to twit the Americans proved irresistible. A pattern that men like Nasser and Sukarno had exploited previously quickly developed. As the United States intensified its pressures on Castro, he turned more and more to the Soviet bloc for support. Unlike Nasser and Sukarno, somewhere along the line, in late 1960 or 1961, Castro decided to become a Marxist-Leninist.

In December 1960, Moscow and Havana issued a joint communiqué in which the Cubans declared their support for Soviet foreign policy. In January 1961, Castro ordered the drastic reduction of American embassy personnel in Cuba. Eisenhower angrily withdrew American recognition of the Castro regime. Plans for the CIA-sponsored Cuban-exile invasion of the island gathered momentum. As he prepared to leave office, Eisenhower was warned that the operation might soon be irreversible. But in a few days, Castro would become John F. Kennedy's problem.

5 Thomas Powers, *The Man Who Kept the Secrets: Richard Helms and the CIA* (New York, 1979).

Clearly, the key player in the interaction between Cuba, the United States, and the Soviet Union, was Fidel Castro. Castro dominated the Cuban revolution and determined its pace and direction. Castro decided correctly that the United States would be an obstacle to his objectives and that the Soviet Union might prove a useful counterweight. Castro needled the Americans and reeled in Khrushchev. It was not a matter of great powers exploiting an underdeveloped country, manipulating its unsophisticated leaders. Castro played the great powers like a virtuoso and once he declared himself a Communist, in December 1961, he made it extraordinarily difficult for the Soviets to abandon him.

American policy might have been wiser. On the other hand, American political culture precluded support for the radical revolution Castro wanted. Friendly relations between Cuban revolutionaries weaned on tales of American imperialism and American leaders convinced of the benign role their country had always played since it liberated Cuba from Spanish brutality in 1898 are not readily imaginable. A less hostile policy, an acceptance of the Cuban revolution, however grudging, without assassination and invasion plots, might have lessened Castro's need for Soviet assistance, and might have left Khrushchev less of an opportunity for mischief. But the odds were not good: The Soviet-American competition was simply too rich a field for a clever leader like Castro to exploit and American responses to a whiff of communism too reflexive.

The election returns were hardly in before Khrushchev began overtures to President-elect Kennedy. The Soviets had given up hope of progress on any of the issues dividing the superpowers in the waning months of the Eisenhower administration. They were eager to signal their desire to work with the new administration, to give and gain assurances on the status quo in Europe, to establish mutually acceptable guidelines for the peaceful competition in the Third World that Khrushchev was confident would result in the triumph of communism. They hoped the new administration would be less prone to using nuclear blackmail, more respectful of Soviet interests, more accepting of the Soviet right to compete for influence around the world, more tolerant of Soviet support for radical regimes in the Third World, of "socialist internationalism."[6]

Soviet hopes for accommodation were matched in Washington, but Khrushchev's terms were not acceptable. No less than its predecessors, the Kennedy administration was committed to containing communism, to preventing the spread of Soviet influence, and to maintaining and capitalizing on American strategic superiority. Kennedy and his advisers were profoundly troubled by Khrushchev's threats regarding Berlin and Soviet activities in the Congo, Laos, and Cuba. Moreover, Khrushchev's signals were often confusing, an unfortunate mixture of appeals for peaceful coexistence and attempts to intimidate. On January 6, 1961, addressing a Communist party rally in Moscow, Khrushchev stressed Soviet commitment to "wars of national liberation," just wars that would ensure communism's ultimate victory in the struggle with the West. Kennedy's Soviet specialists interpreted the speech as an intensely hostile warning of increased guerrilla activity and subversion in the Third World.[7] On February 17, the Soviets resumed pressure on Berlin. However peaceful Khrushchev's intentions may have been, American analysts perceived him as a volatile and dangerous adversary.

Kennedy, in his first days in office, found crises in Laos, where the Western position was deteriorating rapidly, the Congo, where the new nation's disintegration appeared to allow the Soviets a foothold in Central Africa, and Cuba, which seemed to move closer to the Soviets daily. CIA support of the Laotian Right had destabilized a neutralist regime but had proved inadequate to combat the Soviet and Vietnamese support of the Laotian Left it had stimulated. The agency was faring better in the Congo where efforts to eliminate Lumumba were on track. Implementation of the plan for an exile

6 John Lewis Gaddis, *The Soviet Union and the United States* (New York, 1978), 233; William Zimmerman, *Soviet Perspectives on International Relations, 1956–1967* (Princeton, 1969), 133–35, 179–82, 213–25; Marc Trachtenberg, *History and Strategy* (Princeton, 1991), 215–16.
7 Llewellyn Thompson, American ambassador to Moscow, cable, January 19, 1961, John F. Kennedy Papers, President's Office File, Box 127, John F. Kennedy Library. See also Charles Bohlen, draft of approach to Khrushchev, June 1, 1961, and George Kennan, cable, June 2, 1961, Box 126.

invasion of Cuba required the new president's prompt attention. The exiles trained and equipped by the CIA had to be sent in or there would be a "disposal problem." One could not simply send hundreds of armed Cubans back to Miami.[8]

Kennedy and his advisers considered themselves to be supportive of social revolution in the underdeveloped world. They could not conceive, however, of the legitimacy of Communist involvement or Soviet assistance to such a movement. Castro was reputedly a Communist. He had unquestionably allowed known Communists to play an increasingly important role in his government. He had opened the door to Soviet influence in the Caribbean. He had betrayed the dream of freedom that drove the Cuban people when they rose against Batista. The CIA reported that more Soviet-bloc military equipment was headed for Cuba. Castro was unacceptable: His regime had to be destroyed.

In meetings among Kennedy's advisers, the CIA and the Department of Defense pressed for orders to implement the exile invasion plan. Dean Rusk, the secretary of state, skeptical of CIA estimates of a popular uprising in support of the invaders, fearful that American involvement would be exposed, preferred economic sanctions. But in addition to the exile "disposal problem," there was the likelihood that rejection of the CIA plan would be leaked to the public. Kennedy, who had been critical of Eisenhower's "loss" of Cuba, could ill afford the domestic political ramifications of appearing weaker than Eisenhower, of having canceled a plan the Eisenhower administration had devised for overthrowing Castro. To meet Rusk's concerns, the operation was whittled back, the invaders denied air cover the CIA deemed essential. On April 17, 1961, the CIA-trained Cuban exiles were sent ashore at the Bay of Pigs.

Air raids by CIA-operated bombers two days earlier failed to eliminate the tiny Cuban air force, but prompted a Cuban military alert and protest to the United Nations. A second raid, scheduled for the morning of the invasion, was canceled to avoid further implicating the United States. The exile force landed on inhospitable terrain without air cover and without critical ammunition and com-

8 Warren I. Cohen, *Dean Rusk* (Totowa, N.J., 1980), 112–32.

munication equipment, lost in the course of the operation. An attempt to blow up the causeways leading to the beach failed, the Cuban air force pinned down the invaders, and the Cuban army poured into the area to mop them up. The uprising of the Cuban people predicted by the CIA and essential to the success of the plan never occurred. The CIA scheme proved to have been poorly conceived. Implementation, undermined by administration modifications, proved to be a disaster. Only a major assault by the armed forces of the United States could succeed – and Kennedy was not ready for that.

The Bay of Pigs invasion was a humiliating defeat for the United States, equal to that of the British and French at Suez. Having castigated its allies for resorting to atavistic imperialism, for failing to appreciate Egyptian nationalism, American leaders had violated their much beloved principle of nonintervention, to which they were bound by treaty. They attempted to overthrow the Cuban government and they had failed miserably. Adlai Stevenson, the American ambassador to the United Nations, having denied vehemently that his government would ever commit such an act, was greatly embarrassed to discover that the president he served had deceived him. Castro's popularity with his people increased, as did his appeal to Nikita Khrushchev. In July 1961 a Soviet-Cuban alliance was announced, and in December Castro declared himself a Marxist-Leninist. With Washington's assistance, Castro transformed revolutionary Cuba from an irritant to a powder keg.

A month after accepting responsibility for the Cuban debacle, Kennedy decided the time had come for a summit meeting with Khrushchev. The two men met in Vienna on June 3 and 4 where whatever good intentions either may have had evaporated in an atmosphere of confrontation. The desire both leaders had to prevent conflict in areas remote from their nations' vital interests and the hope that they could reduce tensions between the two countries were forgotten as each took a rigid ideological position. Khrushchev, insisting that socialism was on the rise, accused Kennedy of trying to deny the Soviet Union the fruits of impending victory. Kennedy fell back on containment, denying the Soviet Union a right to support any new radical movements that might emerge. Perhaps surprisingly in that context, the two men were able to agree to try to neutralize Laos.

The most troublesome issue to arise at Vienna was Berlin. Once again Khrushchev presented the United States with an ultimatum, threatening to sign a peace treaty with the East Germans that would terminate Western access to Berlin. Kennedy replied that the United States would stand by its commitment. Each man warned that war would follow if the other did not back down. Each went home to take steps to increase the credibility of his threat.

Kennedy's advisers had been preparing for a crisis over Berlin since entering office. Dean Acheson, Truman's secretary of state, had been consulted and his advice was harsh: The Western position on Germany and West Berlin was nonnegotiable; American forces should be mobilized to demonstrate the willingness to fight. Kennedy was dissatisfied with so rigid a posture. He thought de facto acceptance of the division of Germany was sensible, that agreement to negotiate was superior to brinkmanship. Neither Kennedy nor any of his colleagues were willing to surrender anything of substance, but before the Vienna meeting, most were willing to negotiate as a means of easing tensions. Khrushchev's attempt to intimidate Kennedy at Vienna and afterward, however, provoked a more Achesonian, macho response.

On July 25, 1961, Kennedy spoke to the American people on national television, explaining the importance of Berlin and declaring that the American military position there and Western access to Berlin were not negotiable. He then announced a large, 25 percent increase in American conventional military forces, expanding the draft and ordering a partial mobilization of the reserves. Lest the point be missed, he warned the Soviet Union against miscalculating the determination of the United States to preserve its position in Germany. Khrushchev had created the crisis, the United States would not back off. The decision for war or peace would have to be made in Moscow.

Khrushchev retreated immediately. On July 27, he sent assurances through an American visitor that he did not want war. In a speech on August 7, he called for an easing of tension, an end to the war psychosis. He promised to take no military action and softened his position on Berlin markedly: The Soviets would not "infringe upon any lawful interests of the Western powers. Any barring of access to West Berlin, any blockade of West Berlin, is entirely out of the question."[9] In another speech a few days later, he pleaded for negotiation.

The crisis took a new direction as Khrushchev spoke. West Berlin had long been the principal escape route for East Germans fleeing to the West. In July, fearful that the West would surrender to Khrushchev's threats, 30,000 East German refugees slipped into West Berlin. On August 12, 4,000 crossed into West Berlin. The East German regime, faced with imminent collapse, begged Khrushchev for permission to staunch the flow.

Soviet analysts examining Kennedy's July 25th speech noted that he had said nothing of guaranteeing continued access between East and West Berlin. They decided to gamble. They would block access between the Western and Soviet sectors of Berlin, preventing escape from the East – and hope the American response would not be violent. On August 13 barriers started going up. The United States did not respond: The barriers did not infringe on interests Kennedy deemed vital. The Soviet gambit worked and what began as barbed wire obstacles became the Berlin Wall. Quickly the crisis receded. The United States would not attack the barriers, would not take the offensive in a situation in which the stakes were very high for Khrushchev. He had achieved his minimal goal, an end to the bleeding of the East German regime.[10]

In a variety of ways, including the use of a "back channel" line to Kennedy established at the Soviet leader's request, Khrushchev again signaled his desire to reduce tensions between the super-

9 *New York Times,* August 8, 1961.
10 Paul Y. Hammond, *Cold War and Détente* (New York, 1975), 169–70; Robert M. Slusser, *The Berlin Crisis of 1961* (Baltimore, 1973), 93–5; Alexander L. George and Richard Smoke, *Deterrence in American Foreign Policy* (New York, 1974), 436–40; James L. Richardson, *Germany and the Atlantic Alliance* (Cambridge, Mass., 1966), 286; Jean E. Smith, *The Defense of Berlin* (Baltimore, 1963), 258–78.

powers. In September, Secretary of State Dean Rusk met with Soviet Foreign Minister Andrei Gromyko three times and in mid-October, Khrushchev withdrew his deadline for settling the Berlin issue. The Soviet Union had not achieved its goals in Central Europe, but it had dragged the United States into a dialogue over its concerns. Kennedy had shown his administration to be firm on essentials, willing to give a little at the edges.

American strategic supremacy left Khrushchev little room to maneuver. On October 21, Deputy Secretary of Defense Roswell Gilpatric underscored the point in a public address, declaring that the United States could absorb a Soviet first strike and devastate the Soviet Union in retaliation. The United States was not negotiating from weakness. Any Soviet pretense to superiority was brushed aside and Khrushchev's bluster proved unproductive. Indeed, his oscillation between threats and peaceful gestures served to discredit Soviet diplomacy, to serve best those ideologues who argued that changes in Soviet tactics should not obscure the inexorable Communist drive toward world domination.

The failure of Khrushchev's efforts to advance Soviet ends in Germany appears to have weakened him at home. Some of his critics were troubled by his crude threats and embarrassing retreats. Others, echoing Mao's fulminations from Beijing, charged Khrushchev with excessive caution. The historian Robert Slusser has suggested that a Soviet-American tank confrontation on October 26 that came close to starting World War III might have occurred in a moment when Khrushchev's opponents in the Kremlin temporarily controlled the apparatus of government. To prevent further encroachment by East German police, the American military commander in Berlin had ordered tanks into position at a checkpoint between East and West. The East German government called for help and the local Soviet commander sent his armor rumbling forward. The tanks faced each other, with an officer in any one of them capable of starting a war. Suddenly, the next day, Soviet tanks withdrew. Slusser contends that the tank movement had been arranged by Khrushchev's opponents at the Communist Party Congress then in session and that their removal was a partial victory for

Khrushchev and his attempt at peaceful accommodation with the West. [11]

The Soviets increased the pressure again in February 1962, harassing Western flights into Berlin, but once more Rusk and Gromyko talked the tension away. The issue did not disappear: It could not until both sides committed themselves to the status quo in Germany or the two German states had worked things out satisfactorily between them. But the aura of crisis faded once the Soviets concluded the United States could not be persuaded under any circumstances to remove its forces from West Berlin. As Rusk remarked to the Senate Foreign Relations Committee, the Soviets might have postponed the attempt to resolve the issue until they achieved strategic parity, a day toward which they were working frenetically.

In preparation for a meeting between President Kennedy and Soviet Foreign Minister Gromyko on October 18, 1962, the head of the Department of State's Berlin Task Force prepared a memorandum and "talking points on Berlin" for the president. The talking points contained a succinct summary of seventeen months of confrontation and negotiation, describing the talks as useful to both sides, especially as a means of clarifying their respective positions. But "no one could realistically claim . . . that much progress has been made toward an understanding on Berlin which would remove this problem as a point of possible confrontation in which a grave danger of war inheres." [12]

The author of the memorandum and the expert on Soviet affairs who advised Kennedy wanted the president to leave no doubt in Soviet minds that the West was united and would fight, if necessary, over Berlin. What they did not mention – because they did not know – was that the United States and the Soviet Union were on the verge of nuclear war over Cuba. On October 14, an American U-2 flight had obtained unmistakable evidence that the Soviets were

11 Slusser, *The Berlin Crisis of 1961*, 430, 440–1.
12 Rusk for Kennedy, undated [October 17, 1962], drafted by Martin Hillenbrand, obtained from Department of State through the Freedom of Information Act.

building missile sites in Cuba. For Kennedy and other American leaders, Berlin had become a secondary issue.

The Kennedy administration had not been inactive toward Cuba since recovering from the failure of the Bay of Pigs operation. Diplomatically, it had won modest support for its efforts to isolate the Castro regime within the hemisphere and nominal support from its NATO allies for its economic warfare against Cuba. Although Kennedy had declared publicly that a Communist regime in Cuba was intolerable, no further thought was being given to using Cuban exile forces to overthrow Castro. On the other hand, the American government was doing little to suppress piratical acts by exiles against Cuban vessels; and far worse, it was experimenting with a variety of covert operations, some of which were designed to humiliate Castro – and others, to murder him. Perhaps most threatening were contingency plans for American forces to invade the island and the major exercises conducted in the spring of 1962 to test these plans. Soviet and Cuban intelligence services were aware of some of the plots and of the existence of contingency plans for an invasion, which they may have believed imminent. The Cuban government unquestionably had reason to be anxious, to lean more heavily on the Soviet Union, to allow the Soviets to build missile sites directed against the United States.[13]

Although eager to have Soviet protection against the mounting danger to his regime, Castro preferred to perceive his acceptance of the missiles as a Cuban contribution to the Communist cause. He was allowing the Soviets to station missiles on his territory, with the consequent risk of American reprisals, in order to allow the Soviets and the international Communist movement they served to gain a strategic advantage. In short, he was doing Khrushchev a favor. Khrushchev and the generation of Soviet analysts that survived him have insisted, on the other hand, that they had acted to defend the Cubans, that the missiles, the planes, and the Soviet combat troops they sent to Cuba were intended to stave off the American invasion.[14]

13 Raymond L. Garthoff, *Reflections on the Cuban Missile Crisis*, rev. ed. (Washington, D.C., 1989), 6–8.
14 *Khrushchev Remembers*, 493–500; Garthoff, *Reflections*, 11–24.

The Caribbean, 1954-1991

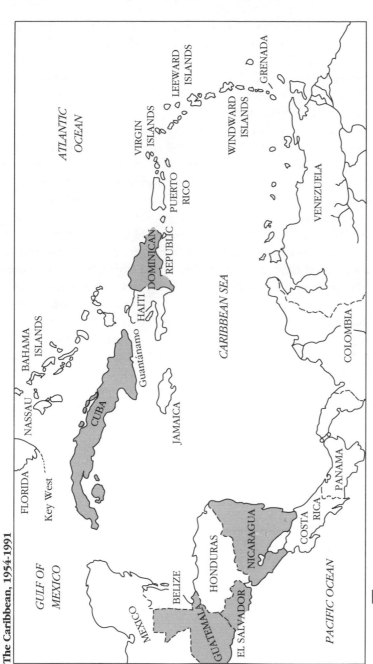

Countries in which U.S. perceived Communist threat

Men and women usually see their self-serving acts as altruistic, their aggressive acts as defensive. The study of motivation is no easier when examining foreign policy decisions than other human endeavors. Khrushchev may well have contrived an explanation for his decision after he decided impulsively to send the missiles. Without doubt he chafed at the fact of Soviet strategic inferiority and its implications for the German question and every other matter at issue with the United States. The Gilpatric speech of October 1961 had revealed to the world the lack of substance behind Khrushchev's claims of Soviet superiority. Something had to be done to redress the strategic balance. In April 1962, Khrushchev was troubled at the news that American intermediate-range missiles (IRBMs) in Turkey, on the very border of the Soviet Union, had become operational. It was at that moment that he apparently conceived of the idea of placing Soviet IRBMs in the shadow of the United States, in Cuba. As Raymond Garthoff, a participant in the events and later scholarly analyst of them, has argued, the most likely reason for Soviet leaders risking the Cuban missile venture "was almost certainly a perceived need to prevent the United States from using its growing strategic superiority to compel Soviet concessions . . . a shared judgment of the leadership that world political perceptions of the strategic balance mattered, and that the Soviet Union's position in 1962 needed shoring up."[15] The fact that Cuba would simultaneously be protected was a likely collateral virtue of the action but, as students of causality might argue, not a "sufficient cause." It is quite clear that the Soviets did not anticipate a crisis: They expected to be able to install the missiles secretly and to present the United States with a fait accompli, to which Washington would acquiesce reluctantly.

In late August 1962, the director of the CIA informed Kennedy and his senior foreign policy advisers that he suspected the Soviets of placing offensive missiles in Cuba. A review of the evidence led Rusk and the others to reject the idea. There was no doubt that the

15 Garthoff, *Reflections,* 21; see also Jack Snyder, *Myths Of Empire* (Ithaca, 1991), 246–7.

Soviets were providing the Cubans with military equipment, but the secretaries of state and defense and their analysts concluded that the buildup was defensive. The Soviets had been warned categorically that offensive weapons would not be tolerated in Cuba and there was no inclination to believe they would take the risk.

As the midterm election of 1962 approached, the Republican opposition was increasingly critical of the administration's failure to eliminate the Communist regime in Cuba. Kennedy's men argued that Cuba was not an offensive threat, that the military buildup was defensive, and that allegations of Soviet missiles were without foundation. Quick to discredit their domestic political opponents, administration leaders discounted the mounting evidence of Khrushchev's gamble. They were further misled by a deliberate Soviet program of deception, of Soviet assurances they would not put offensive weapons into Cuba, a tactic that continued even after the Americans had discovered the missiles. As late as October 14, McGeorge Bundy, Kennedy's national security adviser, assured a television audience that there was no evidence the Soviets were preparing an offensive capability in Cuba. That very day the U-2 returned with unmistakable evidence of a missile complex under construction at San Cristobal. The films were processed on October 15 and by midnight all of the top policymakers except the president were aware that the United States, and especially the Kennedy administration, faced catastrophe.

Briefed as he awoke the next morning, the president called together a group of advisers called the Executive Committee of the National Security Council or "Ex Comm." What were the Soviets up to? How should the United States respond? Contingency plans anticipated an invasion or an air strike and the U.S. military commenced preparations for both. There was considerable support for an air strike but the opposition prevailed. Secretary of Defense Robert McNamara argued that Soviet missiles in Cuba meant little more than Soviet missiles in Russia. Should the Soviets launch an attack, the United States would destroy the Soviet Union no matter where the attack originated. He was unmoved by the contention that Soviet missiles in Cuba might eliminate the strategic advantage the

United States enjoyed. He contended that parity was inevitable and it might be advantageous to American security if the Soviets achieved it sooner rather than later. [16]

After two days of discussion, even McNamara was persuaded that a strong response was required. For domestic political reasons as well as for his image abroad, the president had to demonstrate that the United States could not be deceived and challenged with impunity. The choices of action narrowed to an air strike against the missile sites or a blockade, to be followed by an air strike or an invasion if the Soviets did not respond adequately. Tense debate ensued among the president's advisers, with Dean Acheson, supported by the military leaders, calling for military action. Ultimately, agreement on a blockade was reached, at least in part because Kennedy was not convinced that the air strike would suffice. He very likely suspected the military, dismayed by his equivocation at the Bay of Pigs, of attempting to draw him into the invasion of Cuba. His principal Soviet analyst, Llewellyn Thompson, warned against the possibility of Khrushchev responding irrationally if Soviet troops were killed in an air strike. Kennedy would start with a blockade. American forces began to move into position October 20. On October 22, the Soviets, the American people, and the rest of the world would be informed. [17]

An hour before Kennedy addressed a national television audience, the Soviet ambassador was apprised. He claimed then, and forever after, that he knew nothing of the missiles until Rusk told him. At 7:00 P.M. Eastern Standard Time, Kennedy told Americans of the discovery of the missile sites, spelled out their meaning for the United States, and explained the response he was making. To Americans – to knowledgeable people everywhere – there came an awareness that they hovered on the edge of extinction. The danger of nuclear incineration hung over Rusk's briefing of the ambassadors of nonaligned nations. With a sense that they might never see each other again, each ambassador shook Rusk's hand, perhaps murmur-

---

16 Graham Allison, *Essence of Decision* (Boston, 1971), 195–6; James G. Blight and David A. Welch, *On the Brink* (New York, 1989), 23–4.

17 Elie Abel, *The Missile Crisis* (Philadelphia, 1966), 80–93.

ing a word of hope on the way out. The initiative had returned to Nikita Khrushchev. His choice was war or surrender and his response might come as swiftly as an intercontinental ballistic missile.

Khrushchev and his advisers were taken completely by surprise and badly shaken by the president's address. Soviet intelligence had failed to pick up any indication that the United States had discovered the missiles or that the president and his most senior advisers had spent the week in emergency meetings. Firing the missiles and provoking certain retaliation against the Soviet Union was inconceivable. The central question was what could be salvaged. Might the United States accept the weapons already in Cuba in exchange for an agreement not to send more? How serious was the United States about the blockade? Would the Americans use the opportunity to invade Cuba and, if so, how would the Soviet Union respond?[18]

Initially, the Soviets denied the American charges, condemned the blockade as piracy, sent in submarines to probe the blockade ahead of their surface ships, and ordered Soviet forces in Cuba readied for combat. They were 42,000 strong, far in excess of the numbers estimated by American intelligence, and armed with tactical nuclear weapons, to be used at the discretion of the local commander.[19] The Cubans mobilized their reserves, tripling their forces under arms to a total of 270,000 men. Construction at the missile sites accelerated. World War III was approaching rapidly.

Directed by the president to track Soviet submarines in the area and protect American vessels, the U.S. Navy used low-explosive depth charges to force the Soviet submarines to the surface. On October 24, the Strategic Air Command (SAC) was put on full alert, with the order given "in the clear," leaving nothing to Soviet imagination. Khrushchev could have no illusions about the seriousness of American intent. He chose not to challenge the blockade. On October 25 the last Soviet ships heading for Cuba

18 Garthoff, *Reflections,* 56–9.
19 Raymond L. Garthoff, "The Havana Conference on the Cuban Missile Crisis," in Woodrow Wilson International Center for Scholars, *Cold War International History Project Bulletin* 1 (Spring 1992): 2–4.

stopped and turned back. "Eyeball to eyeball," the Soviets had blinked.[20]

Kennedy and his advisers were enormously relieved by the reports of Soviet ship movements, but they were also aware that Soviet forces in Cuba were still working around the clock to get their missiles operational. One member of Ex Comm noted that the difference between war before the missiles could be used and war afterward would be millions of American lives. The United States would have to attack before any of them were ready, an eventuality estimated to be only two or three days away. The Soviets were informed of the American intent. Castro was so certain the attack was coming that he spent the night of October 26 at a bomb shelter in the Soviet Embassy from whence he urged Khrushchev to stand firm.[21]

On October 26, Aleksander Fomin, the senior KGB officer in the Soviet Embassy in Washington, suddenly contacted John Scali, ABC's State Department reporter, to ask if his friends in the department would be willing to offer a public pledge not to invade Cuba if the Soviets removed the missiles, promised not to reintroduce them, and allowed UN verification. Scali went immediately to a contact in the State Department who passed the message to the secretary of state and the president. Rusk remembered that an unofficial exchange of views had led to the cease-fire in Korea in 1951 and thought a breakthrough possible. Scali was instructed to inform Fomin that time was short, no more than two days, and given a piece of paper with a message from the "highest levels" in the U.S. government indicating that the Americans saw "real possibilities" in the proposal. It was later alleged by Soviet authorities that Fomin was exploring on his own, but in October 1962, the president and his advisers assumed the terms he proposed came from Moscow. Later that day, Kennedy received a long cable from Khrushchev, indicating that he understood the danger of the situation, wanted to avoid conflict, and was prepared to negotiate. He implied that if the United States agreed not to invade Cuba, the missiles could be removed, but he did not specify his terms. Rusk and Llewellyn

20 Garthoff, *Reflections*, 61–2, 67–9.
21 Garthoff, *Reflections*, 91.

Thompson concluded that the settlement outlined by Fomin represented Khrushchev's thoughts, that the Soviets were prepared to back off, that the crisis was over. They guessed that Khrushchev had been struggling with other Soviet leaders eager to challenge the United States and had used Fomin to circumvent them.[22]

That night Robert Kennedy, the president's brother, met secretly with the Soviet ambassador, who indicated that removal of the American missiles in Turkey might help to resolve the affair. Bobby called the president who authorized him to tell the Soviets that he had long considered removing the missiles and that he expected to do so shortly after the crisis was over. Kennedy's message was passed to Khrushchev.[23]

On the morning of October 27, a second cable was received from Khrushchev, this time demanding that the missiles in Turkey be removed as a condition for removal of the missiles in Cuba. Unaware of the meeting between Bobby Kennedy and the Soviet ambassador the night before, most members of Ex Comm argued for rejecting what they perceived as Khrushchev's additional demand. They feared a trade could damage relations with Turkey and other American allies who might fear that the United States would sacrifice the protection it offered its allies whenever it was threatened.

Shortly after Khrushchev's second cable was received, Ex Comm was informed that a U-2 had been shot down over Cuba. Later that morning, for the first time, low-level reconnaissance flights were fired upon. A sudden sense that the Soviet position might be stiffening, that military action might still be necessary swept through the group. Acheson and American military leaders suspected the Soviets were hiding something, that they were stalling until some of the missiles were operational. They still favored air strikes and an invasion. In fact, local Soviet air defense commanders, uninformed of the delicate negotiation underway, had heightened the tension.[24]

That afternoon, Ex Comm agreed to a proposal put forward by Robert Kennedy. Khrushchev's second cable was ignored and the

22 Cohen, *Dean Rusk*, 156–7; Garthoff, *Reflections*, 80–1, is inclined to accept Fomin's claim he was acting on his own.
23 James G. Blight and David A. Welch, *On the Brink* (New York, 1989), 337–8.
24 Garthoff, *Reflections*, 82–85.

president agreed to the terms implied in the first cable, presumably spelled out by Fomin. Robert Kennedy personally took the president's message to the Soviet Embassy and informed the Soviet ambassador that his brother was prepared to give the required assurances that the United States would not invade Cuba. The United States, however, could not unilaterally remove the missiles from Turkey. Nonetheless, the president was confident that NATO would withdraw them shortly. If, on the other hand, the Soviets did not agree promptly to remove their missiles from Cuba, the United States would remove them. Although Khrushchev was not told, plans for an air strike on October 29 or 30 had been developed. Again, the decision for war or peace rested with the Soviet leader — unless one of his officers or an American naval or SAC commander acted precipitately.

On Sunday morning, October 28, it was all over. Khrushchev announced that he had ordered the weapons Americans described as offensive to be dismantled and returned to the Soviet Union. The joy in Washington was not matched in Cuba where Soviet officers wept at the news and Castro was enraged. Castro never permitted UN supervision or verification of the removal of the missiles and there were disagreements about Soviet bombers and troops stationed in Cuba that took weeks to resolve. The United States never gave formal assurances that it would not invade Cuba and remained hostile to the Castro regime long after relations with the major Communist powers improved. But the gravest crisis of the Cold War had ended with a victory for the forces of peace.

In 1962, Nikita Khrushchev brought the world close to nuclear war. It is not necessary to ignore American provocations against Cuba or nuclear blackmail of the Soviet Union to charge that Khrushchev gambled impulsively, putting at risk the lives of hundreds of millions of people. He acted deceitfully, putting the missiles in Cuba while sending Kennedy assurances that he would do nothing of the sort. There can be no doubt that he hoped to score a diplomatic and military coup against the United States.

John F. Kennedy's response to the missiles discovered in October 1962 brought the world a step closer to disaster, perhaps unnecessarily. McNamara was probably right: that strategic parity between the United States and the Soviet Union was inevitable and that the gap was merely being closed sooner rather than later; that Soviet missiles in Cuba were strategically tolerable. By treating the discovery of the missiles as an event of no great import, by accepting Soviet claims that they were defensive, by stressing the enormous retaliatory power of the United States, as Gilpatric had the previous year, the rest of the world might well have been impressed again by American confidence. It might be argued that the only grave threat posed by the discovery of the missiles was to the political future of the Kennedy administration; that Kennedy's greatest fear was that the Republican opposition would use the missiles, the existence of which the administration had consistently denied, to ride the Cuban issue to victory in the congressional elections of 1962 and, yet more troubling, in the presidential election of 1964.

Once the administration decided on a strong response, its plans were conceived carefully and executed with an appropriate balance of courage and flexibility. Perhaps most interesting is the fact that Kennedy chose to keep his flexibility secret from the American people. It was six years before they knew that he had agreed that American missiles would come out of Turkey and more than a quarter of a century before Americans, including Ex Comm members, discovered that the president's brother had discussed the trade in one of a series of secret meetings with the Soviet ambassador before Khrushchev raised it. Apparently obsessed with a need to present a public image of toughness, convinced that it was essential to his political success, Kennedy chose to have the American people believe he had won in a man-to-man showdown with the Soviet premier.

In the months that followed, the missile crisis came to be seen by many analysts as a watershed in Soviet-American relations. Both American and Soviet leaders generally acted with greater prudence and sought détente. Much of the tension drained out of the confrontation in the last year of Kennedy's life. A Moscow-Washington "hot line" was set up, permitting direct and immediate communication between the leaders. Agreement was reached on a treaty banning atmospheric nuclear testing by the superpowers. These arguably were not major steps, but they reversed the direction of the previous two years, suggesting that the future might well be one of peaceful coexistence instead of inevitable conflict, that the bomb shelters being built across the United States might not be necessary. They were steps toward building the mutual trust that had never been possible in Stalin's day and which Khrushchev had precluded by his bluster and deceit. Further improvement of relations would depend on the performance of each country, on the respect and confidence that might develop between its leaders. Unanticipated in 1963 was the rapid disappearance of both Kennedy and Khrushchev, the one murdered and the other forcibly retired by his colleagues in the Kremlin.

To be sure, there were fleeting moments of crisis between the superpowers in the years that followed, but they deterred each other from threatening acts by spending enormous sums on nuclear warheads and delivery systems sufficient to destroy each other's people several times over. Out of this emerged the strategic doctrine of Mutual Assured Destruction (MAD), based on the fact that each side would be vulnerable to destruction by the other side, no matter which one started a war.[25] Given such incentive to avoid direct confrontation, the United States and the Soviet Union indulged in costly games on the periphery, primarily, although not exclusively, in areas where neither had vital interests at stake. There, in countries like Vietnam, Afghanistan, and Ethiopia, they brought misery to the local peoples, squandered the lives of their own young, and expended resources desperately needed for the shoring up of their own societies.

25 See Robert Jervis, *The Meaning of the Nuclear Revolution* (Ithaca, 1989), esp. 74–106.

6. America's Longest War

America's war in Vietnam is the textbook example of great-power arrogance and self-deception, of the abuse and dissipation of wealth and power. American leaders knew and cared little about the people of Vietnam, their history, their culture, their aspirations. Vietnam was of no intrinsic importance to the United States. In the years when the French controlled Indochina, they pursued a mercantilist policy, allowing minimal foreign involvement in the region's economy. American business developed no stake there, and although the area was potentially rich in natural resources, there was nothing there that could not be obtained elsewhere, or that the locals could afford to deny to the world market. Similarly, the region was of minimal strategic importance. A case could certainly be made for keeping Cambodia, Laos, and Vietnam from being controlled by a presumed adversary, whether Japan in 1941 or China or the Soviet Union in the context of the Cold War. But, of course, a case for containing the influence of an antagonist could be made for every corner of the earth – and outer space as well. Friendly control of what had once been French Indochina was unquestionably desirable. But if Cambodia, Laos, and Vietnam were all hostile to the United States, the shift in the world balance of power would be imperceptible. No vital American interest would be threatened. Nonetheless, more than fifty thousand Americans gave their lives in a war in Indochina, as did hundreds of thousands of Cambodians, Laotians, and Vietnamese.

Once a nation develops the ability to project its power to distant regions of the globe, to intervene in the affairs of other peoples, the temptation to do so seems very nearly irresistible – at least until its leaders are sobered by disaster or its ability diminishes. American power in the first two decades after World War II, both relative and absolute, was extraordinary. No place in the world was beyond the reach of the United States. And equally important was the sense Americans had of themselves as "winners," as a people who had never lost a war (most Americans seem to think the United States won the War of 1812), a people who could accomplish anything to which they set their minds. They were an ahistorical people, unable, perhaps unwilling, to learn from the failures of others.

The lessons of the past, insofar as American leaders drew on them, taught that aggressors could not be appeased, that the United States had a responsibility to use its power to thwart those who would extend totalitarian systems, that when the will was there, Americans had found ways to stop Hitler and Stalin and would-be perpetrators of evil in Greece, Iran, Guatemala. Contrary examples, like Indonesia and Cuba, were either forgotten or perceived as negative examples, as occasions when only the will had been lacking. The fact that American "successes" against leftist movements usually resulted in vicious military dictatorships was rationalized by the conviction that military dictatorships were anachronisms, had no external source of support, and might evolve into democracies, whereas Communist regimes, supported by the Soviet bloc, were forever.

American leaders discovered Indochina early in World War II, when the Japanese intruded on the French empire. Japanese pressures on Southeast Asia and the Southwest Pacific worried Franklin Roosevelt and his associates, who were fearful the Japanese maneuvers would distract the British and their allies from the task of containing Nazi Germany in Europe, North Africa, and the Middle East. Toward the end of the war, as victory for the Grand Alliance loomed and the retreat of Japanese forces from Indochina was imminent, Roosevelt, contemptuous of the French generally, suggested that the people of Indochina be put under a UN trusteeship rather than subjected anew to French imperialism. The handful of Americans who reached the area before the end of the war discovered a well-organized resistance movement, which had harassed the Japanese and had no intention of submitting to the French. In Vietnam in particular, the will to independence was strong and deemed worthy of American support. Indeed, the leader of the Vietnamese resistance, Ho Chi Minh, was enlisted as an American agent on the eve of Japan's surrender.[1]

When the war ended, the French returned to Indochina in force, determined to reassert their control. French leaders warned Washington that American opposition to French suppression of the Vietnamese independence movement would alienate the French people, strengthen the French Communist party and, conceivably, drive France into the arms of the Soviets. Ho invoked Thomas Jefferson and the Declaration of Independence, but to no avail. He was, after all, a Communist. More to the point, Vietnam was distant and unimportant. France, on the other hand, might well be a major partner in the new world order American leaders envisaged in the late 1940s; French leaders angered by American opposition to the grandiosity of their imperial vision certainly could undermine American plans for Europe. The United States chose to facilitate the return of French power to Southeast Asia, subordinating traditional American antiimperialism to the exigencies of great-power politics. The responsibility of world leadership took precedence over the principles upon which America's claim to moral superiority had rested.

When the French failed and were forced to come to terms with Ho's Vietminh in 1954, the United States determined to do the job right itself. (See Chapter 3.) Eisenhower and Dulles imagined that the Vietnamese still perceived the United States as the beacon of democratic revolution, that the United States could intervene in Vietnam untainted by colonialism and provide a rallying point for Vietnamese nationalism, an umbrella under which Vietnamese who wanted independence not only from France but from international communism would flourish. For the moment, they were prepared to concede Vietnam above the seventeenth parallel, where the Vietminh had regrouped, to Ho Chi Minh's Communist regime. They intended, however, to build a separate, non-Communist nation to

1 For quick sketches of the initial American encounter with Indochina, see Gary R. Hess, *The United States' Emergence as a Southeast Asian Power, 1940–1950* (New York, 1987); George Herring, *America's Longest War*, 2d ed. (New York, 1986), and George M. Kahin, *Intervention* (New York, 1986).

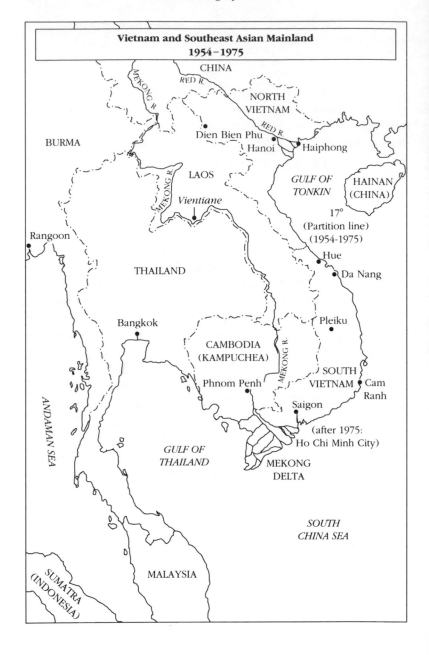

**Vietnam and Southeast Asian Mainland
1954–1975**

CHINA

RED R.

NORTH
VIETNAM

MEKONG R.

Dien Bien Phu

RED R.

Hanoi   Haiphong

BURMA

LAOS

GULF OF
TONKIN

HAINAN
(CHINA)

MEKONG R.

Vientiane

17°
(Partition line)
(1954-1975)

Rangoon

Hue

Da Nang

THAILAND

Bangkok

Pleiku

CAMBODIA
(KAMPUCHEA)

MEKONG R.

SOUTH
VIETNAM

Cam
Ranh

Phnom Penh

Saigon

(after 1975:
Ho Chi Minh City)

ANDAMAN SEA

*GULF OF
THAILAND*

MEKONG
DELTA

*SOUTH
CHINA SEA*

*SUMATRA
(INDONESIA)*

MALAYSIA

the south, where the French, whom they quickly pushed aside, and their collaborators had regrouped. The Americans hoped to use the southern state they would create as a magnet to draw the North out of the Communist orbit.

Indochina became enormously important to the Eisenhower administration primarily because it was perceived in 1954 as the site of the next round in the battle with the Sino-Soviet bloc. The Communists were seeking to extend their influence everywhere. For the moment they were quiescent in Europe. They lacked a toehold in Africa or the Middle East. They had been checked in Korea, but retained an enormous potential for mischief in East Asia. Chinese support for the Vietminh against the French in 1954, as well as Chinese and Soviet recognition of Ho's regime in 1950 helped shape the expectations of Eisenhower and his colleagues. They appear to have overlooked Soviet and Chinese indifference to Vietnamese goals at Geneva, Soviet and Chinese pressures on Ho that forced him to concede to the French far more than they had salvaged on the battlefield. Domestic political pressures, from the Republican Right, also informed Eisenhower and Dulles's conception of the need to draw the line at the seventeenth parallel in Vietnam. Those who found the Truman administration guilty of losing China did not wish to be charged with losing Indochina.

Once Eisenhower had concluded that he had to act in Indochina, he applied his domino theory. Indochina alone may have lacked strategic and economic importance, but if Indochina fell to the Communists, then all of Southeast Asia would follow. Certainly no one would deny the economic and strategic import of all of Southeast Asia, gateway to South Asia and the Southwest Pacific. Laos or Vietnam could each be invested with the value of all of Indochina, Indochina with the value of all of Southeast Asia, Southeast Asia with the value of a large chunk of the globe. Like Truman, Eisenhower seems to have developed his rationale for intervention after he decided to intervene and to have strained to offer something plausible to the American public. In 1956 and 1958 the National Security Council restated the proposition that "the national security of the United States would be endangered by Communist domination of mainland Southeast Asia"; that "the loss to Communist control of any single free country would encourage tendencies toward accommodation by the rest"; that "the loss of the entire area would have a serious adverse impact on the U.S. position elsewhere in the Far East, have severe economic consequences for many nations of the free world . . . and could result in severe economic and political pressures on Japan and India for accommodation to the Communist bloc."[2]

The Ngo Dinh Diem regime created by the Eisenhower administration proved to be an imperfect instrument for achieving American ends. Diem, the prime minister, was suitably anti-Communist but failed to become the popular leader who would draw the Vietnamese people away from Ho Chi Minh. The elections mandated by the Geneva accords for 1956 had to be avoided because of American intelligence estimates that Ho would win 80 percent of the votes. The principle of support for free elections lost its attractiveness in Washington when the victor was likely to be a Communist.

Diem had some initial success in suppressing potential rivals and consolidating his control in the South. His methods, however, alienated much of rural Vietnam and antagonized Buddhist activists, intellectuals, and politicians who might have constituted the loyal opposition. In the countryside, land reform promoted by his American advisers was less attractive to the peasants than the more radical programs that had been instituted by the Vietminh. Provincial and county leaders sent to the countryside from Saigon generally proved more sympathetic to landlords than to peasants and less popular than the local authorities they replaced. Diem's efforts to root out the Vietminh infrastructure in the South included the dislocation of peasants. His "strategic-hamlet" program required villagers to leave their homes and burial grounds to take refuge in fortified encampments. Buddhists were troubled by the preference enjoyed by Catholics, often refugees from the North, both in obtaining government positions and in the freedom to practice their religion. Intellectuals and much of the rest of the politically mobile elite, repressed by Diem's secret police, turned against him. Even before Eisenhower

2 U.S. Congress, House, Committee on Armed Services, *United States-Vietnam Relations, 1945–1967* (hereafter *Pentagon Papers*), Book 9, V.B.3, 1083, 1088.

left office, an insurrection was underway in the countryside and there was minimal support for Diem outside of the Catholic minority in the cities. The American nation-building experiment in Vietnam was in trouble.

John F. Kennedy had visited Vietnam in 1954 and come away with views not significantly different from those of Eisenhower and Dulles: Indochina had to be denied to the Communists; American antiimperialists could succeed where French imperialists had failed; a viable non-Communist nationalist regime could be created with support from the United States. Warned by Eisenhower of the crisis in Indochina, Kennedy, as president, was determined to stop the erosion of the American position there.

Kennedy's first emergency in Indochina came in Laos where Eisenhower's attempts to create a pro-Western, anti-Communist regime had proven counterproductive. American subversion of the Geneva agreements in support of a right-wing general had triggered an increase in aid to the Communist Pathet Lao from Ho's regime in Hanoi and a deeper Soviet involvement in Laos. In January 1961, Washington's man in Laos was on the ropes. Kennedy's advisers concluded that victory for pro-Western forces was improbable, and that the United States would be fortunate if it could induce the other side to accept a return to a neutral Laos. A major military intervention by the United States was rejected by the president when the Joint Chiefs, disinclined to fight another limited war, demanded freedom to use nuclear weapons and to attack China. Instead, Kennedy ordered the carrier U.S.S. *Midway* to the Gulf of Siam, sent a Marine detachment to Thailand, put forces on Okinawa on alert, signaling to the Soviets the apparent willingness of the United States to fight rather than allow the Communists to take over Laos.[3]

American actions may have frightened their allies as much as they did the Soviets. British Prime Minister Harold Macmillan thought the issue could be resolved without war "if the Americans do not suddenly run amok."[4] Khrushchev recognized the risk, did not

3 Warren I. Cohen, *Dean Rusk* (Totowa, N.J., 1980), 125–28.
4 Harold Macmillan, *Pointing the Way* (New York, 1972), 344–5.

consider total control of Laos worth what it might cost to overcome a major American escalation, and indicated a willingness to negotiate. A cease-fire was arranged in May 1962 and negotiations began shortly thereafter. A Soviet-American agreement on a neutral Laos was reached fourteen months later.

Kennedy's willingness to compromise over Laos did not extend to Vietnam. Throughout the early discussions within the administration of appropriate responses to the crisis in Indochina, the president and his advisers indicated a determination to take their stand in Vietnam. The situation there was retrievable, the Vietnamese protégés of the United States would fight. Initially, Kennedy's principal concerns were standing up to Khrushchev and preventing a domestic political disaster. He had been deeply troubled by Khrushchev's strident advocacy of wars of national liberation before and during their meeting in Vienna in June 1961. Subsequently, as the reality of the Sino-Soviet split penetrated their consciousness, he and his advisers were more likely to see the Chinese, working through the Vietnamese Communists, as the evil demons responsible for their distress in Southeast Asia. But no matter whether the initiative came from Moscow, Beijing, or Hanoi, Kennedy was profoundly fearful of being labeled "soft on communism" if he could not prevent a Communist sweep through Indochina. The Republicans had capitalized on the "loss" of China in 1949 and McCarthyism remained a force in the society. Should the Communists prevail in Vietnam, his chances of reelection in 1964 would be slight, the Democratic party would be devastated again, and the forces of reaction would erase the gains of Roosevelt's New Deal, Truman's Fair Deal, and whatever he hoped to achieve with his own New Frontiers program. Success in Vietnam would teach Khrushchev that the indirect aggression constituted by wars of national liberation did not pay, might erase the embarrassment of failure at the Bay of Pigs, and provide the margin necessary to assure Kennedy of a second term.

For Kennedy and his colleagues, Vietnam became a convenient ground for demonstrating America's will and power and credibility to friends and enemies alike. To those around the world who feared that the United States was intimidated by Soviet missiles and nuclear capabilities, there would be proof that the Americans would still ride to the rescue, even in places as distant and inhospitable as the jungles of Vietnam. To those at home who worried that a Democratic president would not stand up to the Communists, there would be evidence to the contrary. To the men in Moscow and Beijing who thought they could accomplish through subversion the conquest they dared not seek through direct, overt acts of aggression, there would be a warning that this, too, would fail. In Vietnam, Kennedy could test the counterinsurgency techniques to which he had become attracted; his Green Berets could be sent into action. There the Pentagon could test a myriad of technological innovations, products of countless billions spent on weapons development. Throughout the Kennedy administration there were brilliant men, the "Best and the Brightest," as the journalist David Halberstam named them, McGeorge Bundy, Robert McNamara, Maxwell Taylor, Walt Rostow, most prominent among them, who were confident that they had the ideas necessary for nation building and that under their leadership the United States had the will and power to succeed in the great-power contest in Vietnam – and ultimately all over the globe.[5]

As they juggled the initial crises inherited from Eisenhower in the Congo, Cuba, and Laos, Kennedy and his advisers found time to focus on the situation in Vietnam. It was deteriorating quickly as the Diem government's influence and support eroded, as the Vietminh became increasingly active in the South and succeeded in obtaining support from Hanoi. American intelligence concluded that the insurgency in the South was indigenous, that the cadres dribbling in from the North were primarily Southerners returning to their homes, and that Ho Chi Minh, while hardly uninterested, was still husbanding his resources to strengthen that part of Vietnam under his control. There was no evidence of Chinese or Soviet involvement. Kennedy's colleagues concluded that the insurgency could be crushed at minimal cost to the United States; that an increase in military supplies and advisers to Diem's forces would be sufficient to compensate for the increase in opposition forces, the men and women Diem called the "Viet Cong." The object was to

5 David Halberstam, *The Best and the Brightest* (New York, 1972).

enhance the performance of Diem's troops. Rostow, who had become the president's principal adviser on Vietnam, argued for using "unexploited counter-guerrilla assets . . . armed helicopters; other Research and Development possibilities; our Special Forces units." He contended that it was "somehow wrong to be developing these capabilities but not applying them. . . . In Knute Rockne's old phrase, we are not saving them for the Junior Prom."[6]

The president began by increasing the number of American military "advisers" in Vietnam, including four hundred members of the Special Forces, in direct violation of the limits placed by the Geneva agreements. He demanded more aggressive tactics and did not flinch when these required Americans to engage in combat, a further violation of the Geneva agreements. In due course Kennedy authorized the dropping of napalm and herbicidal defoliants, the former a jellied petroleum product that clung to the skin while it burned and the latter chemicals that would denude the forest, destroy the productivity of the soil, and have unpredictable effects on humans who came in contact with it.

The Joint Chiefs were less enamored of counterinsurgency operations than were Kennedy, Taylor, and Rostow. They pressed for sending regular U.S. Army combat forces to Vietnam to warn off Hanoi and Beijing. Diem, fearful of losing control of his country to the Americans, apprehensive about being perceived by his people as an American puppet, indicated that American combat troops were not needed. In October 1961, as insurgent successes became more threatening, Kennedy sent Taylor and Rostow to Vietnam to determine whether American troops were necessary. The Taylor-Rostow report, which might have been expected to call for intensifying the counterinsurgency effort, called instead for the introduction of combat forces in the guise of a flood relief team. Kennedy continued to temporize: He did not want to send American troops to take over the war in Vietnam, he did not want to negotiate with the insurgents − and he did not want to risk a Communist victory over Diem.

6 Memorandum to the president from Rostow, March 29, 1961. Quoted in Kahin, *Intervention*, 131.

In response to his perception of the irreducible needs of the Diem regime, Kennedy decided to send American "support" units to Vietnam. These forces dribbled over by the hundreds and then by the thousands. By the end of 1961 there were more than 2,000 American soldiers in Vietnam, roughly three times the number allowed by the Geneva agreements. There were more than 11,000 by the end of 1962, more than 16,000 when Kennedy died in 1963. These support units quickly engaged in combat operations, accompanying Vietnamese pilots on missions, flying the helicopters that carried Diem's troops into battle, killing insurgents as necessary in "self-defense." Despite Diem's opposition and Kennedy's reluctance, the United States had taken an important step toward Americanization of the war.

Kennedy and his advisers had engaged in a sophisticated exercise in self-deception. They considered the alternative of abandoning an unpopular and sometimes difficult ally, but allowing southern Vietnam to fall to the Communists by default was inconceivable. During Kennedy's years in the White House, victory seemed possible if Diem instituted some modest political, economic, and social reforms and if his military was strengthened and provided with more aggressive leadership. And the domestic costs of the "loss" of Vietnam might well be devastating. If sending a few thousand troops to buoy the morale of Vietnamese forces would suffice to turn things around, it seemed a safe, sensible move, less provocative, less dangerous than a major military escalation, politically wiser than withdrawal. They deluded themselves into believing that they were still in control, that they had retained their freedom of action. A little military intervention, however, turned out to be like "a little pregnant." There was no painless way to reverse the process. Kennedy was only a few steps behind the Joint Chiefs.

Throughout 1962, Kennedy was told by his aides that American policy was working, that the insurgents had lost their momentum, that the strategic-hamlet program was succeeding. The American military advisory group in Vietnam began drafting plans to reduce American forces present. The president, pleased with the results of the Cuban missile crisis, pleased with the official reports from Vietnam, reached a new peak of self-satisfaction. He was irritated increasingly, however, by press accounts that suggested the battle in Vietnam was going less well, that the Diem regime was repressive and corrupt, that reports of its strategic successes were exaggerated. Imperiously, the president demanded that the *New York Times* recall its correspondent. He failed in that endeavor but more easily intimidated the television networks.[7]

By January 1963, Kennedy was receiving other indications that all was not well in Vietnam. His friend Senator Mike Mansfield (D.-Mont.) went out to the field at the president's request and confirmed the negative reports of the journalists. Mansfield warned that the Diem regime was less stable and less popular in 1962 than it had been in 1955. The battle against the insurgents was in the process of becoming an American war likely to cost the United States far more in lives and dollars than control of Vietnam was worth to the United States. In mid-January, Diem's troops, supported by U.S. planes and helicopters, were battered by a numerically inferior Viet Cong force they had surrounded in the Mekong Delta near Saigon. The Viet Cong, learning to cope with modern military technology, shot down five American helicopters, and damaged nine others. But the American military advisory group in Vietnam remained optimistic and the president clearly preferred to hear that his policy was working.

A CIA estimate of mid-April 1963 offered fewer grounds for confidence in the administration's course. Although the analysts argued that the Viet Cong drive had been blunted, the enemy had not been crushed by American "involvement." If aid from Hanoi remained minimal, the Viet Cong could probably be contained, but the situation remained "fragile." The CIA was skeptical about the likelihood of Diem carrying out the reforms necessary to convert the military successes of the moment to "lasting political stability."[8]

The "fragile" situation shattered in June 1963. In the years that followed, not even hundreds of thousands of American fighting men could put the Saigon regime back together again. Largely owing to

7 Kahin, *Intervention,* 142.
8 *Pentagon Papers,* Book 12, V.B.4, 524.

the activities of his brother, Ngo Dinh Nhu, Diem's administration had become increasingly repressive in the early 1960s. In May there had been trouble with Buddhists in the city of Hue. Government forces fired on a demonstration, killing several participants. Protests spread through the coastal cities and Americans in Vietnam feared the impact on the struggle against the Viet Cong. They urged Diem to be conciliatory. Nhu urged him to crush the Buddhists. On June 11, a Buddhist priest seated himself crosslegged in a major Saigon intersection, other priests poured gasoline over him, and he set himself afire – an incredible scene that horrified Americans and people all over the world who watched it soon afterward on television.

Under U.S. pressure, Diem and Nhu agreed to end both the special privileges of the Catholic church and the harassment of Buddhists, but the agreement collapsed within weeks. By August the protest movement was out of control, and Diem seemed immobilized by an inability to choose between the advice of his brother and the demands of the American Embassy. On August 21, Nhu sent his security forces into the pagodas. Wielding billy clubs and truncheons, they suppressed the Buddhist movement. Kennedy and his advisers were appalled and embarrassed by the brutality of Nhu's men. They preferred that the United States not be associated with a tin-pot dictatorship that survived by Gestapo methods. They concluded that, at the very least, Nhu should be sent out of the country and that it was time to consider alternatives to Diem's regime.

On August 24, Henry Cabot Lodge, Jr., the American ambassador to Saigon, received a cable from Washington that contained a thinly veiled instruction to encourage a coup against the Diem regime. Lodge was to inform interested Vietnamese military leaders that the United States could not long support a government that included Nhu or suppressed Buddhists. Should the central government collapse, the Vietnamese generals were to be assured of a continued flow of supplies. With the arrogance that only great powers can indulge, the Kennedy administration had decided to invite a coup against a regime that had been created and sustained by the United

States. Heaven, now located on Pennsylvania Avenue, had withdrawn its Mandate from the Diem dynasty.[9]

There was very nearly a coup before the end of August, but the
generals proved timid and Kennedy's advisers had second thoughts.
Kennedy decided to muddle on until the war was won, gradually
increasing efforts to force Diem to liberalize his administration, to
rein in his brother. But reports that Nhu was dallying with the
National Liberation Front (NLF), the political arm of the insurgents,
generated unease in Washington. Kennedy's men feared that Nhu
and Diem might respond to American pressure by coming to terms
with the NLF and Hanoi and demanding that the Americans leave.
Once more advocates of a military coup against Diem prevailed on
the president. Finally, on November 1, the generals launched their
operation. Regrettably, in the course of the coup, Diem and Nhu
were murdered. With their liquidation, however, the American-
supported cause in Vietnam had been purged of the stigma of repression. Now the people of Vietnam would be mobilized to use
American assistance to defend their freedom against Communist-
controlled insurgents.

The United States, a nation whose people long prided themselves
on their adherence to the principles of nonintervention and antiimperialism, had arrogated to itself the archetypal privileges of imperial power. Out of the southern portion of Vietnam it attempted to
build a nation: Southern Vietnam became "South Vietnam." It des-
ignated the leaders of that "nation," funded their programs, armed
their troops, and had them removed when they did not meet American standards of performance. All this was done in accordance with
what was perceived to be in the national interest of the United
States. The best interests of the people of Vietnam were determined
by men in Washington. By preventing the elections scheduled for
1956, the American government consciously denied the Vietnamese
their only chance to express their preferences peacefully. By intro-
ducing American military power into Vietnam, the United States
attempted to deny the Vietnamese the right to overthrow a government they had come to despise. The result was to bring extraordin-

9 Roger Hilsman, *To Move a Nation* (Garden City, N.Y., 1967), 488.

ary misery to the Vietnamese, to come close to destroying their country in order to save it from communism.

Dwight Eisenhower eagerly seized imperial responsibility in 1955 and warned John Kennedy against "losing" Southeast Asia. Kennedy's narrow margin of victory in the election of 1960, his fear of appearing weak, and his own intense anticommunism precluded the alternative of leaving the future of Vietnam to be determined by the Vietnamese. It was Kennedy who began the Americanization of the war, who increased the 600 American military advisers Eisenhower had sent to more than 16,000 – and Kennedy's men in Vietnam were not merely advising. His death, only a few weeks after that of Diem, left a perilous situation in the hands of Lyndon Johnson.

A relatively popular general, Duong Van Minh, headed the junta that replaced Diem's regime. In the closing weeks of 1963, the level of violence in Vietnam declined. The NLF and its allies in Hanoi were eager to explore the possibility of a negotiated peace with Minh, who had a brother active in the NLF. Minh and several of his colleagues were interested, desirous of ending the suffering of their people. They were not willing to turn southern Vietnam over to the North, where Ho and his comrades had demonstrated their ruthlessness, or to accept Communist control, but they were less anti-Communist than Diem and Nhu had been. They could conceive of sharing power with the NLF, of a neutral southern Vietnam free of foreign soldiers, troops from the North, and of the war that had racked their country since 1946. The twin desires for peace and freedom from foreign domination ran fast and deep through Vietnamese society. [10]

Relative quiet in Vietnam suited Lyndon Johnson just fine. Asked by the advisers he inherited from Kennedy what he wanted to do about Vietnam, he told them he wanted it put aside for the moment. He did not want an escalation of the American role; he did not want a wider war. His principal concern in late 1963, early 1964 was the presidential election scheduled for 1964. Nothing would be

10 Kahin, *Intervention*, 182–6.

allowed to interfere with his campaign to be elected in his own right. Toward that end, he wanted to concentrate on his domestic programs, on building the Great Society in America. That was where his vision lay; that was where the votes could be found.

Neither the Vietnamese nor the American military accepted Johnson's timetable. American military men responsible for overseeing the Saigon regime's war effort were disappointed by Minh's lack of aggressiveness. They were deeply troubled by reports of his interest in a negotiated settlement, of his willingness to ask the Americans to go home, and by his resistance to greater American control over the operations of his forces. Moreover, Minh and his colleagues were opposed to the Pentagon's recommendation that the war be taken to the North, fearful of provoking a major attack across the seventeenth parallel by Hanoi's regular army. Before long American military advisers in Vietnam were shopping for a new Vietnamese leader, encouraging creation of a government more responsive to their guidance.

Three months after Minh's group seized power, General Nguyen Khanh mounted a successful coup against it with the knowledge and assistance of American military advisers in Vietnam.[11] As the reins slipped out of Minh's hands, the last chance for avoiding catastrophe slipped away as well. But the United States was delighted with Khanh, particularly with his eagerness to receive American political advice, to increase the number of American military advisers in the country, and to participate in covert operations against Hanoi. American aid increased rapidly. Unfortunately for Khanh and his American sponsors, his popularity among Vietnamese never matched that which he enjoyed in Washington. His government had little support among his own people at the outset and that little eroded quickly.

Johnson did not want any major initiatives in Vietnam before November 1964, but he could hardly accept the loss of Vietnam

11 See Kahin, *Intervention*, 182–202, for a fascinating investigation of the role of the U.S. government in Khanh's coup.

during the campaign. It became increasingly clear that the major danger to his election came from the Right, from men such as Senator Barry Goldwater (R.-Ariz.), who were demanding more vigorous prosecution of the war, who were probably aware of the Pentagon's desire to bomb northern Vietnam. Johnson chose to pose as the peace candidate, the man who would prevent extremists like Goldwater from widening the war and costing the United States tens of thousands, perhaps millions of casualties. But as the collapse of the Saigon regime loomed, the need for American boys to go over there and do the job right, for the full force of American power to be brought to bear on the North, became harder to deny.

Johnson and his advisers, an eye constantly on the American electorate, tried to halt the deterioration of the situation covertly. Rather than bomb the North, Khanh was encouraged to run small-scale guerrilla operations against the Hanoi regime without overt American assistance. Evidence of large numbers of northern Vietnamese regulars in Laos led to secret American bombing runs against suspected Communist positions. Of course, these covert operations were less a secret from their targets than from the American people and Congress. The executive was running its own war in Vietnam.

Pressure to attack the North mounted through early 1964. Some of the president's men thought an attack on the North would demonstrate American resolve; others thought it would bolster Khanh; the Joint Chiefs wanted to provoke Hanoi into acts that would justify systematic bombing; Ambassador Lodge thought nuclear weapons might be necessary. In May, Johnson's advisers agreed to an *eventual* program of using selected and gradual force against the North. The principal barrier to an immediate attack was the president's perception of his domestic political needs. When that perception changed briefly in August and disappeared in November, no one could restrain the application of America's great power against the Hanoi regime.

On August 2, 1964, an American destroyer was attacked by North Vietnamese torpedo boats while patrolling in the Gulf of Tonkin, off the coast of North Vietnam. American analysts suggested the assault was the result of an assumption by North Vietnamese leaders that the ship was involved in clandestine operations such as the South Vietnamese had just completed in the area. The ship was ordered to return to the same area, accompanied by a second U.S. warship, to demonstrate American resolve. On August 4, the North Vietnamese allegedly launched a second attack. The incident came at night, and there was uncertainty about whether it had occurred, but naval authorities assured the president that it had. Almost reflexively, Johnson ordered reprisals against what he called aggression on the high seas. It was an extraordinary opportunity to demonstrate American power and determination, to demonstrate North Vietnamese vulnerability, and to undercut Goldwater's criticism. The peace candidate would leave no doubt that he would respond fiercely to provocation.

The incident in the Gulf of Tonkin not only gave the Johnson administration the desired excuse to attack North Vietnam but also provided the occasion for the president to ask Congress for authority to take whatever steps he deemed necessary, including the use of force, to protect any endangered state in Southeast Asia. His advisers had long agreed that a congressional resolution was an essential part of the preparations for carrying the war to Hanoi. In August, the House voted 416–0 and the Senate 88–2 to give Johnson a blank check. Preparations were completed to cash it after the election.

Although Hanoi's role in the insurrection in southern Vietnam had been marginal – and American intelligence analysts knew that – the United States was preparing to go to war against Ho Chi Minh's regime. The war in the South was going badly. The Khanh government was faring worse than its predecessors. Johnson's advisers, excepting only George Ball, undersecretary of state, could not accept defeat, would not countenance American withdrawal. They could not tolerate the "loss" of southern Vietnam to the Communists, its domestic consequences, its impact on the credibility of the American imperium. They could not believe that the greatest power the world had ever known lacked the means to crush a peasant rebellion in what the president would call some "pissant" country. An attack on the North would probably reduce the rate of infiltration and cut the Viet Cong off from supplies and reinforcements. It would warn the Vietnamese, the Chinese, and the Soviets that the

United States was determined to hold the line. It would raise morale in the South. The decision to attack North Vietnam was born of frustration and arrogance, taken by men who were losing a relatively minor skirmish and could not bear it. They chose instead to invest the revolutionary struggle in Vietnam with weight in the world balance of power, with the potential of tipping the scales in favor of international communism. They chose instead to widen the war, to increase the stakes, to use America's vast power to intimidate the Vietnamese, to impose an American vision of their future on an unwilling and uncomprehending people.

On November 3, 1964, the Americans gave Lyndon Johnson an enormous victory over Barry Goldwater. In much of the world, those men and women who concerned themselves with issues of war and peace rejoiced at what they perceived as a victory for peace. In Washington, preparations for war were complete. In Saigon, the generals were playing at musical chairs again, thwarting American efforts to operate from a stable base in the South. The president resisted a powerful argument for commencing systematic bombing of the North presented by McGeorge Bundy and Robert McNamara. The dogs of war strained at their leashes.

Suddenly, on February 7, 1965, the Viet Cong attacked an American installation at Pleiku, killing seven Americans and wounding more than one hundred others. Johnson immediately ordered attacks on barracks and staging areas in North Vietnam. A few days later he gave the order to implement the full-scale bombing plan, put into effect February 28. Less than a week later, two battalions of U.S. Marines went ashore at Danang to protect the airfields from which the bombing attacks were being launched. Johnson and his advisers hoped that Hanoi and the Viet Cong could be brought to heel without a major combat role for American ground forces. Rusk and Taylor worried that "white-faced" troops would be counterproductive; that they would be viewed with hostility by the local people, discredit the side on which they fought, and have trouble distinguishing between friendly and unfriendly villagers. But intelligence reports soon indicated that the bombing had not affected Hanoi's will, that North Vietnamese regular army troops were beginning to cross into the South. On April 1, the president approved the use of American troops for offensive operations. On election day, in November 1964, there had been 25,000 American military men and women in Vietnam. In July 1965 there were 75,000. In November, a year after the election, there were 165,000 and reports that more were on the way. American boys were trying to do what candidate Lyndon Johnson had promised Asian boys would be allowed to do for themselves. Gradually Americans realized they were at war.

Unhappiness with the American role in Vietnam manifested itself as early as March 1965 as student activists, religious pacifists, and academics specializing in Southeast Asian affairs began to challenge the administration. The first of the antiwar demonstrations was mounted in Washington in April. In May there was a national teach-in involving over a hundred campuses across the country. Opposition to the war grew in intensity as the Americanization of the struggle continued, slowly drawing more and more ordinary middle-class Americans into the antiwar coalition. Attempts by Johnson and his advisers to counter criticism were often disingenuous, increasing rather than allaying doubts. The president's gift for hyperbole served him poorly.

One critical step toward the undermining of Johnson's credibility was his handling of an unrelated crisis in the Dominican Republic in April and May of 1965. The deviousness with which he justified sending in the Marines cost him the trust of a valued and powerful ally, Senator J. William Fulbright (D.-Ark.), chairman of the Committee on Foreign Relations, and much of the foreign policy establishment. Fearing that Communists might be on the verge of turning the Dominican Republic into another Cuba, Johnson responded with characteristic vigor, sending first a small detachment of Marines and then more than 20,000 soldiers to suppress a mutiny by democratically inclined officers against a conservative military junta. The United States intervened in the internal affairs of the small Caribbean country and the president greatly exaggerated both the danger to Americans resident there and of Communist involvement. Skepticism about Johnson's shifting explanations and distaste for his eagerness to assume imperial responsibilities stimulated Fulbright and others to reexamine policy toward Vietnam. They were dismayed by what they found.

Between January 28 and February 18, 1966, Fulbright held six televised hearings on the war. Reflecting the hardening of the administration's commitment to a non-Communist South Vietnam, Rusk insisted that the war was an act of outside aggression by the Hanoi regime, that the United States had commitments to repel that aggression. He argued that what was at stake was not merely Vietnam, but the credibility of American commitments all over the world: "We must make clear that the United States keeps its word wherever it is pledged."[12] Presumably, if the United States did not fight in Vietnam, the whole postwar edifice of collective security would collapse. Others spoke in support of the administration's policy, but of greatest consequence was the appearance of George Kennan in opposition. Consistent with his low regard for the importance of developing countries, Kennan argued that the war was foolish and might well lead to a disastrous encounter with China. He insisted that withdrawal – and, by implication, Communist control of the South – would not hurt any major American interest. The televised hearings, highlighting the doubts of prominent and highly respected observers, assured millions of Americans of the respectability of dissent. Even Robert Kennedy and other intimates of the late president openly criticized the administration.

Johnson and his advisers were unmoved by their critics. The war went on. Every week scores, sometimes hundreds of Americans and thousands of Vietnamese died. Billions of dollars that might have been spent on Lyndon Johnson's vision of a Great Society were drained away for war-related expenses. Slowly the fabric of American society strained, threatened to unravel, and finally was rent apart as the president and his men concentrated their time, energy, and the nation's resources on the war. Around the world men and women of goodwill viewed the United States with a contempt hitherto reserved for Chiang Kai-shek, Franco, and Stalin. America the liberator, the protector was gone, replaced by the brutal oppressor of tiny Vietnam.

12 *Department of State Bulletin* 54 (March 7, 1966), 346–56.

Johnson's advisers saw the criticism as a public relations issue. Without changing course, the administration might have to steer a more sinuous line. The American public and critics all over the world would have to be pacified with evidence that Lyndon Johnson was a reasonable man second to none in his desire for peace. The administration agreed to several bombing halts and accepted or sponsored a series of missions – Canadian, Russian, Hungarian, Polish, British, as well as American – in search of peace. The president offered Vietnam a rural electrification program for the Mekong Valley to rival the Tennessee Valley Authority at home. But it was all a charade. The United States was not interested in negotiations for peace while the momentum in Vietnam was with the insurgents. American terms for peace required the surrender of Hanoi's dream of unifying Vietnam, of the NLF's demand for a share of the government of the South, of everything for which the opposition had been fighting and had every expectation of winning.

The massive use of American air power failed. Johnson lifted a variety of restrictions on targeting, to no avail. Estimates by the CIA and the Defense Intelligence Agency indicated that the bombing had not significantly affected North Vietnamese morale or ability to send men and materials south. Equipment destroyed by the bombing raids was being replaced by the Soviets and Chinese, who vied with each other to win Ho's fealty. The Soviet Union had remained virtually uninvolved until 1965, until the massive attacks on the North began. Accused by the Chinese of abandoning the cause of international socialism, the Soviets demonstrated their commitment by sending Hanoi large quantities of modern military equipment, including surface-to-air missiles (SAMs) and jet interceptors.

To all indications that the military effort of the United States was ineffective, the Joint Chiefs replied with demands for more men, more bombs, and more freedom to choose targets. In June 1966, the president authorized a troop buildup to 431,000. By fall, the secretary of defense, Robert McNamara, began to despair. He, too, came to question the value of the escalation of the war. But he could think of no way to end it.[13]

13 Cohen, *Dean Rusk,* 273–4.

Johnson was determined to win, was irritated by McNamara's doubts, and turned increasingly to those of his advisers who continued to be optimistic. Friends like Clark Clifford and Abe Fortas urged him on. General Earle Wheeler, chairman of the Joint Chiefs of Staff, assured him that the war was going well. Walt Rostow, surpassed by none in his confidence that the United States could win in Vietnam, succeeded Bundy as the president's national security adviser. Doubters lost their influence with the president and the inner circle became one of "yea-sayers," of "can-doers."

In May 1967, with 436,000 American troops in Vietnam, the military was talking of needing 565,000 to win in three years, 665,000 to win in two. The CIA reported, however, that "short of a major invasion or nuclear attack, there is probably no level of air or naval actions against North Vietnam which Hanoi has determined in advance would be so intolerable that the war had to be stopped."[14] The Communist regime was confident of victory and the Pentagon's own analysts contended that more American troops would do little good and probably great harm, especially to the economy of South Vietnam.

The United States could not win and could not seem to end the war. Popular dissatisfaction grew. As American casualties multiplied, demonstrations, draft resistance, and desertions from the military increased. In the field the phenomenon of "fragging," of the murder of American officers by men resisting being led into battle, spread ominously. In July 1967, riots exploded in Newark and Detroit. Scores were killed, thousands arrested, millions of dollars in property damage sustained. The anger of the black ghettos was not related directly to the war in Vietnam, but the riots added to the sense of a society breaking apart. There were demands that funds being used to kill in Vietnam be used for saving lives at home, for a war on poverty. The war was now costing the American people $20 billion per year. It was becoming clear that the government lacked the resources for both the Great Society and Vietnam. In August, Johnson averted financial disaster by agreeing to a 10 percent surcharge on income taxes. The response in the public opinion polls was immediate: For the first time a plurality of Americans, most of

14 Cited in Cohen, *Dean Rusk,* 277.

those with an opinion, thought the war in Vietnam was a mistake. Pressure on the United States to end the war intensified. Even the pope called for suspension of the bombing. Senator Eugene McCarthy (D.-Minn.) stepped forward as a peace candidate to challenge Johnson for the Democratic party presidential nomination.

Johnson's reaction was to start 1968 with a new team, on which there were no doubters in evidence. The military braced for a major North Vietnamese attack on a U.S. Marine garrison near the Laotian border, at Khesanh, perceived as a replay of the 1954 battle of Dienbienphu. There the Americans intended to demonstrate to the Vietnamese the difference between the United States and France. American military leaders were convinced they were on the verge of victory: All they needed was another 100,000, perhaps 200,000 men and a little more freedom to attack the North. They assured the president that the Viet Cong had been weakened to the point where they lacked offensive capability without support from the North.

The president and his aides received a rude shock on the morning of January 30, while most Vietnamese relaxed during the Tet or lunar new year holiday. As Americans focused on the base at Khesanh, the Viet Cong penetrated the American Embassy compound in Saigon, besieging it for six hours before they were overcome. But the attack on the embassy was only a symbol of what was happening across the length and breadth of South Vietnam. In Saigon the airport, the presidential palace, the headquarters of the general staff all came under attack. Simultaneously, the Viet Cong attacked four of the other five major cities, capturing the ancient Citadel in Hue, and scores of provincial and district capitals. An insurgent force alleged to be on the verge of liquidation launched a brilliantly conceived attack that demonstrated, most obviously at the American Embassy, that no one was beyond its reach. [15]

The Viet Cong and North Vietnamese took very heavy losses in their Tet offensive, suffering as many as forty thousand deaths. Viet Cong main force units did most of the fighting, suffered most of the casualties, and never recovered. All the territory they held during

15 See the book-length study by Don Oberdorfer, *Tet!: The Turning Point in the Vietnam War* (Garden City, N.Y., 1971).

the attack was regained by South Vietnamese and American troops, although it took three weeks to recapture Hue. The people in the cities did not rise to welcome their Communist liberators. The American military command expressed pride in the performance of the Vietnamese troops it had trained and claimed victory. In terms of kill ratios and territory controlled, the Americans were unquestionably correct.

The primary target of the North Vietnamese planners, however, was American public opinion and with that audience they were strikingly successful. The optimism expressed by the president and military leaders just weeks before seemed absurd. The war would be endless, a bottomless pit. Every week in February at least four hundred Americans were killed in Vietnam with no indication of what had been accomplished, of when it would all be over. Walter Cronkite, the most respected of American television news commentators, declared the war a hopeless stalemate: "To say that we are closer to victory today is to believe, in the face of the evidence, the optimists who have been wrong in the past."[16]

In the United States, not only the public but the government evidenced profound shock at the demonstration of Viet Cong capability and the failure of American and South Vietnamese intelligence to anticipate the attacks. The ability of the Saigon regime to recover from the onslaught, to capitalize on its military victory, was widely doubted. Support for the war eroded not only among the unwashed masses, but within the establishment, among the "in and outers," to whom presidents and cabinet officers were most responsive. The Communists won the psychological victory they sought. Johnson could not hold course. The military would not get the additional 206,000 men requested. There would have to be changes in American policy.

On March 12 the domestic political context in which Johnson acted began to change radically. On that day, Eugene McCarthy, the quixotic peace candidate for the Democratic nomination, received a stunning 40 percent of the votes in the New Hampshire primary,

16 Quoted in Marilyn B. Young, *The Vietnam Wars, 1945–1990* (New York, 1991), 226.

very nearly defeating an incumbent president. Four days after Mc-Carthy demonstrated Johnson's vulnerability, Robert Kennedy reassessed his chances and declared his candidacy. Massive "Dump Johnson" rallies were organized by antiwar activists. The president was in political trouble. Peace in Vietnam was likely to provide his best chance of recovering.

Moreover, the economy was verging on disaster. To mobilize the reserves and deploy two hundred thousand additional men overseas would exacerbate long-standing balance-of-payments difficulties. Gold was flowing out of the country at an alarming rate, largely to finance the war in Vietnam. Unless there was a tax increase, difficult to obtain in an election year, there would be serious inflation in the United States, panic in Europe, and possibly a collapse of the international monetary system. The president's advisers groped for a way out.

On March 25, a group of leading establishment figures, the so-called Wise Men, highly prominent former government officials including Dean Acheson, McGeorge Bundy, Douglas Dillon, John McCloy, and Matthew Ridgway, assembled in Washington to be briefed on Vietnam and to advise the president. With few exceptions, they concluded that the war was absorbing too much of the nation's energy, too much of its resources. They urged a scaling down of American objectives and of the American effort. Two, George Ball and Arthur Goldberg, insisted on a bombing halt. A few months earlier, most of these men had supported the war. No one had anticipated so radical a change of attitude. The "Wise Men" were deeply troubled by the divisions in American society, by the decline of American standing in the world, by the gold drain, and most concluded it was time to find a way out. Johnson was shaken by their response. [17]

On March 31, the president addressed the American people. He spoke of his efforts to achieve peace in the past and he announced the cessation of attacks on North Vietnam except for staging areas just north of the demilitarized zone – and those attacks would cease if

---

17 Herbert Y. Schandler, *Unmaking of a President* (Princeton, 1977), 262–4; Gabriel Kolko, *Anatomy of a War* (New York, 1985), 316–20.

Hanoi showed restraint. Then he shifted suddenly to a discussion of the accomplishments of his presidency and to his concern for national unity. Contending that the stakes were too high to allow the presidency to become involved in election-year partisanship, he announced dramatically, "I shall not seek, and I will not accept, the nomination of my Party for another term as your President." It was a striking bid for national unity and a signal to the North Vietnamese of the seriousness of his peace initiative. Three days later Hanoi agreed to negotiate, but Lyndon Johnson had not run up the white flag, was still unwilling to accept defeat, and peace in Vietnam remained many years away. Indeed the air war in the South soon intensified, almost mechanically. The air force had the planes, the pilots, and the bombs. Deprived of targets in the North they simply concentrated on the South.

On April 4, Martin Luther King was murdered in Memphis, Tennessee. Hours later Washington was in flames. Riots followed across the nation. In June, Robert Kennedy was murdered in Los Angeles. In August, antiwar demonstrators outside the Democratic National Convention in Chicago were attacked viciously by the police, in what a subsequent investigation labeled a "police riot." When Governor Abraham Ribicoff of Connecticut protested on the convention floor against police action, Mayor Richard Daley led his claque in chanting "kike, kike." This was not the America God had blessed, liberator of oppressed people. The war had changed all that, and another side of American life surfaced, ugly, brutal, reminding some of the rise of fascism. In Vietnam, American boys were destroying villages "to save them," committing unspeakable atrocities against an alien people whose savage struggle for independence frightened and confused them. At home, Americans were turning on each other, divided by the war, by race, by class. The Great Society had become a sick society. The tension caused by the war in Vietnam and racism at home had infected almost every aspect of American life. Nerves were taut and international affairs had to be conducted in this atmosphere. Johnson and his advisers were pitted against the sweep of the hour hand. Could they find an acceptable peace in Vietnam before the bell tolled for America?

It was May before Washington and Hanoi agreed on a site for the talks, May 13 before the first formal session was held. That week 562 Americans were killed in Vietnam, the highest weekly total of the war. It was July before the American negotiators perceived a breakthrough and a chance for peace. Johnson was not convinced by their reports and continued the military pressure. By late August, supporters of Richard M. Nixon, Republican presidential candidate, had persuaded the South Vietnamese to reject any peace terms the Johnson administration might be prepared to accept. They assured the Saigon regime they would obtain better terms after the election, after Richard Nixon became president. Saigon became increasingly recalcitrant, especially on the place of the NLF at the talks. [18]

In October, Johnson's negotiators finally convinced him that an agreement was in reach. He authorized them to try and they succeeded with astonishing speed – and the help of the Soviet Union. Rusk worked with the Soviet ambassador in Washington and the American negotiators in Paris worked with the Soviet embassy there. The Soviets took it upon themselves to make sure that the Vietnamese knew what was expected of them and pressed them to agree to the American terms. Issue after issue was ironed out and on October 31, Johnson ordered the cessation of all attacks on North Vietnam. But that was only a part of the war. The struggle for the control of the South continued. Johnson was still determined to deny it to the Communists. The Saigon regime, convinced Nixon would gain more for it, charged Johnson with betrayal, and refused to participate in the talks if the NLF was present as a separate delegation. Nixon's victory had the opposite effect on Hanoi: The North Vietnamese were eager to reach a settlement before facing the Nixon administration. Concessions by Hanoi produced a formula that won Saigon's consent to sending a representative to Paris, but nothing came of the expanded talks. The war went on – and on.

Nixon had indicated that he had a plan for ending the war in Vietnam, but once elected he was no more willing than Johnson to be "the first American president to lose a war" – and victory was

---

18 Lyndon B. Johnson, *The Vantage Point* (New York, 1971), 517–18; see also William P. Bundy, Lyndon B. Johnson Oral History Collection, Lyndon B. Johnson Library.

nowhere to be found. "Peace with honor" became the administration slogan. Nixon was alleged to have interpreted that to mean leaving the Saigon regime strong enough to survive his tenure in office, so that its inevitable collapse would be blamed on Teddy Kennedy, by whom he expected to be succeeded.

The new president and his principal foreign policy adviser, Henry Kissinger, had no illusions about the importance of Vietnam to the security of the United States. Both were ruthless practitioners of great-power politics, eager to be relieved of the burden of an unpopular war, eager to concentrate their intellectual energy on relations with the Soviet Union and China. But the president had to be perceived as strong at home and abroad. His dilemma was to find a way to get out of Vietnam short of surrender, yet quickly enough to stay ahead of antiwar sentiment at home. The basic formula was a reversion to elements of the Eisenhower administration's New Look, reliance upon American air power and local forces, in this instance called "Vietnamization." Gradually, on a fixed schedule, American troops were pulled back from combat and out of the country. In support of South Vietnamese troops, the air war was stepped up and extended to infiltration routes in neutral Cambodia and to staging areas in Laos. The killing went on, but fewer of the corpses were American. With declining American casualties, Nixon and Kissinger assumed the American people would give them more leeway to negotiate an acceptable settlement. Successful manipulation of domestic opinion was essential. Kissinger's staff at the National Security Council referred to the efforts to end the war as "political theater."

Hopes for a quick decisive end to the American military presence faded as the North Vietnamese stubbornly held their ground, confident that one day the American people would tire of the war and bring their children home, leaving the future of Vietnam to be determined by the Vietnamese. But there was reason for satisfaction with the "Vietnamization" policy. The performance of Saigon's forces improved markedly, largely because the Viet Cong had suffered enormous casualties during their Tet offensive, and by 1970, the countryside was securer than at any time since the insurgency began. The balance of forces in the South had shifted in favor of the government. More and more the burden of fighting Saigon and its American supporters fell to North Vietnamese regulars. Supplied with Soviet SAM ground-to-air missiles that took a heavy toll of American bombers, the Northerners resisted American pressures. Shipments of the latest Soviet tanks gave Ho Chi Minh and his colleagues confidence that they could counter any invasion. Infiltration rates increased. It was clear to Nixon and his advisers that infiltration routes had to be blocked.

Cambodia was a tiny, weak country, whose volatile leader, Prince Norodom Sihanouk, had been remarkably adept at protecting his people from the war in neighboring Vietnam. To accomplish this, he was forced to tolerate the presence of North Vietnamese bases on his territory. The United States frequently urged him to drive the Vietnamese out of his country, but he lacked the means. An assault on the Vietnamese by the weaker Cambodians would be suicidal. The Vietnamese affront to Cambodian sovereignty seemed a small price to pay for peace and survival.

The American military had long advocated a strike at Vietnamese sanctuaries in Cambodia, including what they believed to be the headquarters for the Communist insurgency in the South. Johnson had refused, but Nixon immediately authorized secret bombing raids in 1969. The secret, of course, was to be kept from the American people, not from the recipients of the bombs. Early in 1970, to the delight of the American government, Sihanouk was overthrown by a military coup led by officers friendly to the United States. In May, American troops invaded neutral Cambodia, determined to destroy the Vietnamese sanctuaries. The results were unbelievably disastrous for Cambodians, led to anti-American demonstrations around the world, and death on American college campuses.

Caught between the Americans and the Vietnamese, hundreds of thousands of Cambodians died. Their country was devastated, and control gradually passed to a murderous group of Communist insurgents known as the Khmer Rouge, who subsequently, in an act of extraordinary depravity, slaughtered hundreds of thousands more, perhaps as many as two million of their countrymen. Whatever joy Americans may have felt at Sihanouk's departure was short-lived. The May 1970 invasion also resurrected the antiwar movement in the United States. Protesters at Jackson State and Kent State were shot and killed by police and National Guardsmen. The president was besieged in the White House, with troops posted on the premises in case of an attack.

The Nixon administration withstood the aftermath of the invasion of Cambodia, but the situation in the field and on the home front deteriorated. In February 1971, South Vietnamese forces supported by American planes and helicopters struck at North Vietnamese sanctuaries in Laos, another major expansion of the war – and another disaster. Apparently Hanoi's intelligence operatives had advance notice of the operation and hit the South Vietnamese hard, using some of their new Soviet tanks. Saigon's troops suffered a casualty rate of 50 percent and fled ignominiously from the battlefield, in some instances clinging to the skids of helicopters. At home, Lieutenant William Calley was convicted for his role in the massacre of women and children at the village of My Lai and other veterans came forward to reveal that such atrocities were not isolated incidents. Then, in June 1971, the *New York Times* began publishing a secret Defense Department documentary history of American decision making in Vietnam, revealing many of the ways the Kennedy and Johnson administrations had deceived the American people. Polls taken soon afterward indicated that 71 percent of the American people thought it had been a mistake to go to war in Vietnam. Even more striking was the fact that 58 percent thought the war was immoral. Nixon knew he had to find a way out before he ran for reelection in 1972 – and so did his adversaries in Hanoi.[19]

Intensive efforts to reach an agreement in late 1971 failed, largely because of the inability to agree on the disposition of the Saigon government. But Nixon and Kissinger succeeded in their efforts to move closer to the Soviet Union and the People's Republic of China, ultimately gaining the support of Moscow and Beijing for the peace process. They assumed that they could isolate North Vietnam and force it to come to terms. The initial response from Hanoi, in March 1972, was a conventional attack across the demilitarized zone that caught the Americans and their Vietnamese protégés by complete

19 Herring, *America's Longest War*, 243.

surprise. The United States responded with yet more massive air attacks on the North and ultimately the mining of Haiphong harbor. The North Vietnamese were stopped well short of the collapse of the Saigon government.

Renewed military stalemate, additional American concessions, pressure from its Soviet and Chinese allies, both now eager to improve relations with the United States (see Chapter 7), and the realization that Nixon was likely to be reelected finally led Hanoi to accept a diplomatic arrangement short of victory in the fall of 1972. The Saigon regime rejected the agreement, but the exigencies of the election campaign led Kissinger, a few days before the voters decided, to announce that "peace was at hand." His aides readily admitted that they could have achieved the same agreement at any time in the previous year: The announcement was designed to help bury George McGovern, the Democrats' peace candidate.

After the election, Nixon proved more responsive to Saigon's cries of betrayal and demanded changes in the agreement. The North Vietnamese balked. Nixon ordered the most devastating bombing of the war, the "carpet bombing" of parts of the North, a series of raids in which more bombs were dropped in twelve days than had been dropped in the two years between 1969 and 1971. At the same time massive supplies of military equipment were delivered to the Saigon regime with Nixon's personal assurance that the United States would return if the North violated the agreement. Finally, in February 1973, the war ended for the Americans.

Nixon continued efforts to sustain Saigon after the peace agreement led to the withdrawal of American forces but the Watergate scandal soon crippled him and ended, at least temporarily, the "imperial presidency." Congress reasserted itself in foreign affairs and restricted the president's power to reinvolve the United States in the war in Vietnam. American support for the Saigon regime declined and with it so did one of the regime's principal reasons for existing. Although the military initiative appeared to rest with the South Vietnamese Army throughout 1973, by mid-1974 operations had to be curtailed for lack of adequate supplies. The departure of the Americans and the reduction of American aid affected morale in Saigon adversely and the will to fight had ebbed palpably by early

1975. Enormous numbers of government troops deserted. When the North Vietnamese struck in March 1975 with the first in what was supposed to be a two-year series of major attacks, the South Vietnamese army panicked and then disintegrated. Calls for help from the United States were to no avail. Richard Nixon was gone in disgrace, and his secret promises to the authorities in Saigon could not be honored by President Gerald Ford. A few weeks later the fighting stopped. The Communists controlled all of Vietnam and Saigon became Ho Chi Minh City. After a war of roughly thirty years, the Vietnamese revolution had triumphed over the French, the Americans, and all internal opposition. Unhappily for the men in Washington, the revolution was dominated by Communists, by men and women with ties to America's adversaries in Moscow and Beijing, by men and women who had watched their countrymen suffer terribly because of American intervention in their affairs. But it was over.

Fifty-five thousand Americans and millions of Vietnamese died in the American phase of the Vietnamese revolution. It was a struggle in which the United States should never have intervened, in which a weaker power could not have intervened so massively and for so long. No vital American interest was threatened by events in Indochina. Defeat in Vietnam was of little consequence, without impact on the strategic balance between the United States and its adversaries. Indeed, before the war ended, the United States had taken major strides toward reconciliation with the Soviet Union and the People's Republic of China, the very nations Americans had sought to contain by killing and dying in Vietnam. The dominoes of Southeast Asia did not fall. To be sure, the Khmer Rouge triumphed in Cambodia shortly before the fall of Saigon and the Pathet Lao seized control of Laos not long afterward, but the remaining nations of the region remained independent and non-Communist, friendly to the United States, ultimately creating in the Association of Southeast Asian Nations (ASEAN) an important force in world affairs.

But if losing the war had little impact on the strategic position of the United States, the cost of fighting the war hurt the nation badly, accelerating its decline as a hegemonic power. The achievement of strategic parity by the Soviet Union and the regaining of their economic edge by Japan and Western Europe were all but inevitable, but the disastrous economic policies of the 1960s and early 1970s, including the means of financing the war in Vietnam, contributed mightily to the timing and depth of the slide.

The dollar had been weak since the late 1950s and balance-of-payments deficits had troubled Kennedy, but the deficit did not get out of control until 1964. After Eisenhower, no president gave adequate consideration to the cost of American security. Kennedy, Johnson, and Nixon proudly refused to put a price tag on the foreign policy goals they chose to pursue. Balance-of-payments concerns were consistently subordinated to security concerns. There was a sharp increase in the rate of inflation in the 1960s as the government printed more and more dollars to pay for its imperial activities. Both the Johnson administration and the Nixon administration tried to export the cost of the war, export inflation, to their trading partners. The French rebelled in 1965, demanding gold for the dollars they held, and the British and Germans objected to American international monetary policy in 1971. The world had grown tired of collecting inflated American dollars in return for protection against a Soviet threat they perceived as much diminished or to support an American war in Vietnam of which most Europeans disapproved. Tensions grew as currency issues began to compete with security concerns in the minds of allied leaders. The political scientist Robert Gilpin explains that "for both foreign policy and domestic reasons, successive American administrations pursued expansionary and inflationary monetary policies that eventually undermined the dollar and destabilized the monetary system. [The United States had become] the rogue elephant of the global economy."[20]

The inflated dollar priced U.S. goods out of overseas markets and, in 1971, the United States ran its first trade balance deficit of the century. In the course of the year, to staunch the outflow of gold, the Nixon administration refused to redeem dollars for gold. Nixon's men chose to end the dollar's status as a reserve currency and to destroy the Bretton Woods system Harry Dexter White and John

20 Robert Gilpin, *The Political Economy of International Relations* (Princeton, 1987), 149, 153.

Maynard Keynes had designed in the 1940s and which had brought striking prosperity to those who participated in it. Many of the economic problems facing the United States in the late 1960s and 1970s would have existed without the war, the result of inflationary domestic programs to provide jobs and services to the American people, but they were exacerbated by the billions spent in Vietnam. Stagflation, a stagnant economy with rapidly rising prices, hit the United States in the 1970s. Germany and Japan, denied the opportunity to play the great-power game by defeat in World War II, became the principal beneficiaries of American decline. The Japanese, who spent 99 percent of their research-and-development budget on civilian production, easily captured markets from the United States, which devoted 50 percent of its research-and-development expenditures to armaments. Richard Rosecrance, another political scientist, points to the rise of the "trading state," of nations like Germany and Japan who have chosen, however involuntarily, trade over military means to acquire wealth and power.[21] Without denigrating the brilliance of the Japanese industrial planning, we cannot ignore the fact that by its senseless struggle in Vietnam the United States at the very least hastened the day when the world had to confront the idea of "Japan as number one." The opportunity for the United States to fashion a new, posthegemonic style of leadership, along with American wealth and power, had been squandered.

21 See Richard Rosecrance, *The Rise of the Trading State* (New York, 1986).

7. The Rise and Fall of Détente

In 1969, when Richard Nixon, Cold Warrior personified, entered the White House, it was clear that most Americans had had their fill of war and confrontation. The country was eager to end the wasting of American lives abroad, no longer persuaded that a hostile world would deny Americans their freedom if they stopped spending billions to support the appetite of the military-industrial complex. The endless war in Vietnam had changed American attitudes, led the people to question the wisdom of their leaders, eroded support for overseas military adventure. The United States had to disengage from the Vietnamese conflict. Perhaps the time to end the Cold War had arrived as well. No one was quicker to perceive the new public mood than Richard Nixon. No one was better able to free the country from the tyranny of hysterical anticommunism than the man who had contributed so much to fanning that hysteria. As one Washington wit remarked, he was the first president since the end of World War II who did not have to guard his flanks against attack by Richard Nixon.

Nixon and his national security adviser Henry Kissinger, like all postwar American leaders, sought a stable world order in which American interests would be preserved. Like their predecessors, they considered the containment of Soviet influence central to that end. But they confronted a Soviet Union that had gained strategic parity with the United States and whose leaders believed their country to be on the verge of becoming the world's preeminent power. Moreover, as Soviet strength and assertiveness grew, Nixon and Kissinger found themselves constrained by public and congressional weariness with the battle, and by a fragile economy seriously weakened by Lyndon's Johnson's attempt to provide guns *and* butter. Their strategy had to overcome these domestic handicaps in order to cope with increased Soviet capabilities.

Central to the Nixon-Kissinger approach was their determination to control foreign policy from the White House, to prevent opposition in the bureaucracies, the press, Congress, or the streets from interfering. Rather than attempt to educate the public, they chose to circumvent the weaknesses of the American political system by finessing constitutional restraints on the president. They wanted to end the asymmetry between Washington and Moscow, to be free to act as quickly and ruthlessly in pursuit of American interests as they imagined the Soviet Politburo acted. Neither man had great respect for traditional American political culture. At home and abroad they were practitioners of power politics. When the interests of the United States or their personal interests were at stake, no holds were barred.

To contain the Soviet Union at a time when the relative wealth and power of the United States were in decline and public support at low ebb was the task that confronted them – and Nixon and Kissinger were almost equal to it. Their negotiating strategy was often labeled "linkage." They offered the Soviets recognition of their strategic parity, tolerance of the aberrant political philosophies and human rights abuses of which the Soviets and their satellites were guilty, and a promise of access to Western capital and technology. In exchange they asked Moscow to recognize the mutuality of superpower interest in stability, especially in maintaining order in the Third World. They wanted Soviet assistance in extricating the United States from Vietnam. Nixon and Kissinger were telling Leonid Brezhnev and his colleagues that the Soviet Union would benefit more from cooperation with the United States than from attempting to capitalize on unrest on the periphery. They were asking the Soviets to contain themselves at a time when America's will to hold the line was in doubt.

Simultaneously, Nixon and Kissinger were striving to restore the public consensus in support of the leadership role the United States had played in world affairs throughout the postwar era. Ending the war in Vietnam would contribute mightily toward that goal. Easing tensions with the Soviet Union could help, although there was always a risk that if the public concluded that the Cold War was over, willingness to make the sacrifices necessary to lead abroad would decline further. But the risk had to be taken in the hope that the demonstration of the administration's new approach to Soviet communism, its acceptance of peaceful coexistence, would regain supporters alienated by the war in Vietnam. Finally, there was the tactic the president liked to have called the "Nixon Doctrine," a devolution of American responsibilities in the Third World upon regional powers like Brazil, Iran, Indonesia, and Zaire. Rather than use American troops to intervene, the United States would arm surrogate forces to do the fighting and dying for it. Presumably, the reduction in American casualties, the "lower profile" of the United States would be more acceptable to the American people: They would rather pay taxes to arm and train friendly foreign troops than send their own children into combat abroad.

From the Kremlin, Brezhnev and his colleagues looked at the United States with growing disdain. Racial unrest, antiwar demonstrations, chaos in the streets, all confirmed their estimate of the weakness of democratic society. Americans were tearing their society apart and the government lacked the power or the will to impose order. Clearly, the United States was in decline. Soon, in their lifetime, Soviet leaders anticipated supplanting the Americans as the world's hegemonic power. [1]

In the years since they had deposed Nikita Khrushchev, the members of the Brezhnev Politburo had not waited passively for the Americans to self-destruct. They did what they could to hasten the process with large-scale aid to Ho Chi Minh's regime, by seeking to undermine the American position in the Middle East, and by expanding their own military power enormously. They had continued the rapid buildup of their strategic nuclear forces to the point where they could claim parity with the United States. They had also expanded their conventional forces and capabilities to the point where they could contest American power in most parts of the Third World. Not even the Western Hemisphere would be left as an American preserve. These were not impulsive men such as Nikita Khrushchev. They were cautious and they were conservative, but

---

1 Harry Gelman, *The Brezhnev Politburo and the Decline of Détente* (Ithaca, 1984), 135–7.

they were also convinced that the "correlation of forces" in the world had shifted in their favor and they were prepared to act aggressively to achieve a position of dominance.

Requests from the United States for Soviet pressure on Hanoi to allow the Americans to extricate themselves from Vietnam through "peace with honor" could hardly be taken seriously in Moscow. Except for 1968, when the Soviets aided the peace process in an apparent attempt to preclude the election of Nixon, there was little incentive for the Soviet leadership to betray its commitment to support "wars of national liberation." America's war in Vietnam could not have been more advantageous for the Soviets had it been planned in the Kremlin. The war drained American resources, exacerbated tensions within American society, alienated NATO allies as well as Third World countries, and heightened Vietnamese dependence on the Soviet Union. In blood, in treasure, in the sullying of America's image in the world, the war in Vietnam was enormously costly to the United States and a great boon to the Soviet Union. The Soviets increased their aid to Vietnam and ultimately facilitated Hanoi's victory.

At no time were Brezhnev and his colleagues willing to end their efforts to expand Soviet influence in the world, preferably at the expense of the United States. Like Khrushchev before them, they saw American efforts to place the Third World outside the arena of superpower competition as an effort by the United States to maintain its advantage, to deny the Soviets their coming victory. Similarly, Soviet leaders were skeptical of Nixon's interest in arms control, suspecting the Americans of attempting to halt the arms race before the Soviets overtook them. They had the power to deter a nuclear attack by the United States and they perceived the momentum to be on their side. This was no time to commit themselves to the existing world order. Certainly the Soviet military saw little to be gained by an easing of superpower tensions, by the détente for which the Americans were striving.

The Soviet Union did have a few problems that might be alleviated through better relations with the United States. Although excellent weather in the late 1960s had meant good crops, there were bound to be lean years ahead. The leadership had maximized its commitment to agriculture, was subsidizing food prices in the cities, and could spare no more without reducing military spending. Industrial growth was slowing and capital for new investment in industrial infrastructure was not available. The Soviet standard of living had risen in the late 1960s, and consumer expectations had grown, but the prospects for the 1970s were less reassuring. Like Lyndon Johnson, Brezhnev was trying to provide both guns and butter, trying to project Soviet power abroad while improving the lot of Soviet citizens, and the economy was beginning to strain. The Soviet Union could benefit from an infusion of capital and technology from West Germany, Japan, even the United States. The Germans and the Japanese seemed interested, but were too timid to act without American approval. A reduction of tension between the United States and the Soviet Union seemed to be a prerequisite.[2]

Similarly, Soviet efforts to drive a wedge between the United States and its European allies on political issues had fallen short. The Soviets were eager for formal European acceptance of their World War II gains and of the status quo in Europe, especially the borders of the two Germanys. Again, the West Germans were very interested, but some resolution of the Berlin issue would be necessary. That, too, involved the United States. Détente with Western Europe, desired primarily as a means of separating the United States from its allies, was unlikely without an improvement in Soviet-American relations.

And, of course, off to the east, there was Mao Zedong, forever sticking his finger in Brezhnev's eye. A series of efforts to conciliate the Chinese had proved unsuccessful. Soviet military intervention to crush an heretical reform movement in the Communist party of Czechoslovakia in 1968, followed by the Brezhnev Doctrine claiming the right to use force in defense of "socialism," failed to intimidate the Chinese. Incidents along the Sino-Soviet borders increased in number and intensity. As Soviet leaders considered their options for punishing the Chinese, it seemed advisable to neutralize the United States. A Chinese-American connection might not be in the interest of the Soviet Union.

2 Gelman, *Brezhnev Politburo*, 85–6; Raymond L. Garthoff, *Détente and Confrontation* (Washington, D.C., 1985), 87–90.

From the perspective of the men in the Kremlin in 1969, an improvement in bilateral relations with the United States might have value after all, provided the Soviet Union remained free to outmaneuver the Americans throughout the Third World. The Soviets were satisfied with the situation in Europe and sought only to ratify it. They were interested in Western trade and investment. Arms control appealed to them less, but there were areas in which they might reap advantage, or be spared disadvantage through an agreement. And perhaps through bilateral ties to the United States some new leverage could be obtained. American capitalists profiting from business in the Soviet Union might prove useful in mitigating anti-Soviet sentiment in the United States. Washington might acquiesce in whatever sanctions the Soviets applied against the Chinese. But for none of these possible gains were the Soviet leaders prepared to cease their efforts to extend Soviet influence around the world. Now, with Soviet power ascendant, was not the time to accept restraints.

Meanwhile, in Beijing, the turmoil of the Great Proletarian Cultural Revolution did not blind Chinese leaders to the danger from the Soviet Union. In November 1968, Zhou Enlai called for talks with the newly elected Nixon administration, but more radical leaders, determined to struggle against both superpowers simultaneously, forced cancellation of a scheduled meeting. In the months that followed, Sino-Soviet tensions erupted in serious border incidents, provoked by the Chinese, over Chenbao Island in the Ussuri River, followed by a sharp retaliatory strike by the Soviets in Xinjiang. Fearful of a preemptive attack on their nuclear installations in the region, the Chinese backed off. Their hostility toward the Soviets greater than ever, they proved receptive to overtures from the Nixon administration. Ambassadorial-level talks began anew early in 1970, but the year was almost over before Zhou persuaded the aging Mao that the United States was no longer a threat to China and might prove a valuable counter to Soviet pressure.

Nixon and Kissinger were eager to engage China diplomatically, primarily to seek help ending the war in Vietnam, but also to use China as a possible lever against the Soviet Union. Further, rapprochement with the Chinese would facilitate the withdrawal of American forces from East Asia. American troops would no longer be required to prepare to fight major wars in Europe and Asia simultaneously, reducing force requirements. The Chinese could contain the Soviets and Vietnamese in East Asia and American resources could all be focused on the Soviet Union. In sum, détente with China fit magnificently with the Nixon-Kissinger approach to the Soviet Union and with the Nixon Doctrine.[3]

Secret cables flew back and forth between Beijing and Washington through a variety of sources, friendly signals were raised, and one day the world discovered that Kissinger had just returned from Beijing. On July 15, 1971, without warning to friend or foe, Nixon announced that Kissinger had met with Zhou and that he, the president of the United States, had accepted an invitation to visit China. Brezhnev and his fellow Soviet leaders were not amused.

In August and September the United States accepted the seating of Beijing's representative in the United Nations while giving nominal support to the effort by the Guomindang regime in Taibei to retain a seat for itself. An American motion to seat both delegations failed to obtain a majority. An Albanian motion to substitute Beijing's representative for Taibei's won easily. It was one of the least painful diplomatic defeats the United States had ever suffered. In February 1972, Nixon flew to China, where the old Red-baiter enjoyed a personal audience with Mao. An astounded worldwide television audience watched the American president sit through and then warmly applaud a dreary ballet heavily laden with Communist propaganda. A new era in Chinese-American relations had begun.

As the two sides talked during that memorable week, it was clear that the principal obstacle to regular diplomatic relations, to "normalization," was American policy toward Taiwan. The Chinese stressed their opposition to all variations on the idea of two Chinas and insisted that all American forces be withdrawn from Taiwan. The Americans conceded that Chinese on both sides of the Taiwan Straits insisted that Taiwan was part of China, that there was but one China. The United States would not challenge that position. Washington had moved to a "one China, but not now" policy: It would accept the idea of one China, with a tacit understanding that the

3 Henry Kissinger, *The White House Years* (Boston, 1979), 163–82, 191–4.

future of Taiwan would be determined later, by the Chinese themselves, in their own peaceful way. The Americans agreed to the ultimate withdrawal of their forces and installations from Taiwan, promising to do so progressively as tension in the area subsided. In short, if Beijing helped the United States out of Vietnam and refrained from threatening action in the straits, it could speed the attainment of its objective.[4]

In Moscow, Brezhnev and his advisers watched uneasily. Their worst fears had not been realized: There was no indication of any military understanding between the United States and China. The United States had not wiggled out of its commitment to Taiwan and the Kremlin's specialists on China were certain that Sino-American relations would not advance appreciably until the Americans abandoned Chiang's regime. To the Soviet leaders, it was apparent, however, that they would have to include the Sino-American relationship in their calculation; they would have to try to control the strategic triangle that had emerged. The Soviet Union could not appear so indifferent to American overtures for détente as to drive Washington and Beijing closer together. Nixon's trip to China enhanced the possibility of success in Moscow significantly.[5]

The Soviets correctly estimated that an arms control agreement would be the most effective instrument for demonstrating their surpassing importance to the United States. Once such an agreement was reached, the Americans were unlikely to jeopardize it by entering into a military alliance with the Chinese. Moreover, the Soviets were troubled by the Nixon administration's effort to obtain funding for deployment of an anti–ballistic missile (ABM) system. This was not only an area in which Soviet technology was inferior; at least as worrisome was the potential cost of an extensive ABM system. Military expenditures already stretched the Soviet budget to the limit. Further cuts in expenditures for consumer goods might be dangerous. Military leaders were not eager to reallocate resources committed to existing programs, especially in areas where the Soviet

---

4 Harry Harding, *A Fragile Relationship: The United States and China Since 1972* (Washington, D.C., 1992), 40–7.
5 Garthoff, *Détente and Confrontation*, 240–3.

technology was equal to or superior to that of the United States. Despite Nixon's decision to bomb Hanoi and mine Haiphong harbor a few days before his scheduled visit to Moscow, the Soviet leaders let the invitation stand. They were ready to deal on strategic arms limitations.[6]

Soviet and American arms control negotiators had been talking to each other since 1969, but Nixon and Kissinger were not much interested in an arms control agreement for the sake of limiting the development and deployment of weapons systems. The particulars of an agreement concerned them less than the fact of accord. They wanted to signal a change in the superpower relationship from one in which differences prompted confrontations to one in which resolution was achieved through negotiation. Secretly, Kissinger and the Soviet ambassador bypassed the official negotiators, spared themselves mastery of the technical details, and helped their respective principals come up with a document they could both sign, achieving their political goals. Efforts to reach a comprehensive settlement, limiting all strategic weapons, were put aside by a skeptical and impatient Kissinger.[7]

The first SALT agreement, signed by Brezhnev and Nixon in Moscow in May 1972, contained an important agreement on limiting the deployment of ABM complexes, saving both sides enormous sums for systems deemed of marginal utility. Arrangements for offensive weapons were less satisfying, reflecting pressures on the Soviet and American leaders from their respective military-industrial elites. At home and abroad, Brezhnev and Nixon reaped the political capital they sought. The Soviet ruling class was pleased by the indication that the United States had conceded strategic parity and was satisfied that little had been sacrificed. A few months later, a Soviet-American trade agreement brought closer the economic gains the Soviets expected. The American people warmed to the prospect of ending the Cold War and the "new" Nixon glowed with the aura of a man who had achieved rapprochement with his nation's two

6 David Holloway, *The Soviet Union and the Arms Race,* 2d ed. (New Haven, 1984), 44–6; Gelman, *Brezhnev Politburo,* 131–3.
7 Garthoff, *Détente and Confrontation,* 148–50.

principal adversaries. Around the world there was a perception of a new and less dangerous era dawning.

One likely glimpse of the future emerged when tensions developed between the United States and Japan over issues of trade. Sato Eisaku, Japan's foreign minister, failed to respond promptly to Nixon's 1969 request for restraints on textile exports. Washington retaliated in 1971 with the "Nixon shocks," acts designed in part to undermine Sato. First, the president announced his opening to China without consulting the Japanese, who, out of loyalty to their American allies, had long resisted internal pressures to recognize the Beijing government. Second, Nixon unilaterally declared that dollars could no longer be converted into gold and that a 10 percent surcharge would be levied on all imports. Japan was forced to revalue the yen and to limit exports to the United States. Economic issues, long subordinated to security concerns, were becoming paramount in Japanese-American affairs. The tacit arrangement whereby the Japanese accepted American political and strategic dictates in exchange for a privileged position in their bilateral trade relationship was unraveling. The success of Nixon's overtures to the Chinese and Soviets had reduced the urgency of security matters and increased the relative importance of domestic economic issues.

There was, of course, that dirty little war in Vietnam in which the United States was still engaged. If it had ever made sense for American resources to be so deeply committed to Indochina, Nixon's maneuvers in Beijing and Moscow obviated two imperatives. And, of course, it was 1972. Richard Nixon, who in 1968 had argued that anyone who could not end the war in four years did not deserve to be president, was up for reelection. On the eve of the election, Kissinger announced that peace was at hand. It took an incredibly ruthless bombing campaign in December to wrap up the agreement with Hanoi, but the last American troops left in February 1973. For Americans, the ordeal was over. For the Vietnamese there were two more years of fighting and dying. For the Cambodians the worst was yet to come.

For a few months, Nixon basked in the glory of his landslide victory over George McGovern. Americans, with the atrocities of Southeast Asia relegated to the back pages of their newspapers, disappearing from their television screens, might well have imagined a world at peace. In June 1973, Leonid Brezhnev traveled to the United States where he and Nixon signed the Agreement on the Prevention of Nuclear War. But the Watergate scandal that was to destroy Nixon had already surfaced to distract him and trouble was just over the horizon, as usual, in the Middle East.

The Middle East has long been – and perhaps always will be – an area of exceptional volatility. Communal strife, primarily religious, plagues the region. The great-power decision to grant the Jews a homeland in Palestine and the creation in 1948 of the state of Israel overshadowed all prior grievances, especially among Arab Muslims. And Israel survived the first onslaught against it, in 1948, in large part thanks to Stalin facilitating Czech arms shipments to the embattled Jews. As the Soviet leader anticipated, the Jewish nation was perpetually at odds with its Arab neighbors, creating difficulties first for the British and then for the Americans who succeeded the British as the principal Western influence in the area.

Stalin had paid little further attention to the Arab Middle East, but his successors extended Soviet influence to those states confronting Israel, most importantly Egypt from 1955 to 1974. Soviet bloc arms had buoyed Nasser en route to the Suez crisis in 1956 and the closing scenes of that engagement included Khrushchev rattling rockets at the already humbled British and French imperialists. The historic Russian claim to influence in a region which it bordered was reasserted by Moscow in the 1950s and remained a major irritant in Soviet-American relations throughout the Cold War.

In 1967, under Brezhnev's leadership, the Soviet Union threw a match into the powder keg. Soviet agents in Syria spread false allegations of an impending Israeli attack. The Syrians appealed to Nasser for support. Shortly afterward, the president of the Soviet Union repeated the allegations to the Egyptians, who regarded Soviet information as independent confirmation of Syrian fears. Nasser, attempting to intimidate the Israelis with the threat of a two-front war, demanded the withdrawal of UN peacekeeping forces that separated his troops from the Israelis, and sent his forces toward the

Gulf of Aqaba where they could harass the vital port of Elat. Thus provoked, the Israelis attacked preemptively and, in what came to be known as the Six-Day War, routed Egyptian, Jordanian, and Syrian troops, seizing control of the Sinai Peninsula, the west bank of the Jordan River and Jerusalem, and the Golan Heights. At that point, when the Israelis seemed likely to continue on to Damascus, the Soviets threatened to intervene, a hardly credible threat given the limits of Soviet ability to project its power into the Mediterranean and the presence of the American Sixth Fleet. But Moscow's capacity for mischief had been demonstrated anew, and the Soviets quickly resupplied their Syrian and Egyptian friends and sent thousands of military advisers. In return, the Soviets obtained naval rights in Arab ports and air bases from which they could counter the operations of the Sixth Fleet in the future.[8]

In 1969, Nasser began a "war of attrition" against Israel, to which the Israelis responded after nine months of restraint with air attacks that penetrated deeply into the Egyptian heartland. The Israeli air force demonstrated anew that it could fly where it pleased against its Arab enemies. Humiliated again, Nasser asked the Soviets for air-defense support. This time, in 1970, the Soviets were ready and sent missiles, planes, and thousands of air-defense personnel, including fighter pilots. Soon Soviet warplanes, flown by Soviet pilots, changed the nature of the war — although in one engagement the Israelis shot down five Soviet interceptors. As the war escalated and the Israelis threatened to invade Egypt to knock out the Soviet missile sites, the Soviets proved more amenable to American calls for a cease-fire, achieved in August 1970. But now the Soviets had approximately twenty thousand military "advisers" in Egypt and more credibility with the Arab states.[9]

A month after the cease-fire went into effect, Nasser died of a heart attack. His successor, Anwar Sadat, called upon the Soviets for the support he considered necessary to regain the territory lost to

---

8 William B. Quandt, *Decade of Decisions: American Policy Toward the Arab-Israeli Conflict, 1967–1976* (Berkeley, 1977), 37–71, is a useful introduction to the "Six-Day War." See also Gelman, *Brezhnev Politburo*, 111.
9 Quandt, *Decade of Decisions*, 94–102; Gelman, *Brezhnev Politburo*, 112.

Israel. Although the Soviets were generous with their supplies, Sadat did not get everything he wanted as quickly as he wanted it. He resented Soviet skepticism about his plans. He suspected Brezhnev of betraying Egyptian interests as he moved toward détente with the United States. Abruptly, in July 1972, two months after Nixon and Brezhnev met in Moscow, he expelled his Soviet advisers. The American leaders viewed Sadat's actions as evidence of the wisdom of their policy. Staunch support of Israel had demonstrated that the Arabs could achieve their goals only through the United States. The spread of Soviet influence had been checked and there would be peace in the Middle East.

The Soviet government knew the extent to which Sadat and his Syrian counterpart, Hafez Assad, had armed for war and were aware, by 1973, that the Egyptians and Syrians were serious about taking action to force the Israelis to disgorge the spoils of the Six-Day War. In July, Brezhnev failed to get Nixon to force the Israelis to be more forthcoming and felt no obligation to warn the Americans of the likely result of continued Israeli intransigence. The U.S. government had similar information available to it, including Egyptian war plans. It had been warned by the State Department's intelligence analysts. But Kissinger underestimated Sadat's determination and Soviet willingness to see the United States embarrassed once more by its ties to Israel. [10]

The Israelis, too, were surprised by the attack, which caught them as they observed the holiest of the Jewish holidays, Yom Kippur. Initially, the Egyptians punched through Israeli defenses in the Sinai and the Syrians scaled the approaches to the Golan Heights. A few days into the war, the Soviet Union, attempting to retain influence in the region, launched a massive airlift to resupply its Arab clients. At the same time, the Soviets appealed to other Arab states to join in the fray. For a week, the United States left the Israelis to their own devices, until Golda Meir, the Israeli premier, threatened to use nuclear weapons to save her country. Then the American airlift to Israel began, followed immediately by the Israeli

10 Garthoff, *Détente and Confrontation*, 360–8; Quandt, *Decade of Decisions*, 165–70.

counteroffensive. Quickly the Israelis drove back the attackers on both fronts and in a few days were in position to annihilate the Egyptian army. Sadat, who thought his forces were still winning, resisted suggestions of a cease-fire until the Soviets provided him with satellite photographs to demonstrate the precariousness of his position. At the initiative of the Soviets, Brezhnev and Kissinger worked out the terms of a cease-fire acceptable to both the Israelis and their Arab adversaries.

The Israelis, however, took advantage of relatively minor Egyptian provocations to justify further advances. Sadat appealed to both Washington and Moscow to send troops to enforce the cease-fire. An angry Brezhnev called upon the United States to join the Soviets in sending troops to stop the Israeli violations. Ominously, he warned that Soviet troops would be sent in alone if necessary, and mobilized airborne troops to demonstrate the seriousness of his intent. Nixon and Kissinger responded by putting American forces on strategic alert to hold the Soviets in place and compelling the Israelis to comply. A Soviet-American confrontation was averted, but neither side was satisfied with the actions of the other.[11]

The October 1973 war in the Middle East dispelled some of the illusions both American and Soviet leaders may have had about the meaning of détente. In Washington, there was disappointment in the obvious Soviet effort to undermine the American position in the Middle East. The Soviets did not warn the United States that war was imminent. They worked assiduously to incite the Arab world against the United States, disseminating lies about the American role in the conflict and applauding the oil embargo when it finally came. In Moscow, the outcome of the war was probably the major source of frustration, but the American strategic alert and the implication that the United States had forced the Soviets to back down rankled Brezhnev and his colleagues. Subsequent attempts by Kissinger, largely successful, to exclude the Soviets from efforts to resolve Middle East problems, and Sadat's decision for rapprochement with the United States could only be interpreted as a serious

11 Henry Kissinger, *Years of Upheaval* (Boston, 1982), 569–99; Garthoff, *Détente and Coexistence*, 374–85.

setback. The United States might have conceded strategic parity to the Soviet Union, but it clearly had no intention of allowing the Soviets to play a major role in the Middle East. The great-power rivalry seemed little changed. [12]

The most stunning event of the mid-1970s was, of course, the forced resignation of Richard Nixon from the presidency in August 1974. It was the culmination of years of illegal activities directed from the White House designed to destroy political opponents, uncover possible acts of disloyalty to the president among his supporters, and, in particular, to preserve the secrecy with which he and Kissinger conducted foreign policy. Hearings on the Watergate scandal, the incident in which the White House "Plumbers" unit broke into and searched the headquarters of the chairman of the Democratic party, began in mid-1973. As the weight of the evidence of wrongdoing grew heavier against the president, his power ebbed and Congress reasserted itself in the realm of foreign policy. The once troubling "Imperial Presidency" faltered and the system of checks and balances created by the Founding Fathers came back into play.

In 1973, Congress passed the War Powers Act, designed to restrain the president's use of military force without a declaration of war – and demonstrated its determination by overriding a presidential veto. Before the year was out Congress ordered an end to the merciless bombing of Cambodia, passed a law preventing American troops from returning to Vietnam, and signaled its intent to hold trade relations with the Soviet Union hostage to Soviet performance on human rights issues, specifically the freedom of Soviet Jews to emigrate. These limits on the ability of Nixon and Kissinger to manage foreign affairs brought about the collapse of the intricate schema they had contrived. Their "game plan" for Indochina and détente could not be executed. They could not deliver on promises to their allies in Indochina or their adversaries in Moscow. Once again, the United States served as an illustration of the strong-state, weak-government paradigm. The Nixon administration and its re-

12 Gelman, *Brezhnev Politburo*, 151–6.

placement, the administration of Gerald Ford, successive governments of the most powerful state in the world, were not strong enough to act as they wished in world affairs. In Nixon's mind, the United States was in danger of becoming "a pitiful giant."

Whether the weakened presidency was a boon or tragedy will depend on the perspective of the beholder. When the North Vietnamese launched their final assault on the Saigon regime and the United States did not ride to the rescue, a war of thirty years' duration came to an end. The suffering of the Vietnamese people did not end, as thousands of refugees demonstrated in the years that followed, but peace was a blessing for most and the country could begin the arduous task of reconstruction. Cambodians, relieved of the terror of American B-52s, enjoyed little respite before facing horrors of far greater magnitude at the hands of their new Communist leaders, the Khmer Rouge. The Jackson-Vanik amendment to the Soviet-American trade agreement and the Stevenson amendment to the Export-Import Bank authorization indicated that Congress would not provide the economic rewards Brezhnev had anticipated and reduced the likelihood of moderating Soviet behavior. The unraveling of the fabric of détente Nixon and Kissinger had woven seems more likely, however, to have been an inevitable outcome of the many deceptions they practiced, their general contempt for democratic practices, and the mistrust their high-handedness provoked in the bureaucracy, in Congress, and ultimately among the American people.

Chinese-American relations also fell victim to Nixon's disgrace. Liaison offices had been opened in Beijing and Washington with the expectation that they quickly would be elevated to embassies, that the United States would abandon the pretense that Taiwan was China, disengage from Chiang's regime, and establish normal diplomatic relations with the People's Republic. Fighting to stave off impeachment, the president became increasingly dependent on the support of conservative congressmen, many of whom were long-time supporters of Chiang's "Free China," implacable enemies of "Red China." Unable to risk alienating them, Nixon chose not to abrogate the defense treaty with Taiwan. Recognition of Mao's China was not quite equal in importance to the preservation of Richard Nixon's presidency. His successor, Gerald Ford, likewise needed the support of the Republican right wing, especially after he was challenged for party leadership by Ronald Reagan, long the first choice of the Right. Recognition of the People's Republic would have to wait. And in China, American delays undermined advocates of rapprochement with the United States and a dying Zhou Enlai lost control of policy. Succession crises in both countries precluded decisive action in the mid-1970s.

Perhaps the most serious problem the United States faced in the 1970s was posed by the decline in its economic power, especially as aggravated by the policies of the Johnson and Nixon administrations. It is important to stress that the decline was relative, that although the United States ceased to dominate the international economic order as it had in the first two decades after World War II, it remained an enormously wealthy and powerful country. The American economy was troubled and mismanaged but never in danger of collapse.

The American economy had been the engine that drove the nations linked to it to extraordinary prosperity in the 1950s and 1960s. The United States had accepted the imperial burden of protecting its friends and allies while they reconstructed or developed their economies. The patchwork system that evolved out of Bretton Woods (see Chapter 1) had worked. Real wealth had increased among the countries participating in the American-led liberal order. But, by 1960, a number of problems, some systemic, some specific to the United States emerged. First, European countries and Japan recovered from the impact of the war and became more competitive and more assertive in their trade policies. They were prepared to continue cooperation with an American-led system, but demanded a voice in its direction. Second, the American people became increasingly sensitive to the inequities within their society, the persistence of poverty amid plenty. The Kennedy administration, faced with a serious balance-of-payments problem, a declining trade surplus, and demands for social justice at home, conceived a series of innovative steps to expand the economy, but a simultaneous increase in defense and foreign assistance spending precluded success. Keynesian methods of achieving full employment might well have succeeded in a quiescent world; added to the expense required to meet the challenge of a Khrushchev-invigorated Soviet Union, they meant excessive federal deficits, inflation, and a balance-of-payments deficit that threatened the stability of the international economic order established at Bretton Woods.

Lyndon Johnson was even more committed to social justice for his countrymen. His reforms rivaled those of Franklin Roosevelt's New Deal for boldness of vision and presidential skill in obtaining the necessary legislative action. But Johnson was also committed to winning the war in Vietnam and squandered billions of dollars in that benighted cause. A powerful president who dominated the executive branch, manipulated the legislative branch with ease, he lacked the strength and courage to tax the American people to pay for his Great Society programs and his war. The budget deficit grew, inflation increased, the rate of economic growth declined, and the domestic and foreign economic policies of the United States were left in disarray for Richard Nixon.

Nixon, Kissinger, and their aides much preferred to focus their attention and hone their skills on the pursuit of political and military advantage over their adversaries. But they were confronted with a politically damaging recession in 1969 and concluded that inflationary tactics, including devaluation of the dollar, were essential. The United States had run out of devices for maintaining the Bretton Woods system. The Germans and Japanese were resisting American pressure to revalue the mark and the yen, unwilling to allow the United States to devalue the dollar, and gold was leaving the country at alarming rates. The huge balance of payments deficit meant foreigners held more dollars than could be redeemed in gold. The system had always been costly to the United States but it had borne the cost for political reasons, to enable its friends to reconstruct and to preserve vital security relations. By 1971, Nixon had decided the price was too high, the system too restrictive. He was confident that Germany and Japan would not stray, and that the United States could change the rules, and destroy the system at acceptable cost. Contrary to the commitment to convertibility, the president decreed that the gold would not be given in exchange for the excess dollars of countries with balance-of-payments surpluses. He placed a surcharge on import duties to meet protectionist demands in Congress

and instituted wage and price controls in an effort to control inflation. Before the year was out, agreement was reached on a devaluation of the dollar. These steps, however disruptive of the international economic order, helped stimulate a boom in the United States
in 1972, easing Nixon's path to reelection. Again, it should be
noted that despite the decline of American economic power in the
1960s, the United States remained strong enough to determine the
shape of the new international economic order. In order to increase
its freedom of maneuver, the United States wrecked the system it
had created. [13]

But in the new era that began in the 1970s, the United States no
longer dominated the international financial system. In 1971, the
United States recorded its first balance-of-trade deficit of the twentieth century. Increasingly, it required the acquiescence of Germany
and Japan, German and Japanese capital, to maintain domestic prosperity and to project its military power across the world. Both
countries became increasingly assertive, the Germans on monetary
issues and the Japanese on trade. Gradually American leaders discovered they no longer had the freedom of action their predecessors had
enjoyed in the quarter of a century following World War II. Increasingly, the United States needed foreign capital to maintain the
living standards of its people and its influence abroad, and that
capital did not come without strings. German and Japanese ideas
about what the United States did at home and abroad had to be
considered. If, as seemed likely, the United States became a debtor
nation, it might have to defer to its creditors as France had had to
defer to the United States to obtain needed funds in the 1920s.

The relative decline of American power had also been underscored
in the oil crisis of the mid-1970s, induced by the Organization of
Petroleum Exporting Countries (OPEC). Until then the United
States had controlled the world energy market as well as the monetary system. But as American automobiles and industry consumed
more and more of the world's oil each year, American reserves de-

13 See Joanne Gowa, *Closing the Gold Window: Domestic Politics and the End of Bretton
Woods* (Ithaca, 1983); Robert Gilpin, *The Political Economy of International Relations* (Princeton, 1987), 139–41.

clined. The United States, for the first time, became dependent on foreign suppliers. It could no longer use its own once vast petroleum reserves to keep world prices down, and to assure Americans an endless supply of inexpensive fuel. In the midst of the Arab-Israeli war of 1973, the presumably friendly shah of Iran extorted an enormous price increase while Arab suppliers withheld shipments, and the Saudis replaced Americans as the arbiters of world oil prices. Unable to assure its friends of essential supplies at affordable prices, the United States lost the ability to influence their policies, as was exemplified by American inability to prevent the Japanese from shifting from a pro-Israel to a pro-Arab policy in 1973.

The year Nixon resigned the presidency, 1974, was a particularly bad year for the American economy. Gerald Ford entered the White House confronted with a stagnant economy and a high rate of inflation, the unusual combination economists called "stagflation." Ford and Kissinger found the American people much more concerned about jobs and the cost of living than competing with the Soviets on the periphery. With the collapse of the Saigon regime in 1975, there was a widespread unwillingness, in Congress and across the country, to throw scarce resources into endlessly draining, relatively unimportant, probably hopeless causes abroad. The war in Vietnam had denied Americans the Great Society Lyndon Johnson had promised. It was hard for them to imagine any place in the Third World that was worth a further lowering of their standard of living.

Kissinger was deeply troubled by the message that American ennui sent to the Soviets. He never doubted that the Soviets would seek any advantage they could; that an indication that the United States was withdrawing from the field would be perceived in Moscow as an opportunity to expand Soviet influence without risk. Détente depended on the stick as well as the carrot. Congressional action on trade and credit issues had left him little in the way of carrots. Now it began to appear that the administration lacked the support it required to continue three decades of containment. When in May 1975, Cambodian Communists seized an American vessel, the *Mayaguez,* the Ford administration reacted muscularly, sending in the Marines. The operation proved to have been unnecessary. The captives had been released before it began, and more lives were lost among the would-be rescuers than there had been prisoners. But Ford and Kissinger had demonstrated, to their satisfaction, that the United States was not to be trifled with.

Angola, an African nation in which the United States had little interest, emerged as the major point of contention in Soviet-American relations during the Ford administration. A bewildering array of indigenous groups, each with external sources of support, had been seeking to wrest independence from the Portuguese, who abandoned the field after their own revolution in the spring of 1974. As might be expected, there was a Marxist-Leninist organization, the MPLA, supported primarily by Cuba, with intermittent support from the Soviet Union, the Congo, Algeria, the Communist party of Portugal, and some West European governments. A second group, the FNLA, won the support of a odd assortment of backers, including the CIA, Zaire, North Korea, China, Algeria, Morocco, Romania, Libya, India, several West European governments, the Ford Foundation, the AFL-CIO, and, eventually, South Africa. A third important force, UNITA, also received aid from China and wooed South Africa. Tribal as well as ideological differences separated the Angolan revolutionary factions.[14]

In January 1975, the Organization of African Unity brokered an agreement among the three leading organizations: They would work together and with the Portuguese in a transitional government to which Portugal would transfer power in November. The Chinese, determined to prevent a regime friendly to the Soviets, moved first to strengthen the FLNA. The CIA followed suit. In due course the Soviets and Cubans stepped up their aid to the MPLA. By mid-1975, heavy fighting initiated by the FLNA had resulted in unexpected MPLA successes. A Soviet-supported Marxist-Leninist regime seemed likely to emerge in Angola.

Additional aid from the United States, China, Zaire, and South Africa enabled the opponents of the MLPA to regain the advantage by late September. A major South African intervention in October

14 Garthoff, *Détente and Confrontation*, 502–8, makes the tangle comprehensible.

allowed the FNLA and UNITA to close in on the Angolan capital, still held by MPLA forces. In November, Cuba raised the stakes, sending combat forces to assist the MPLA. Quickly, the MPLA turned the tide again, routing FNLA and Zairian troops in the north and halting the South African advance.

Unwilling to be tainted by association with South Africa, the Chinese withdrew from the Angolan tangle before the Cubans arrived in large numbers. Kissinger, however, was less interested in local issues, less concerned about alienating black Africa, and willing to ally with the devil to stop a regime friendly to the Soviet Union from controlling Angola. The decision to intervene in force appeared to have been made in Havana, but there was no reason to doubt that it pleased Moscow. Moreover, there was evidence of Soviet involvement in the airlifting and supplying of the Cuban troops. Angola was not important to the United States, but the Cubans and Soviets could not be allowed to act unopposed. The administration turned to Congress for more money for its Angolan revolutionaries.

To Kissinger's horror, Congress said no. In January 1976 it banned further covert aid to Angola. Congress was unwilling to step into another morass on the periphery. Money would not stop the Cubans and, as American prestige became more intensely involved in the struggle, American troops would be required. Not so soon after Vietnam; not in the midst of the domestic fiscal mess, which Kissinger did not deign to consider.

Freed of the risk of confrontation with the United States, the Soviets deepened their involvement and the Cubans sent more troops. Unable to count on American support, the South Africans abandoned the field. The People's Republic of Angola, beneficiary of South African hostility, quickly won recognition from other black-African states and by March 1976 had reached agreements with Zaire and South Africa to relieve most of the external pressures on it. Soviet influence in Angola increased briefly, but the dominant foreign influence was Cuban. In 1977, Cuba and the Soviets backed different factions within the Angolan regime with the Cuban-backed government forces prevailing over pro-Soviet dissidents. Neither Cuban nor Soviet-backed members of the Angolan government could be restrained from reaching out to the West, including the United States, for trade and investments.

The Soviets had gained little in Angola, but that was not Kissinger's perception. The victory of the Soviet-backed MPLA sharply reduced his tolerance for Soviet competition in the Third World. As long as the Chinese- and American-backed FNLA seemed likely to prevail, the Soviet role had not been troublesome. When the tide of battle shifted, the United States declared Soviet intervention unacceptable, inconsistent with détente. Efforts to persuade the Soviets to back off were ultimately unsuccessful and the administration, for better or worse, lacked the means to respond more forcefully. Kissinger feared that the Soviets would be emboldened to further interventions, further demonstrations of their growing ability to project power abroad. Perhaps worst of all, he feared that Americans had lost the will to meet the Soviet challenge.[15]

To Brezhnev and his colleagues, Kissinger's strictures seemed the rankest hypocrisy. The American interpretation of the rules of détente allowed competition so long as it resulted in success for the Americans. Now that the Soviets were able to do what the Americans had been doing throughout the Cold War, the Americans declared such action unacceptable. They might make gestures toward compliance with American wishes, but there is no indication in the statements of Soviet leaders or in their actions in the Angolan situation that they were prepared to surrender in the contest for influence on the periphery.

The Soviets, moreover, were confronted by an additional challenge, that of the Chinese. Not only did they have to prove to themselves and the rest of the world that their country was a superpower as deserving of deference as was the United States, but they also had to demonstrate to Communists and radicals in and out of power all over the world that Moscow and not Beijing was their mecca, that the Soviet Union would do more for them than would China. In the unlikely event that the Politburo had concluded that its potential gains in Angola were not worth the possible increase in

15 William Hyland, *Mortal Rivals: Superpower Relations from Nixon to Reagan* (New York, 1987), 142–6.

Soviet-American tensions, Chinese involvement likely would have drawn the Soviets into the fray. Moreover, Chinese-American collusion in Angola seemed to touch a raw nerve among Brezhnev's colleagues. Too much had been invested in building Soviet military might to allow the Chinese and Americans to intimidate or outmaneuver Moscow. [16]

Finally, it is clear that as American willingness to use military power abroad declined, Soviet willingness increased. In part, as Kissinger feared, the Soviets perceived a clear field in Angola. Congressional action suggested there was little risk of confrontation. Like the Americans before them, the Soviets did not easily resist the opportunity to test their newly developed air- and sealift capabilities. The Soviet military was eager to experiment with new equipment and new techniques. Despite the evidence of how the cost of America's Third World interventions had eroded the power of the United States and contributed to its relative decline, the Soviets were determined to defy the lessons of history. Starting with a far weaker economic base, the Soviets wanted to believe that their great military power, the one area in which they excelled, would enable them to succeed where the Americans had failed, to gain advantage on the periphery.

In the central arena, Europe, détente held. Europeans, especially German leaders, were less concerned with Soviet-American rivalry in the Third World, and eager to take steps to reduce the likelihood of their homelands becoming battlegrounds for testing Soviet and American tactical nuclear weapons. Willy Brandt, chancellor of West Germany, had made enormous strides with his *Ostpolitik*. Trade burgeoned between Eastern and Western European countries. In 1970 West Germany and the Soviet Union signed a nonaggression pact. They declared the boundaries of Poland, the Soviet Union, and Germany, as determined by Churchill, Roosevelt, and Stalin at Tehran and Yalta during World War II, to be inviolate. In 1971, accord was reached on Western access to Berlin, to be guaranteed by the Soviets. By 1972, East and West Germany had recognized each

16 Garthoff, *Détente and Confrontation*, 527–30.

other. Uneasy about the German initiatives, but preoccupied by Vietnam, Nixon and Kissinger could do little but follow suit.

The Soviets pressed hard for détente with Western Europe. They sought technology not easily obtained from the United States and hoped to be able to drive a wedge between the Americans and their NATO allies. Brezhnev and his colleagues wanted formal acceptance by all European countries of their post-1945 borders and proposed a conference from which they hoped to exclude non-European nations, most obviously the United States. By 1973, the Soviets succeeded in bringing about a Conference on Security and Cooperation in Europe, but had to accept American participation – and that of Canada and the Vatican.

Two years of negotiations resulted in the Helsinki Agreements of August 1975, giving the Soviets the assurances they wanted on the European status quo. To get those assurances, the Soviets were forced to commit themselves to improve their record on human rights, specifically to allow the free movement of peoples and ideas. Were they to honor their Helsinki commitments, the political system from which Brezhnev and bloc leaders derived their power would be destroyed. Perhaps little of substance had been achieved, but like the American Declaration of Independence, the Helsinki Agreements established a standard toward which the signatories might strive and to which they might be held. They symbolized the extent to which the Iron Curtain had been penetrated from both sides.

Nixon and Kissinger remained apprehensive about the easing of tensions in Europe. They feared Europeans would relax their vigilance, that they would be unwilling to support military preparedness, that they might think the Cold War over and turn away from the United States. While Europeans were heartened by the Helsinki accords, the decision of President Ford to sign them was derided by his political opponents as evidence of his naïveté in foreign affairs. Ford, a popular Midwestern conservative, fought off the Reagan challenge from the right wing of his party and won the Republican presidential nomination in 1976, but lost the election to Democrat Jimmy Carter, whose views on most issues seemed vague and elastic. It was Carter who had to determine how the United States would respond to Brezhnev's opportunism in Africa, and whether efforts toward extending détente would continue.

The election of Jimmy Carter as president of the United States in 1976 illustrated the best and worst of the American political system. The American people were weary of the sacrifices demanded of them – the lives of their children spent senselessly in distant wars, the inroads of stagflation on their standard of living. Not unreasonably, they blamed their government, the men in control in Washington. And unlike their counterparts in the Soviet Union, China, and many other parts of the world, they had a remedy: They voted out their rulers and started fresh, with a new government headed by a man completely uncontaminated by previous contact with Washington, and unassociated with any of the tired policies of the past. America would remake itself. A new president would remove all of the irritants and set the country back on course toward a liberal democratic utopia.

Unfortunately, the new American president, however well he had once run the state of Georgia, was ill-prepared to manage the foreign policy of the world's greatest power. He was bright and he was able, but he had to learn on the job. In the nuclear age, in the volatile world of the late 1970s, it was terrifying to think that the man who had his hand on the levers of American power, the man responsible for American policy, had no experience in international relations. It was not a job for an amateur; it was not a time for an amateur. But Jimmy Carter was the people's choice.

The result was four years of disarray. A good and decent man, Carter was also sufficiently arrogant to think he could put aside the misguided efforts of his predecessors and start anew. Like Woodrow Wilson more than a half century before, he denounced the selfish realpolitik of the preceding administration and proclaimed America's intention to return to its ideals. Insistence on respect for human rights would be the centerpiece of his administration's foreign policy. He was determined to alleviate tensions with the Soviets and to end the Cold War, but was slow to comprehend that his criticism of Soviet performance on human rights complicated his efforts. Eager to accelerate the arms control process, he disrupted it by putting aside proposals resulting from years of Soviet and American negotiations and substituting a more radical plan, the implications of which were unclear and were ultimately perceived as threatening by the Soviets. His principal advisers on foreign policy, Cyrus Vance, secretary of state, and Zbigniew Brzezinski, national security adviser, pulled him in opposite directions on Soviet issues in particular, but on many others as well. The president attempted to construct a policy out of ideas offered by both and succeeded only in confusing friends and enemies alike, provoking contempt at home and abroad.

For Vance, the principal objective of American policy was to revive and strengthen Soviet-American détente, to work closely with the Soviets both to reduce bilateral tensions and to resolve some of the world's less tractable problems, like those of the Middle East. He was persuaded that beneath the geriatric leadership of the Brezhnev Politburo was a generation of Soviets free of Stalinist dogma, as eager as any American to end the Cold War and desperately anxious to modernize their country.[17]

Specifically, Vance sought further arms control agreement, a SALT II treaty, to slow and, if possible, reverse the arms race. Such an agreement might also serve to permit the United States to reduce the defense expenditures that strained the nation's resources and contributed mightily to inflation. He was prepared to accept a Soviet role in the Middle East, convinced that admitting the Soviets to partnership was the only way to persuade them to act responsibly, that giving them a stake in the peace of the region was the best way to stop malicious Soviet agitation of radical Arab forces. Vance was troubled by aggressive Soviet behavior in Africa, but perceived no threat to any important American interests. In due course the men in the Kremlin would learn the lesson the United States had learned in Vietnam: The ability to project power on the periphery was double-edged, its exercise as likely to sap national strength as to increase it.

Vance was not particularly interested in China and apprehensive lest the Chinese manipulate the United States toward their own

17 See Cyrus Vance, *Hard Choices* (New York, 1983).

ends, exacerbating Soviet-American tensions to maximize China's room to maneuver. To Vance, the best hope for the future, for the world as well as for the United States, was to encourage the modification of Soviet behavior. Change would not occur overnight, but if détente were back on track, the next cycle of Soviet leaders might accelerate the process.

Brzezinski never doubted that the Soviet Union was central to American concerns. He did not believe, however, that solutions to the problem could be found in Moscow. He perceived no prospect for a voluntary improvement in Soviet behavior. The Cold War could only be ended with the defeat of one of the superpowers. To defeat the Soviet Union the United States had to strengthen itself and its allies and maintain relentless pressure on the Soviets. SALT II was less important than seeking strategic advantage over the Soviets, revitalizing NATO, enlisting the Chinese on the side of the United States, weakening Soviet control over Eastern Europe, promoting dissent within the Soviet empire, and countering Soviet interventions anywhere in the world. He insisted that the competition between the United States and the Soviet Union was ordained by history and geography, as well as conflicting political cultures. The United States could only play to win.[18]

Vance was clearly right about the imminence of change in the Soviet Union. The forces Khrushchev had unleashed in the late 1950s, the reinvigoration of the social sciences, the serious scholarly study of the world, had proved their worth to the Soviet leadership. The "new thinking" leaking through the dikes of ideological dogmatism had increased from a trickle to a flood by the late 1970s. Nonetheless, the dikes held. Brezhnev and his colleagues in the top echelons of Soviet government remained largely impervious to the intellectual turmoil that Vance's advisers had noted. The party elders were not receptive to fresh ideas, new approaches. They held on to power and exercised it as they always had and the Soviet people had no recourse. Vance's vision was probably not realizable in the 1970s.

Brezhnev perceived a United States weakened by Vietnam and Watergate, led by an irresolute and uninformed president. The mo-

18 See Zbigniew Brzezinski, *Power and Principle* (New York, 1983).

ment was opportune for the Soviet Union to press its advantage, as it did in the fall of 1977, airlifting Cuban forces to the Horn of Africa, and winning the allegiance of America's longtime Ethiopian ally. Brezhnev could only be heartened by the Communist seizure of power in Afghanistan in April 1978 and his Vietnamese protégé's easy victory over the Chinese-backed Khmer Rouge of Cambodia in December of that year. In January 1979, the shah of Iran, the American surrogate in the Middle East and Southwest Asia, fled his country and the ensuing civil strife undermined the strategic position of the United States in the region. Even on the doorstep of the United States, first in tiny Grenada and then in Nicaragua, forces friendly to Cuba and the Soviet Union seized power.

From the perspective of the Kremlin, Carter had been ineffectual in responding to each of these situations. Soviet power could no longer be checked anywhere. The men of the Politburo were quite satisfied with themselves and saw no need for new approaches. They ignored the probable repercussions of their policies on American behavior and functioned much as Brzezinski had anticipated. Forsaking their usual prudence, Soviet leaders undermined Vance and drove Carter into Brzezinski's arms. [19]

Although ground was lost in the all-critical effort to end the Cold War, the Carter administration enjoyed important successes in Latin America, the Middle East, and East Asia. Unfortunately, none of these successes could be achieved without affecting Soviet-American relations adversely. In 1977, Carter signed several treaties that ultimately would permit Panama to gain control over the canal, an eventuality to which some American conservatives were unalterably opposed. The administration won a bruising battle for ratification by the Senate, but the process cost it votes it would need for acceptance of the SALT II treaty. Some of the conservative senators who helped the administration on the Panama treaty would have to renew their conservative credentials by voting against arms control.

The Camp David accords, enormously important agreements between Israel and Egypt, facilitated by Carter, angered the Soviets, who had been excluded from the process. Sadat had lost faith in the

19 Gelman, *Brezhnev Politburo*, 145–6.

ability of the Soviets to aid his cause before the 1973 war and relied increasingly on American leverage with the Israelis. In 1977, aware that Carter needed help overcoming Israeli rigidity, Sadat heroically traveled to Israel to demonstrate to American friends of Israel, as well as Israelis, his willingness to live in peace with his erstwhile enemies. Carter succeeded in brokering the agreements by means of which Egypt regained its Sinai territory and, by making peace with Israel, by recognizing the state of Israel, broke the back of the Arab coalition against Israel.

Egypt's rapprochement with the United States and Israel deprived the Soviets of their most important friend in the Middle East. Exclusion of the Soviets, who were trusted by neither the Egyptians nor the Israelis, from the peace talks disparaged their claim to superpower status. The affairs of one of the most vital regions of the world were being arranged without them. Moscow did not sanction the accords and gave encouragement to those forces in the Arab world that continued to reject's Israel's right to exist. The odds on Israel's survival had increased greatly, but without at least a gesture toward Soviet interests in the region, there was little chance for an enduring peace. And again, Soviet support of Arab belligerence against Israel intensified anti-Soviet attitudes in the United States, creating a political climate unreceptive to the strengthening of dé-tente. As long as the Soviet Union was excluded from the peace process, it would stir trouble in the Middle East. As long as it stirred trouble in the Middle East, it would be difficult to improve Soviet-American relations. Until Soviet-American relations im-proved, it would be difficult for the men in Washington to share influence in the region with the Soviets. It was a conundrum from which there seemed no escape short of surrender by the Soviets, for which the Politburo was not quite ready.

The long-overdue normalization of relations between the United States and the People's Republic of China was also one of Carter's accomplishments. Regrettably, the issue of when and how to achieve this goal was caught up in the Vance-Brzezinski rivalry and in the two men's conflicting view of how to cope with the Soviet Union. Vance was convinced that showing any kind of favoritism toward the Chinese would aggravate Soviet-American relations, that relations with China were less important than relations with the Soviets. Brzezinski, of course, demonstrated less concern for Soviet sensibilities and thought frequent jabs to the head reminded Soviet leaders of the need to conciliate the United States. Brzezinski prevailed.[20]

Chinese ends were not congruent with those of the United States. There was, to be sure, a shared interest in containing Soviet power, but the Chinese were apprehensive about improvement in Soviet-American relations. Historically, a weak China had used barbarians to control barbarians and in the 1970s they perceived an interest in playing the Soviets and Americans off against each other. Deng Xiaoping, who emerged as China's leader in the late 1970s, was quick to recognize the Vance-Brzezinski rivalry and to use it to China's advantage. Eager to bloody the Vietnamese for challenging Chinese influence in Cambodia, Deng wanted an American connection that would neutralize the Soviets, reduce the possibility of Soviet intervention when China attacked Vietnam. Whenever and wherever they could, Chinese leaders attempted to stir trouble between the Soviet Union and the West. Deng was at least as successful at using the Americans as they were at using the Chinese.

Recognition of the Beijing regime in 1979 as the government of China was unquestionably sensible and an important achievement for American diplomacy. If, however, it was to be accomplished in a way that increased tensions with the Soviet Union, the one nation in the world with the capacity to destroy the United States, the price was too high. Whereas Vance was unappreciative of the opportunity for rapprochement with the Chinese, Brzezinski was indifferent to the cost of antagonizing the Soviets. Indeed he rarely missed an opportunity to taunt Moscow. But it was Brzezinski's approach that appealed to the American electorate, and to which Carter was drawn.

Despite Vance's opposition, Washington persistently signaled interest in strategic cooperation with the Chinese against the Soviets. When the Soviets reacted angrily, American critics of détente were

20 Michel Oksenberg, "A Decade of Sino-American Relations," *Foreign Affairs* 61 (1982): 175–95; Harding, *Fragile Relationship,* 67–81.

appeased momentarily. On the other hand, if the American public was led to believe that getting tough with the Soviets was the appropriate course, there were men like Senator Henry Jackson (D.-Wash.) and Ronald Reagan who were better cast for the role of helmsman than was Jimmy Carter.

Carter's last effort to salvage détente came in 1979 when, despite anger at Chinese-American collusion over China's attack on Vietnam, the Soviets agreed to a summit meeting and the signing of the SALT II agreement. Certainly Vance was genuinely interested in regaining momentum toward accommodation with the Soviet Union and Brzezinski thought that Brezhnev's willingness to meet Carter and sign the treaty was evidence of the success of his efforts to intimidate the Soviets. SALT II was not a great breakthrough in arms control, but most of the professionals who examined it thought it better crafted than SALT I and very much in the interest of the United States. The Soviets, for their part, had an intense need to reduce military expenditures. Although Brezhnev and the other party elders seemed unmindful of the alarms being sounded by Soviet midlevel analysts, the economy of their country was beginning to disintegrate and the cost of their empire was greater than their people could bear. Briefly, the possibility of revitalizing détente seemed to exist, but it was not to be.

Soviet actions in the Third World, the Kremlin's suppression of dissidents at home, combined with Carter's inept leadership, allowed Senator Jackson and other anti-Soviet elements in American society to seize the initiative. In late summer 1979, Frank Church (D.-Idaho), a senator friendly to détente, inadvertently doomed the SALT II treaty by calling attention to a Soviet combat brigade in Cuba and demanding its immediate removal. Church, widely considered too liberal for his constituents, was attempting to ward off conservative attacks in his fight for reelection. In fact, the brigade had been in Cuba for years with the acquiescence of the American government. When Carter, in response to the domestic political furor caused by Church's revelation, demanded that the Soviets withdraw their troops, it was Brezhnev's turn to be outraged. The Soviets had done nothing wrong. They had honored their promise not to reinforce their forces in Cuba. They were being asked to retreat from a position they had held since the early 1960s to assist the American president with his domestic political problems. They refused. Carter and the Soviets thus gave additional ammunition to the anti-SALT forces in the Senate.[21]

The issue of the Soviet combat brigade discovered in Cuba was quickly overshadowed by the hostage crisis in Iran that began in November 1979 and the Soviet invasion of Afghanistan in December. The shah of Iran, reestablished in power by the CIA-directed coup of 1953, had fled in January 1979, as forces hostile to his far from benevolent rule became increasingly threatening. Hopes for a moderate democratic successor regime were quickly buried by powerful Islamic fundamentalists who looked to the Ayatollah Khomeni as their leader. In November, Khomeni's followers seized the American Embassy and took those inside it hostage, ultimately holding fifty-seven of them for fourteen months, for the remainder of Carter's presidency. The inability of the Carter administration to obtain the freedom of the hostages, through negotiations or a bizarre rescue attempt, intensified public frustration with the president's leadership – or lack thereof. Gulliver tormented by the Lilliputians was not an image of their country acceptable to Americans. They wanted their leader to act forcefully to command the respect due the world's greatest power. They could not understand why he could not get the Soviets out of Cuba, or the hostages out of Iran. They were ready to find someone who could – and would. The president had to run before the mob.[22]

In December, the Soviets gave Carter an opportunity to act assertively, to assume the mantle of greatness Brzezinski held out for him, at the cost of détente. In Afghanistan, the Communist regime that had come to power in April 1978 was disintegrating, partly under pressure of Islamic fundamentalist opposition, but largely because of ethnic factionalism within the Afghani Communist party. Soviet advisers and pressures had failed to ameliorate the situation. Unrest in a nation on its border, among people ethnically related to

21 Garthoff, *Détente and Confrontation*, 828–48.
22 Gary Sick, *All Fall Down* (New York, 1985), is the most useful starting point for the study of the Carter administration and Iran.

restive Soviet peoples in Central Asia, boded ill. The triumph of Islamic fundamentalism in Iran threatened Soviet interests as well as American. Whereas the American concern was primarily for control of Persian Gulf oil, the Soviets feared for the security of their border regions. When political pressure failed, the Soviets resorted to force, another classic example of the arrogance of power. The mighty Red Army, feared all over Europe and America, marched into Afghanistan to teach what Lyndon Johnson would have called a "pissant country" not to defy the will of a superpower. Again, Brezhnev and his colleagues underestimated the American reaction to steps they considered vital to their security.[23]

Carter responded vigorously. With striking hyperbole, he called the Soviet action the gravest danger to world peace since World War II. He imposed a grain embargo against the Soviet Union, infuriating American farmers. In due course he decided to have American athletes boycott the summer Olympics scheduled for Moscow, outraging the athletes and all those who considered athletics more important than politics. He declared the "Carter Doctrine," a warning to the Soviets that the United States considered the Persian Gulf a vital interest and would not tolerate a Soviet advance toward the Gulf. Of greatest consequence, he called for an arms buildup in the United States to meet the new Soviet threat.

The Soviets were shocked by the forcefulness of Carter's response and were put on the defensive in the court of world opinion. They surrendered hope of cooperating with the Carter administration and hunkered down for a new era of confrontation. The war in Afghanistan drained resources from their already profoundly troubled economy.

The glorious achievement of parity with the United States, the exhilarating sense that the correlation of forces in the world favored the Soviet Union, the joy of traveling the road to world leadership, had hardly been savored before the foundations of the Soviet empire began to give way. The army, no matter how brutally it performed its duties, could not crush Afghani guerrilla forces, supplied primar-

23 Garthoff, *Détente and Confrontation*, 887–965, is easily the best explanation of Soviet behavior in Afghanistan.

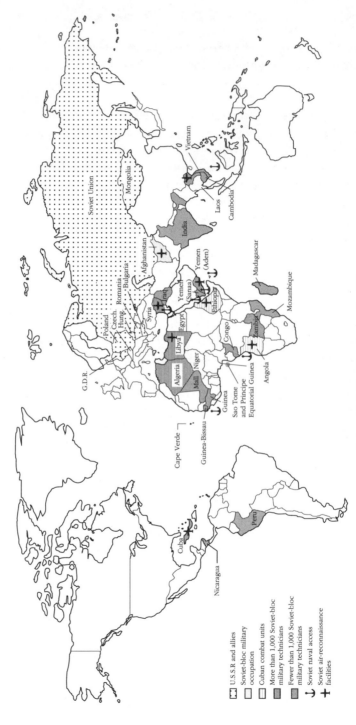

Soviet and Soviet-Bloc Military Presence, Circa 1985

Soviet Union

Mongolia

Afghanistan

Poland
Czech.
Hung.
Romania
Bulgaria
Syria
G.D.R.

Libya
Algeria
Mali
Niger
Guinea
Sao Tome
and Principe
Equatorial Guinea
Guinea-Bissau
Cape Verde

Egypt
Yemen
(Sanaa)
Yemen
(Aden)
Ethiopia
Congo
Angola
Zambia
Mozambique
Madagascar

India
Vietnam
Laos
Cambodia

Cuba
Nicaragua
Peru

U.S.S.R and allies

Soviet-bloc military
occupation

Cuban combat units

More than 1,000 Soviet-bloc
military technicians

Fewer than 1,000 Soviet-bloc
military technicians

Soviet naval access

Soviet air-reconnaissance
facilities

ily by the Chinese and Americans. The economy, ramshackle at best, could not stand the strain of subsidies to allies like Cuba and Vietnam, the price of empire. And now there was likely to be a new and costly arms race with the United States. Fearful of Soviet communism, Americans had long exaggerated the threat posed by the Soviet Union. In 1980, many Americans perceived the Soviet Union on the offensive, poised to achieve its goal of world domination. Brezhnev and the other party ancients reveled in that vision, but the reality was a regime everywhere on the defensive.

The years 1969 through 1980 were years of erratic, halting steps by the superpowers toward the end of the Cold War. The euphoria of Nixon's openings to Moscow and Beijing in 1972, the widespread hopes for peace, were dashed in the closing months of the Carter administration. But the forces propelling the superpowers toward accommodation remained powerful. Foremost among them were the domestic economic realities from which no American or Soviet leader could escape. The empires built at such great cost in the years since World War II had placed unacceptable burdens on both societies. America's relative decline had begun in the 1960s, but the Americans had achieved a standard of living that remained out of the reach of the people of the Soviet Union. The agricultural and industrial foundation of American power remained stronger than anything the Soviet system could construct. The Soviets kept straining to equal, to surpass the United States, but what they succeeded in doing militarily, they could not accomplish in their consumer economy. The United States might be in decline, but the Soviet Union could not overtake it.

Neither Soviet nor American leaders were willing to surrender hegemonic visions, and the structure of their respective societies continued to erode. The competition continued into the 1980s. The strains were obviously greater on the Soviet side and advocates of the "new thinking" in the Soviet Union knew the race could not go on much longer. Americans, however, were not willing to give up their nation's place in the sun and their system was stronger, more flexible, their people living farther from the edge. Under the leadership of Ronald Reagan, the American people were prepared to mortgage the future of their children in a renewed effort to win the Cold War. Brezhnev's successors had nothing to mortgage. If wise leaders could not find a way to end the mutually debilitating confrontation, bankruptcy might.

8. In God's Country

If anyone ever doubted that America was God's chosen country, the events of the 1980s should have been reassuring. Electing Ronald Reagan, a onetime movie star, to lead them, to determine their future in a world of extraordinary complexity, with nuclear holocaust a hair's breadth away, was the ultimate act of faith by the American people. Their faith did not go unrewarded.

Reagan was a man of unusual charm, with an appealing self-deprecating sense of humor. He was a likeable man, who shared the nostalgia many Americans felt for the days of American hegemony. He offered himself as their leader at a time when their economy was a shambles, when they were still heartsick from defeat in Vietnam and from the humiliation of the Iranian hostage crisis. Once in the White House, he restored the nation's confidence in itself and its future. He was the charismatic leader his people wanted. His impact was reminiscent of that of his early idol, Franklin Delano Roosevelt, who had assured hungry Americans, frightened by the grinding misery of the Great Depression, that they had "nothing to fear, but fear itself," that they had "a rendezvous with destiny."[1]

Unlike Roosevelt, Reagan knew little about the world in which the United States had long been the dominant power. He was uninformed – and not terribly interested. Details, such as the political orientation of various governments, bored and eluded him. Efforts by foreign policy specialists to explain were often futile. He ignored briefing books and dozed while the intricacies of military strategy were presented to him. He was generally uncritical of stories that fit his presuppositions and seemed to lack a capacity for analysis. And yet, most of those who worked with him as governor of California or

---

1 Lou Cannon, *President Reagan: The Role of a Lifetime* (New York, 1991), is the most balanced study of Reagan as president.

president of the United States argued that he was not stupid. Lou Cannon, a reporter who followed him for much of his political career, wrote of Reagan having a different kind of intelligence, more common to actors than to lawyers and professors.[2]

Perhaps more troubling than the peculiarities of his mind was Reagan's disinterest in governing. He had wanted to be president, to provide his vision to Americans, to ride into Washington on his white horse and rescue his country. Once there he had little interest in how things were done. He did not know enough, or care enough, about how government worked to exercise his presidential powers. On most issues, he was quite content to delegate his authority, to let others make decisions and determine how they would be implemented. Once the script had been prepared by his advisers, he would perform for the public. His was an unusual conception of presidential power, but there were surely times when Jimmy Carter envied him.

Reagan was not without ideas relevant to foreign affairs, however many came from movies that he had seen or in which he had acted. He perceived a world in which the forces of good led by the United States were pitted against the "evil empire," the Soviet Union. The Soviet Union and its allies were adversaries with whom "we are at war," a war he intended to win. Opposition to the Soviets was the central focus of all he knew or thought about foreign policy. He contended that the Soviets had achieved military superiority in the 1970s as a consequence of détente and he was critical of arms control agreements in general and Carter's SALT II accord in particular. The Soviets, he argued, had cheated on all those agreements; Soviet leaders would always lie and cheat. Confronted by such an opponent, the United States could depend only upon its military power. He was determined to rebuild that power, regain for the United States the capability to wage war successfully against the Soviets, to act with impunity against Soviet Third World clients, and to regain

2 See Cannon's fascinating application of the theories of Harvard psychologist Howard Gardner to his analysis of Reagan's mind in Cannon, *President Reagan*, 137–40.

its status as the world's dominant military force. Not until then could the Soviets be expected to keep their agreements, if ever. He despised the Soviet political system and doubted whether the United States could ever reach an accommodation with it.

Despite the extraordinary military buildup over which he presided and the confrontational rhetoric for which he was notorious, Reagan had an intense emotional horror of nuclear weapons. He was appalled when he realized that American security was dependent on the concept of deterrence, on having a sufficient number of strategic nuclear weapons, deployed at sea, in the air, and on land, to deter a first strike by the Soviets. In theory, no matter how the Soviets attacked, American weapons sufficient to retaliate and destroy the Soviet Union would survive and vice versa. The security of both superpowers had come to rest on the idea of mutually assured destruction. A fraction of each side's strategic force would survive a first strike and destroy the other; there was, therefore, no point to an attack. Deterrence had been central to American defense strategy at least since the Soviets developed a credible strategic force in the 1960s, but it was not good enough for Ronald Reagan. He equated nuclear war with Armageddon, the destruction of the world. He wanted nuclear weapons eliminated rather than controlled. Short of their elimination, he wanted some means to prevent them from being used against Americans. In the 1940 movie, *Murder in the Air,* Reagan, as Brass Bancroft, had protected an American secret weapon, an "inertia projector" capable of destroying enemy planes before they could reach their targets. He would have to do something like that again to stave off the apocalypse. Absent nuclear war, the strength of the American free-enterprise system would ultimately leave the Soviets light years behind.

Once settled into the White House, Reagan and the men and women who accompanied him lacked a blueprint for action. Indeed his administration required two years to produce a document outlining its policy toward the Soviet Union. In 1981, the United States was slipping into the worst economic decline since the Great Depression. The president and his aides, like Herbert Hoover and Franklin Roosevelt in the early 1930s, were preoccupied with the domestic crisis. The Soviets and the rest of the world could wait.

In the interim, the president's rhetoric was inflammatory, but American actions were contradictory. Carter had imposed an embargo on grain sales to the Soviet Union as punishment for the Red Army's invasion of Afghanistan. Despite his vows to be much tougher with the men in Moscow, Reagan's first major foreign policy act was to lift the ban. American farmers had voted for Ronald Reagan and he had made promises to them, too. For all his ideological rigidity, Reagan had little trouble rationalizing compromises dictated by political exigencies, foreign or domestic. His determination to abandon SALT II evaporated when he discovered that the Joint Chiefs of Staff were quite content with its provisions and angered by his charges of American military inferiority. Reagan decided he could live with its provisions.

Similarly, the president found he could not so easily dispense with arms control negotiations. In response to European anxieties over new Soviet intermediate-range missile deployments in the late 1970s, Carter had agreed to station a new generation of American Pershing and cruise missiles in Europe in the 1980s. Unabashed by the threat their weapons posed to Western Europe, the Soviets were outraged by the threat the proposed American deployment constituted to them. They organized a major propaganda campaign against it among Europeans. Indeed, keeping the new American missiles out of Europe became the principal task of Soviet diplomacy in 1981 and 1982. To protect themselves from antimissile political activists, the European potential host governments needed to demonstrate a good faith effort to achieve security through arms reduction: They needed to have the United States negotiate with the Soviets for the removal or reduction of intermediate missiles from Europe prior to accepting the necessity of deploying new weapons. Reagan had no choice and he sent his negotiators to talk to their Soviet counterparts in what were known as INF (intermediate-range nuclear force) talks. Shortly afterward, Reagan was forced by Congress to back away from his refusal to resume strategic arms limitation talks (SALT). He disguised his retreat by calling these strategic arms *reduction* talks (START). His predecessors had been content to control the arms race by agreeing to limits on their new weapons. He claimed he would reverse the process by eliminating weapons.[3]

The crisis in Poland in 1981 provided another example of Reagan being forced to retreat under pressure from his European allies. As the growing strength of Polish workers and intellectuals united in the Solidarity movement promised to sweep away the Communist regime, Soviet pressures prompted the Polish army to seize power. The United States responded with economic sanctions against Poland and the Soviet Union and insisted that its NATO allies follow suit. In particular, the Reagan administration demanded that Europeans stop assistance to the Soviet construction of a gas pipeline to facilitate the sale of Soviet natural gas to Western Europe. When the Europeans failed to respond to Reagan's satisfaction, American firms licensed in Europe were ordered by Washington to withhold essential parts, an act of dubious legality guaranteed to infuriate host governments. In the ensuing uproar, the United States retreated once more and the pipeline construction resumed.

Reagan seemed content to accelerate the arms race and bash the Soviets verbally. His secretary of state, the volatile Al Haig, wanted to demonstrate American resolve in other ways, by striking at Soviet friends around the world, particularly in Central America. Although Haig was reputedly desirous of turning Cuba into a parking lot, he focused his attention on El Salvador, where murderous right-wing army officers contended with leftist guerrillas across the helpless shell of a would-be democratic government. The leftists were receiving aid from the Sandinistas, who had wrested power from the Somoza family dictatorship in Nicaragua, and from Cuba. The rightists, despite their responsibility for the assassination of the popular and politically moderate Archbishop Romero, and their complicity in the murder of American nuns, received aid from the United States. It was not a happy choice of fields for liberal democ-

---

3 Michael Mandelbaum and Strobe Talbott, *Reagan and Gorbachev* (New York, 1987); Raymond L. Garthoff, *Détente and Confrontation* (Washington, D.C., 1985), 1023.

racy to contend against authoritarian socialism, but it was accessible, and American operations there were relatively inexpensive and risk-free. If American intervention in El Salvador was not especially troubling to Moscow, it did prove to the American Right that the Reagan administration's anticommunism would be demonstrated with more than words.

Further comfort to those whose mistrust of the Soviets knew no bounds came when the administration repudiated an informal agreement reached between Soviet and American arms control negotiators in July 1982. Paul Nitze, who had long since established his anti-Communist credentials as principal author of NSC-68 in the Truman era and as the driving force behind the Committee on the Present Danger, created to alert Americans to the threat Carter's arms control programs posed to their security, was the American negotiator. He and his Soviet counterpart went for a walk in the woods near Geneva, Switzerland, and worked out a compromise on intermediate missiles, to the chagrin of the White House, which wanted no agreement. Repudiation upset European leaders but the president was spared substantial embarrassment by Soviet rejection of the arrangement.[4]

Reagan sent one further message to the world early in his administration. In a "don't tread on me" signature gesture, U.S. Navy pilots intercepted and destroyed two Soviet-built Libyan jets that dared to challenge them over the Gulf of Sidra, an area claimed by Libya. Carter may have been the sort of president who would turn the other cheek and invite disrespect from Third World countries; Reagan most definitely was not. American power would not be reined in. "Let friend and foe alike know that America has the muscle to back up its words," the president warned.[5] Additional evidence of Reagan's willingness to project American power came in 1982, when, against the advice of the secretary of defense, he ordered U.S. Marines to Lebanon in an attempt to create order out of the chaos resulting from the Israeli invasion of that benighted country.

Despite Reagan's hostile campaign rhetoric and anti-Soviet reputation, Soviet anger at Carter had been so great in 1980 that Soviet

4 Strobe Talbott, *Deadly Gambits* (New York, 1984), 116–51.
5 Quoted in Garthoff, *Détente and Confrontation*, p. 1060.

leaders had welcomed Reagan's election. They assumed that once in office Reagan, like Nixon, would shed his Red-baiting garb and work toward détente. The years of détente had been good for the Soviets and they were unwilling to see that era end. They had been granted formal recognition of equality with the United States, had been able to expand their influence in the Third World, and, in the ABM treaty, had obtained a measure of restraint on the technological advantages of the Americans. Brezhnev, too enfeebled to devise a new policy, allowed the hope of renewed détente to obscure the reality that Reagan's approach would be radically different from Nixon's, an intensification of all the Soviets had disliked of Carter's confrontational policies of 1980. Brezhnev died in 1982, never to see a glimmer of hope that Ronald Reagan would accept accommodation with the Soviet Union.[6]

By the time of Brezhnev's death, surviving Soviet leaders recognized Reagan's intransigence and were ready to give up any expectation of working with the United States. They saw little choice but to wait him out, to hope that dissatisfaction with his belligerence, both in Europe and the United States, would bring a new, more reasonable American president in 1984. But of greater long-term consequence was evidence that the men to whom Yuri Andropov, Brezhnev's successor, looked for advice, were beginning to recognize that Soviet actions contributed to American militance; that the Soviet military buildup in the 1970s, Soviet expansionist policies in the Third World might be perceived as threatening by the United States; that the Soviet quest for "absolute" security might have forced the United States to resume the arms race; that changes in Soviet behavior might be necessary to obtain the desired changes in American policy. And Andropov and his advisers, analyzing the results of Brezhnev's ineptitude, reviewing the strains on the Soviet economy, the costs of the war in Afghanistan and their overseas adventures, began to realize that their empire was overextended.[7]

Andropov, slowly dying of kidney failure, presided over the worst

---

6 Seweryn Bialer and Joan Afferica, "Reagan and Russia," *Foreign Affairs* 61 (1982–3): 249–71.

7 Mandelbaum and Talbott, *Reagan and Gorbachev*, 24–5; Bialer and Afferica, "Reagan and Russia."

year in Soviet-American relations since the Cuban missile crisis of 1962. The Soviet Union's diplomatic offensive to prevent the deployment of new American intermediate-range missiles (INF) resulted in a humiliating failure. In the arms control negotiations, the United States offered only propagandistic proposals markedly disadvantageous to the Soviets. One by one the European governments that were to provide sites for the missiles overcame internal opposition and approved their installation. In November 1983, hoping to place blame on the United States, the Soviets walked out of the INF talks. They accomplished nothing.

Most threatening to the Soviet leadership was the apparent intention of the United States to begin a new "high-tech" race for defensive weapons. In March 1983, Reagan's interest in preventing the use of nuclear missiles led him to announce suddenly, with minimal warning to the secretaries of state and defense, that the United States would seek to create a strategic defense system (SDI or "Star Wars"). The idea had intrigued the president for years and he was delighted when he found both scientists and military leaders who thought it feasible. Although those of his advisers who supported the plan saw it either as a bargaining chip to trade for Soviet arms reductions or as a limited antimissile defense to reduce the chance of a Soviet first strike, the president imagined a shield that would prevent any missiles from striking the United States. His conception may have been undiluted science fiction, but SDI came to be the critical element in arms negotiation for the remainder of his administration. Soviet scientists, like most American scientists, thought the idea preposterous, but Soviet leaders could not take the risk of ignoring it. SDI had to be stopped, or the Soviets would have to compete in its development, a task for which they were ill-equipped.

The worst political disaster of the year, the incident that probably had the most adverse effect on any movement toward Soviet-American accommodation, came late in the summer. On August 31, the U.S. government learned that a Soviet plane had shot down a Korean jetliner, KAL 007, en route from Alaska to Seoul. The crew and all passengers, including several Americans, were killed. The Soviets initially denied shooting the plane down, then charged that it was a spy plane. American intelligence intercepts determined that the plane had indeed strayed into Soviet air space, and that the Soviets had indeed mistaken it for a spy plane. Reagan, angered by the outrage, attacked the Soviets sharply, alleging falsely that they had knowingly fired on a civilian plane. In the context of Soviet-American tensions, and given the fact that the United States did fly spy planes in the area, the tragic Soviet action was understandable, perhaps even inevitable. Andropov's unwillingness to accept Soviet responsibility, to express regret for the tragedy, is less easily explained. Similarly, Reagan's deliberate abuse of the evidence to belabor the Soviets – who for years afterward persisted in believing that KAL 007 was being used by American intelligence – was needlessly inflammatory.

The principal American defeat of the year came in Lebanon, but the Soviets failed to gain from American blunders there. In June 1982, the Israelis had invaded Lebanon, with the acquiescence of Secretary Haig, who saw Israel as an American surrogate against the Soviets and their friends. They were determined to eliminate sanctuaries of the Palestine Liberation Organization (PLO) and to turn southern Lebanon into a buffer zone to shield Israel against Arab attacks. Syria, supplied with Soviet arms, failed to contain the Israeli advance.[8]

Reagan, like much of the world, was appalled by Israeli aggression, and unmoved by Israel's insistence that it was acting defensively, clearing out terrorists. When the Israelis failed to prevent their Lebanese Christian allies from massacring Palestinians trapped in refugee camps, Reagan sent in the Marines to attempt to maintain order in Beirut. Slowly the Americans were drawn into the civil strife as various Lebanese factions, Muslim and Christian, backed variously by Syria, Israel, and Iran, struggled to control the country. One morning in October 1983, a terrorist with a truckload of explosives evaded American security, attacked the Marine barracks, and killed 241 Americans. The president then withdrew the remaining Marines to ships offshore.

American forces had been put in an untenable position in the

8 Garthoff, *Détente and Confrontation,* 1062.

midst of a war and lives had been lost. Intervention had accomplished nothing. The Soviets, apprehensive about American and Israeli intentions, had avoided direct involvement, but resupplied the Syrians, who became the dominant force in Lebanese politics. The Israelis, trapped in a quagmire, spent many months and many lives, Israeli as well as Arab, before extricating themselves. Lebanon ceased to exist as a viable country and the world's attention shifted elsewhere.

Two days after the American Marines were withdrawn from Beirut, American forces attacked the Caribbean nation of Grenada, ostensibly to rescue American medical students trapped between rival Marxist factions vying for control of the island. Vastly superior American forces overwhelmed local resistance, including that of several hundred Cubans and a handful of North Korean advisers. Pro-Western forces seized power. The Soviets, skeptical of Cuban testimonials on behalf of the self-styled Marxists of Grenada from the outset, did not attempt to counter the display of American force. But again, Reagan's signal to Andropov could not have been clearer: The eagle was screaming. American pressures on the periphery of the Soviet empire would increase.

SDI, the aftermath of the KAL 007 incident, the American use of force in Lebanon and against Grenada, the deployment of new missiles in Europe, all suggested to the Soviet leaders that a sharply increased level of confrontation was ahead for them and would continue as long as Reagan remained in the White House. The correlation of forces was shifting against them and they prepared their people for a crisis. In fact, as Soviet apprehensions began to crystallize, George Shultz, who had replaced Haig as secretary of state in mid-1982, had already begun the process of moving the president toward a less apocalyptic vision of how to cope with his adversaries. More fortunate than Brezhnev, Andropov did catch a glimpse of a more hopeful relationship before he died in February 1984.

Shultz discovered that Reagan was interested in traveling to China and the Soviet Union. He indicated to the president that an improvement in relations would have to antedate a visit to either nation. Reagan remarked that he was not unwilling to reduce tensions. Shultz arranged for the president to have a surprise talk with the Soviet ambassador, Anatoly Dobrynin, in February 1983. Reagan demonstrated interest in a more constructive relationship. The Soviets responded by allowing a group of Pentecostal Christians who had taken refuge in the American Embassy in Moscow – and for whom Reagan had expressed concern – to leave the country in April. But distrust of Reagan was overwhelming in the Soviet leadership and the remainder of the year provided little hope that he was changing. Still, Shultz pushed internally for conciliatory moves, arguing that the United States had recovered economically, was rebuilding militarily, and was in a strong position to negotiate. Shultz's hand was strengthened by polling data revealing that foreign policy was Reagan's one weak point with the electorate. In January 1984, Reagan made a relatively amiable speech about future Soviet-American relations and Shultz persuaded Soviet Foreign Minister Andrei Gromyko that the president was in earnest. Andropov responded with a secret letter manifesting interest in developing communications between the two leaders.[9]

The death of Andropov and his replacement by the ailing Konstantin Chernenko precluded any dramatic moves by Moscow. Reagan continued to offer friendly gestures, and efforts to resume arms control talks began, but no significant change in Soviet-American relations was likely until the Soviets had a leader as strong as the American president. Shultz and Reagan turned their attention to the other corner of the strategic triangle, China.

The tensions that had developed in relations with China were partly a result of the inability of Reagan, prior to taking office, to understand that China had become a strategic asset to the United States. Chiang Kai-shek and "Free China" (i.e., the Republic of China on Taiwan) were important symbols to the American Right and candidate Reagan had surrounded himself with men and women who saw Nixon's rapprochement with the People's Republic of China as a gross betrayal. Reagan talked of restoring recognition of the Taiwan regime, withdrawn when the Carter administration recognized Beijing in 1979. He frequently offered gratuitous remarks and

---

9 Don Oberdorfer, *The Turn: From Cold War to the New Era: The United States and the Soviet Union, 1983–1990* (New York, 1991), 15–77.

gestures offensive to the government of Deng Xioaping. Reagan's behavior aggravated disagreements over the continued sale by the United States of weapons to the Taiwan regime. The advantages Nixon, Ford, and Carter had gained by drawing China closer to the United States in opposition to the Soviet Union were in danger of evaporating. [10]

Vice-President George Bush and Secretary of State Haig had both traveled to China to reassure Chinese leaders of American interest in a cooperative relationship. The Chinese continued to separate themselves from the United States and to be unsupportive in public forums like the United Nations. In August 1982, an agreement on arms sales to Taiwan merely papered over unresolved differences. Shultz never shared the Kissinger-Brzezinski estimate of China's strategic importance, but he recognized the value of good relations, especially if tension could be reduced easily by muzzling the president. Gradually he brought Reagan to an understanding of the extent and value of Chinese-American collaboration, especially in gathering intelligence information about the Soviet Union. The president learned to swallow most of his notorious one-liners. In April 1984, Reagan visited China, his first foray into a Communist country. The Chinese greeted him with the extraordinary hospitality for which they are justly renowned, and they never had any trouble with him again. He enjoyed the trip and his reception enormously and came away with a more sanguine view of life in China than was probably justified. Trade and cultural relations prospered. The political relationship never regained the closeness of the late 1970s, but with the resurgence of American power it was not likely to be as important again.

In November 1984, the American people once again chose Ronald Reagan to lead them. At the peak of his popularity and power, he turned to the Soviet Union to look for possible accommodation as the centerpiece of his second administration. Arms control negotiations began in Geneva in January 1985. In March, however, Chernenko died. Enter Mikhail Gorbachev, destined to

---

10 Harry Harding, *A Fragile Relationship* (Washington, D.C., 1992), 107–19; Warren I. Cohen, *America's Response to China* (New York, 1990), 204–6.

become one of the most important political figures of the twentieth century.

Soviet leaders had realized since Brezhnev's dying days that their economy was in trouble, that their society was on the verge of crisis, that their system was not working. The research institutes of the Academy of Sciences had produced an avalanche of papers pointing to the need for reform and offering blueprints for change. Andropov had begun the process of reform, but his failing health precluded significant progress. Chernenko was less active. By March 1985, the Politburo was ready to select a young, vigorous man to lead the country. The goal was the modernization of the Soviet economy.

Gorbachev understood that to revitalize the Soviet economy, radical changes were probably necessary, but the fragility of his support in the Politburo, the resistance of the military and the civil bureaucracy, and the skepticism of ordinary Soviet workers required him to move slowly. The support of Soviet intellectuals was enormously helpful, but the Soviet Union of 1985 was not a state in which the power of the pen seemed likely to prevail.

Gorbachev (and his wife) had traveled in the West as tourists and he had no illusions about the superiority of the Soviet model of development. He knew that apart from its great military power, conditions in the Soviet Union were more like those of a Third World country than like one of the developed societies of the West: It was "Upper Volta with missiles." He understood that to modernize, the Soviet Union could not just buy technology; it would have to accept some Western ideas and values as well. He would have to dismantle the Stalinist obstacles to Western civil society, to complete the task Khrushchev had begun. The job would have to be done with extraordinary care to avoid either a conservative backlash or a rush to democracy that would undermine the Communist party, which was, after all, the source of his power.

Modernizing and strengthening the Soviet Union would also be costly. Virtually the entire infrastructure was rotten or outdated and would have to be replaced. His colleagues, especially in the military, were greatly agitated by Reagan's SDI program, and frightened by "high-tech" defensive equipment already a part of NATO's force structure. Where would they find the assets, material or intellectual, with which to compete? Gorbachev could ill afford to increase military expenditures.

Then there were Soviet commitments to the Third World, a tremendous drain on existing Soviet resources. One American analyst estimated the Soviets were spending $40 billion annually on their friends abroad.[11] Gorbachev and his advisers saw little economic, strategic, or ideological advantage deriving from the overseas commitments of the 1960s and 1970s. They were not only an extravagance, but they were also a major irritant in Soviet-American relations. Although some Soviet leaders still clung to the vision of their nation as the protector of socialist revolution against capitalist imperialism, Gorbachev was skeptical. He saw little potential for revolutionary change in the Third World. The experts to whom he turned for advice noted that in the 1980s most of the national liberation movements in the Third World were anti-Communist and anti-Soviet.[12]

Not least of his problems was the war in Afghanistan. It was expensive in both blood and rubles. It was increasingly unpopular at home. The Soviets had learned little from the American experience in Vietnam, but Afghanistan was teaching them firsthand how difficult it was to win or to extricate themselves from a civil war in an undeveloped country. Moreover, the invasion had brought upon them nearly universal condemnation, intensifying Soviet isolation. He had to find a way out.

In brief, Gorbachev needed a respite from the Cold War to be able to devote his energies and his nation's resources toward building a more modern, efficient Soviet state. He thought he could win one from the United States, from Ronald Reagan, archenemy of communism and the Soviet Union. First of all, Gorbachev was persuaded that the Soviet Union was secure from external threat. That much Brezhnev had willed to his successors. More nuclear weapons were

11 William Hyland, *Mortal Rivals* (New York, 1987), 227–60.
12 Elizabeth K. Valkenier, "Revolutionary Change in the Third World: Recent Soviet Assessments," *World Politics* 38 (1986): 415–34; Seweryn Bialer, "The Soviet Union and the West: Security and Foreign Policy," in Seweryn Bialer and Michael Mandelbaum, *Gorbachev's Russia and American Foreign Policy* (Boulder, Colo., 1988), 457–91.

unnecessary. More was not better: Soviet accumulation of missiles aroused apprehension in the United States, left American leaders feeling insecure, and triggered a new cycle in the arms race. He was the first Soviet leader to understand the security dilemma, to understand that there could be no security for the Soviet Union without security for the United States. Second, he was aware that Reagan's first-term military expenditures had resulted in an intolerable deficit in the United States budget, and that Reagan was unlikely to be able to maintain the pace of the arms race. The Americans would probably be receptive to Soviet overtures for an arms control agreement, for a mutual reduction of military spending. Finally, he recognized that the Soviet obsession with secrecy, initially born of the need to hide weakness, created anxieties abroad, because it allowed for exaggerations of Soviet military capabilities and misperception of Soviet intentions. He was ready to open up the society a little, even to consider the on-site inspections the Americans always demanded. [13]

Reagan and the rest of the world were not quite ready for the extraordinary course Gorbachev was about to undertake. Nor, as the Soviet leader's plans unfolded, were Americans sure that it was in the interest of the United States to help him to build a modern, efficient Soviet economy, a stronger Soviet Union. The skeptics waited. In the interim, Reagan persisted in his efforts to roll back Soviet influence. Implementation of the "Reagan Doctrine," American assistance to forces attempting to overthrow Communist or pro-Soviet regimes in the Third World, intensified. The CIA had gone to war against the Sandinista regime in Nicaragua in 1982, beginning with the training and equipping of "contras" or, as the president preferred to describe them, "freedom fighters." Nicaragua was the central front in the campaign, but American aid in various forms went to opponents of the Soviet-backed governments of Afghanistan, Angola, Cambodia, and untold other distant lands. When Congress tried to restrain the executive branch, the president's men raised money in the private sector and lobbied for finan-

13 Bialer, "Soviet Union and the West"; Valkenier, "Revolutionary Change in the Third World"; Celeste A. Wallander, "Third World Conflict in Soviet Military Thought: Does the 'New Thinking' Soviet Grow Prematurely Grey?" *World Politics* 42 (1989): 30–63.

cial support from wealthy friends abroad, like the Saudis or the sultan of Brunei. Even the Israelis and ultimately the Iranians became involved as zealots in the National Security Council decided to sell arms secretly and illegally, with Israeli collusion, to the Iranians. They used the proceeds to support the contras, thus subverting the intent of Congress and the Constitution of the United States. Reagan seemed only vaguely aware of what was being done in his name, but was to be weakened gravely when the Iran-Contra scandal became public knowledge in 1986.

The Soviets continued the struggle in Afghanistan, supported the Vietnamese in Cambodia and the Angolan government against its enemies, but backed off from sending MIGs to Nicaragua and suggested Cuban restraint as well. Gorbachev had higher priorities. He wanted an arms control agreement with the United States and he wanted a meeting with Reagan to accelerate the process, to try to persuade the American president to give up the expensive fantasy of strategic defense. In November 1985, Reagan and Gorbachev traveled to Geneva for the first meeting between Reagan and a Soviet leader.

Reagan despised and mistrusted Communists and hated the "evil empire" in the abstract. But he responded differently to contact with people, with individual Soviet citizens, like Dobrynin and Gromyko. In Gorbachev he found a man as personable and confident, as determined to protect his nation's interests, and as eager to avoid nuclear holocaust as he was himself. At Geneva, and in the meetings that followed, the two men found common ground. From time to time each grew angry or impatient with the stubbornness of the other, but the antagonism between them and their countries gradually diminished. Summitry, so often derided by professional diplomatists and scholars as sheer puffery, proved to be remarkably useful in the late 1980s. Reagan could not have come to trust Gorbachev had he not met him, argued with him, shared his hopes and fears.[14]

Little besides the establishment of a personal relationship resulted from the first meeting between Gorbachev and Reagan. The Americans were not ready to take the dramatic Soviet proposals seriously

14 See especially Oberdorfer, *The Turn*, 139–54.

and Reagan left no doubt of his commitment to SDI. In the months that followed, however, Gorbachev electrified the world with the changes he began to institute in the Soviet Union and the ideas he was offering for ending the arms race. Most striking were his professed willingness to drop the rigid stance of his predecessors on intermediate-range missiles and to sign an INF agreement largely on American terms; his apparent willingness to accept limits on previously nonnegotiable intercontinental ballistic missiles, so beloved of the Soviet military and worrisome to their American counterparts; and his indications that he was also ready to adjust the balance of conventional forces in Europe, to redeploy Soviet forces from their traditional offensive posture, so threatening to the West, to a defensive one. He explained to the Soviet people that the struggle against capitalism was no longer decisive in world affairs, and that a way had to be found to permit both the United States and the Soviet Union to feel secure, that the goal of the superpowers had to be common security. Gorbachev was prepared to take risks that appalled his military. He was determined to end the Western perception of a Soviet threat, to obtain an arms control agreement with Reagan, and to avoid a struggle for advantage in strategic defense.[15]

The American response had to be profoundly disappointing to the Soviet leader. In April, American planes attacked Libya with the intention of killing Qaddafi, the Libyan leader with whom the Soviets had ties, presumably in retaliation for Libyan complicity in a terrorist act in Europe. At approximately the same time, Reagan ordered the CIA to provide the Afghan resistance with Stinger shoulder-fired antiaircraft missiles with which the Afghanis promptly began downing Soviet helicopters. The United States was increasing the pressure on Soviet friends in the Third World. And in May, Reagan announced that the United States would no longer be bound by the terms of the unratified SALT II agreement. As the Soviet leader waved the olive branch, seeking to shift to the defensive, the United States became more threatening.

At virtually the same time, late April 1986, the Soviet Union was

---

15 Robert Legvold, "War, Weapons, and Soviet Foreign Policy," in Bialer and Mandelbaum, *Gorbachev's Russia and American Foreign Policy*, 118–19.

devastated and Gorbachev distracted by a nuclear catastrophe, an explosion at the Chernobyl nuclear power plant. Soviet leaders handled the crisis badly and most Soviet citizens learned of the explosion and of the danger to them from foreign broadcasts. It took Gorbachev nearly three weeks to issue a statement – in which he petulantly rejected Western estimates of the magnitude of the disaster. The episode did little to encourage Western faith in the Soviet leader's promise to open his society, his talk of *glasnost*.

In August, another Cold War incident, a reminder that Stalinism was not dead in the Soviet Union, disrupted the Soviet leader's efforts to establish his credibility in the West. Gennadi Zakharov, a Soviet UN official, was arrested in New York in the act of purchasing classified documents. It was hardly a major incident. Indeed, there had been several more shocking revelations of American CIA, FBI, and military personnel betraying their country to the Soviets in 1986. But a week after Zakharov's arrest, Soviet authorities retaliated by framing Nicholas Daniloff, the highly respected Moscow correspondent of *U.S. News and World Report*. Americans were outraged, and movement toward a summit was temporarily derailed when Gorbachev brushed aside a letter from Reagan giving the president's personal assurance Daniloff was not a spy. Shultz and Eduard Shevardnadze, the Soviet foreign minister, struggled mightily before coming up with a formula that resulted in charges being dropped against Daniloff and Zakharov being deported after pleading no contest to the charges against him.

By October, the two superpower leaders were in need of some dramatic breakthrough to enhance their domestic political fortunes. Gorbachev had little to show, at home or abroad, for his efforts. Reagan was beginning to lose his magic. The American people still loved him, but Congress cut his defense budget sharply and then overrode his veto of sanctions against the racist regime in South Africa. If the Democrats gained enough seats to take control of the Senate in the November election, his remaining two years in office would likely prove frustrating. His efforts to achieve an "October surprise," a triumph that would galvanize the electorate, by selling arms to Iran in exchange for the release of American hostages held by pro-Iranian terrorists in Lebanon, was floundering. Both Gorbachev and Reagan stood to benefit politically from a major agreement at their meeting at Reykjavik, Iceland.

Gorbachev had asked for the meeting, hoping that in direct talks with Reagan he could reach agreement on limiting SDI. He was prepared to offer major concessions. He whetted Reagan's interest by suggesting 50 percent reductions in strategic missiles over a five-year period, the removal of American and Soviet intermediate-range missiles from Europe, and the elimination of all ballistic missiles in ten years. He dropped a number of previous Soviet conditions for an agreement, even accepted SDI laboratory research. Reagan indicated his willingness to accept Gorbachev's proposals – until he understood that SDI testing would be limited to the laboratory.

Reykjavik collapsed over SDI, but it was apparent that SDI had motivated the Soviets to take the initiative in arms control. For the first time, it was evident that they were ready to move forward. Reagan's obstinance on SDI and his inability to comprehend some of the issues involved – as when he agreed to surrender the missiles on which European security arguably depended – muddied the waters temporarily, but the American negotiators sensed that historic agreements were virtually within reach. [16]

The next few months were difficult for Reagan. The Republicans did lose control of the Senate in the midyear elections, and the Iran-Contra scandal broke, revealing the president's willingness to enter into deals with terrorists, the disregard of his men for the law, and the extent of his detachment from the operations of his government. Reagan never lost the affection of his people, but they came to hold a more realistic estimate of his limited competence. His presidency had lost its moorings in the early days of 1987. The president was adrift.

Gorbachev, on the other hand, had to drive harder and faster to stay in control of the apparatus of power in the Soviet Union. He had failed to achieve anything by insisting on halting Reagan's SDI program as a price for Soviet concessions. In February he proposed the elimination of intermediate-range missiles *without* mentioning SDI. Those of Reagan's advisers least amenable to an arms control

16 Mandelbaum and Talbott, *Reagan and Gorbachev,* 163.

agreement had the president respond to Gorbachev's offer favorably, contingent on the Soviets accepting highly intrusive verification procedures, which the Soviets had always rejected. They were astonished and appalled when the Soviets proved amenable. It took several months of haggling, with Gorbachev fighting off opposition in Moscow, maneuvering constantly to strengthen his forces in the Politburo and the military, but in November Shultz and Shevardnadze reached agreement on verification procedures and in December, Gorbachev went to Washington where he and Reagan signed a momentous agreement (INF) to destroy more than 2,500 intermediate-range missiles. The arrangements for verification were so thorough that American officials became apprehensive about Soviet inspectors learning too much about what was going on in the United States. [17]

Signs that the Soviet Union was on a radically new course multiplied. At home, human rights abuses declined and political dissidents and would-be Jewish emigrants were released from exile or prison. The Russian Orthodox Church, with the support of the government, marked the thousandth anniversary of the introduction of Christianity into Russia. Churches were refurbished and reopened all over the country. Criticism of the Soviet system became more acceptable. Gorbachev chose the seventieth anniversary of the Bolshevik Revolution to denounce the Stalinist heritage and to praise some of Stalin's victims. Denunciation of the 1939 Nazi-Soviet pact surfaced in the Baltic republics. Gorbachev won approval for reforms that pointed toward a less centralized economy. And in foreign policy, the Soviets reached out to the Israelis and indicated their intention to withdraw their forces from Afghanistan.

In March 1988, Soviet troops began to pull out of Afghanistan. In May, they began coming back from Mongolia and, incredibly, there was even talk of the Red Army withdrawing from Eastern Europe. Also in May, Ronald Reagan traveled to Moscow to exchange ratifications of the INF treaty. Polls showed that only 30 percent of the American people still perceived the Soviet Union as an enemy, and Reagan readily acknowledged that it was no longer an

17 Oberdorfer, *The Turn*, 233–4.

"evil empire." In December, after the heir apparent, George Bush, was elected to succeed Reagan, Gorbachev flew to New York and before the United Nations announced that he would reduce Soviet forces by 500,000 — *unilaterally* — and that he would eliminate units then stationed in Germany, Czechoslovakia, and Hungary. The structure of the remaining elements of the Red Army in Eastern Europe would be altered to put them on the defensive, eliminating the threat to the West. As further evidence of his good intentions, Gorbachev added Soviet pressure to that of the United States to persuade the Cubans to withdraw their forces from Angola. As he explained to President-elect Bush, the crisis within the Soviet Union left him no choice. The Soviets could no longer afford an empire. [18]

The collapse of the Soviet empire came faster than anyone had imagined possible. The United States had little to do with conditions in Eastern Europe and within the Soviet Union as the dominoes toppled on the Kremlin. One after another, events the world's leading analysts considered inconceivable occurred. Freedom came to much of Eastern Europe, to much of the Soviet Union, the two Germanys were reunited — and one day, the Soviet Union disappeared. The Cold War was surely over and the United States, greatly weakened, staggering, but still on its feet, claimed victory.

Gorbachev's domestic policies heartened reformers throughout the Communist world. In 1968, Brezhnev had crushed the Prague Spring and intimidated all movements toward "communism with a human face." Now it was the turn of the old-line Stalinists to tremble as the Kremlin encouraged emulation of Gorbachev's *glasnost* and *perestroika*. In March 1989, the Soviet Union conducted the freest elections in its history, and many Communist party regulars were defeated in the competition for seats in the Congress of People's Deputies. In April, Andrei Sakharov, the great Soviet physicist and Nobel Prize–winning symbol of the fight for human rights in the Soviet Union, freed by Gorbachev from exile, was chosen by

18 Oberdorfer, *The Turn*, 294–318.

the Academy of Sciences to sit in the Soviet Chamber of Deputies. It was not democracy, nor was democracy Gorbachev's goal, but the Soviet Union was changing, and the signals were clear. And to underscore the message, Soviet troops and tanks began to pull back from Poland, Hungary, and East Germany.

In May, Gorbachev traveled to Beijing to deepen the rapprochement he had effected with China. But he was upstaged by thousands of Chinese demonstrators who, chanting his name, demanded political reform from their own leaders. They had assembled in the vast Tiananmen Square before he arrived and they continued their vigil after his departure, ignoring government demands that they disperse. The world, watching the demonstrations on satellite television, dared to imagine that the Chinese leaders might yield, that China too might be verging on a democratic revolution. But on June 4, the aging Chinese leaders responded with force, sending the People's Liberation Army to crush the people. Hundreds, perhaps thousands, died; and many more were imprisoned. China, the Communist nation whose successful economic reforms had won widespread admiration in the 1980s, would not join the march to freedom in 1990. Instead, the "Chinese solution" came to signify the choice of repression in response to the cries of the people.

The Communist governments of Eastern Europe were also forced to choose. In July, the communiqué issued after a meeting of Warsaw Pact nations declared that "there are no universal models of socialism." Gorbachev indicated that the Soviet Union would not interfere in Poland, where a resurgent Solidarity movement was on the verge of overwhelming the Communist regime, or in Hungary, where reform Communists were moving the economy away from socialism and opening the political system to opposition parties. In August, when the Communists of Poland reached out frantically to Gorbachev for help in salvaging their power, he advised them to let go.

As astonishing as the events in Poland were, East Germany provided yet greater drama. In September, Hungarian authorities made the critical decision to allow East German refugees to cross their borders to flee to the West, in violation of an agreement with the East German regime. A German appeal to Moscow was brushed aside. No new wall was built to contain freedom-seeking Germans. Gorbachev's spokesman reported that the Hungarian decision was not a Soviet concern. The Soviets would not interfere. The Hungarian Communists quickly transformed themselves into democratic socialists and opened the floodgates for East Germans to pass through. Massive demonstrations swept East Germany. Hundreds of thousands of Germans took to the streets demanding democracy, freedom, and unification with West Germany. Erich Honecker, the German Communist leader, chose to emulate Deng Xiaoping. He would replicate Tiananmen in Leipzig if necessary. But his subordinates rejected the order to turn their guns on their own people. The regime was forced to open the gates of the Berlin Wall in November, and that hated symbol of the Cold War, of the division of Germany and of Europe, was destroyed. The Soviet Union did not interfere.

Soon the Czech people were back in the streets. The Communist regime evaporated. Alexander Dubcek, leader of the 1968 liberalization, returned and was elected chairman of the national parliament. The dissident playwright Vaclav Havel, released from prison only months earlier, was elected president. In Bulgaria and Romania, the people also rose against their Communist rulers. In Romania, the Communist dictator, Nicolae Ceausescu, attempted the Chinese solution. Although the people did not prevail over the party apparatus, Ceausescu and his wife were executed as an earnest of the new regime's allegedly reformist intentions.

The Soviet sphere of influence in Eastern Europe, conceded by Roosevelt at Yalta, long perceived as Moscow's most vital interest, had vanished. In Poland, Hungary, Germany, and Czechoslovakia, the people had freed themselves, but it was Gorbachev who had opened the door to freedom by signaling his willingness to see the old-guard party leadership replaced. To be sure, he had not anticipated the utter rejection of the Communists, most likely assuming that reformist Communists like himself would prevail. But he made no effort to resist radical change until it began to threaten the very survival of the Soviet Union.

Across the vast Soviet empire, ethnic tensions were common. Racial, linguistic, and religious differences had been submerged in a harsh minorities policy through which little more than lip service was paid to the multiplicity of existing cultures. Conflicts arose from time to time and were suppressed more or less ruthlessly by the Soviet leaders. As Gorbachev attempted to open Soviet society, to give a degree of legitimacy to pluralism, long smoldering separatist movements as well as interethnic violence erupted. The Baltic republics – Estonia, Latvia, and Lithuania – comprised a special problem. They had enjoyed independence between World Wars I and II, but were occupied and then annexed by Stalin as part of the agreement with Hitler in 1939, the notorious Nazi-Soviet nonaggression pact. By 1989, discussion of the pact was no longer forbidden and the Soviet government admitted its culpability – or rather Stalin's. The obvious next step was for the Baltic peoples to denounce the pact and demand their independence. Here Gorbachev drew the line: If the Baltic republics were allowed to claim their independence, how could Ukraine, Georgia, or any of the other republics with strong separatist movements be denied? Gorbachev might well have paraphrased Winston Churchill: He had not become president of the Soviet Union to preside over its demise.

As Gorbachev attempted to threaten and cajole the Baltic republics into remaining part of the Soviet Union, complications with the United States arose. There were substantial and vocal Lithuanian, Latvian, and Estonian populations in the United States. There were still Americans who mistrusted the Soviets. The use of force against the Baltic republics would undermine much of the goodwill Gorbachev had generated and bring considerable anti-Soviet pressure to bear on George Bush, who had proved much more tentative in his acceptance of the new Soviet image than had Reagan. Gorbachev's attempt to hold on to the Baltics without alienating the United States was probably doomed from the outset by the intransigence of the Lithuanian independence movement and the anti-Lithuanian belligerence of Russian elements in the Soviet military.

For a year, amid this incredible turmoil, amid the dissolution of the Soviet empire and the unraveling of the Soviet Union itself, Gorbachev tried with minimal success to reach out to the new American president. He indicated his willingness to effect disproportionately large cuts in Soviet conventional forces to highlight the absence of any hostile intent. Shevardnadze went fishing in Wyoming with Bush's secretary of state, James Baker, and bared his heart, admitting Soviet wrongs and errors, promising to do the right thing. Gorbachev expressed the desire to integrate the Soviet Union in the world economy, to join GATT and the IMF, to accept the offer Stalin had rejected in 1945. Bush temporized. Finally, in December, the two men met at their first summit, in Malta.

Bush seized the initiative and assured Gorbachev of American support. The essential gesture from Bush was his indication that he was ready to begin negotiations on a Soviet-American trade agreement without restrictions on most-favored-nation treatment. The United States would support various Soviet efforts to participate in the international economic order. The economic warfare that had begun in the 1940s would end in 1990. And the United States was also ready to respond to Gorbachev's desire for rapid progress in arms control and force reductions. In turn, Gorbachev stressed his desire for partnership with the United States: The Soviets now *wanted* an American presence in Europe, most likely to contain the Germans. It was not quite a resurrection of the grand alliance of World War II, but the United States and the Soviet Union had ceased to be enemies. [19]

Tensions over Germany and the Baltic republics continued into 1990. Neither the United States nor the Soviet Union was eager to confront a unified Germany, but they lacked the power to resist the *Anschluss*. The economic and political power of West Germany dictated the timing and the terms of unification. German leaders allowed the Big Four – Britain, France, the Soviet Union, and the United States – to participate in discussions of the external modalities and gave appropriate assurances of satisfaction with Germany's existing borders. The Germans also indicated their willingness to provide the Soviets with desperately needed economic assistance. Reluctantly, Gorbachev accepted first reunification and then participation of a united Germany in NATO. The question of independence for Estonia, Latvia, and Lithuania continued to be troublesome, but Bush, understanding Gorbachev's dilemma, the mounting pressures on him from the military and ultranationalists, restrained his criticism. Gorbachev, appreciating the demands on Bush, did what little he could to minimize the irritation.

19 Oberdorfer, *The Turn,* 374–83.

The decisive test, which the new Soviet-American relationship passed successfully, came in the confrontation with Iraq that began in August 1990 with Iraq's invasion and occupation of Kuwait. Haltingly, but conclusively, the Soviet Union abandoned its long-time Arab ally and aligned itself with the United States. The Soviet-armed and -trained Iraqi army was left to confront and be decimated by the full fury of the United States and its European and Arab allies. Even George Bush, who prided himself on his lack of the "vision thing," was inspired to promise a New World Order.

For Gorbachev, the end of the Cold War brought a well-deserved Nobel Peace Prize, but the great statesman won little honor at home. Neither his diplomatic exploits nor his *perestroika* put food on the plates of his people, or did anything to alleviate the miserable economic conditions of the Soviet people. Buffeted from the right and the left, he sailed first one way, then the other, in a desperate and ultimately unsuccessful effort to ride out the storm. In August 1991, he was deposed in a coup led by conservatives and held prisoner in the Crimea. A few days later, the coup leaders found the military unwilling to crush a few thousand demonstrators who had rallied around Boris Yeltsin, a onetime Gorbachev supporter who had come to personify the demand for more radical change. Gorbachev returned to Moscow, but events had passed him by. Communism, however reformist, was finished in the Soviet Union. Indeed, the Soviet Union was finished. The Baltic states immediately declared and achieved their independence, without resistance from Moscow. One after another, the constituent republics declared their independence, the Communist party was outlawed, and Gorbachev had no empire, no country, and then no government to rule. Before the year was out, Boris Yeltsin, popularly elected president of the Russian Republic, moved into the Kremlin and Gorbachev was forced into early retirement. On December 31, 1991, the Soviet Union officially ceased to exist, succeeded by a loosely organized Commonwealth of Independent States.

The United States of America was the only superpower to survive the Cold War. It had triumphed economically, ideologically, and politically. It had been spared the ultimate military test of a direct confrontation, probably nuclear, with its principal adversary. Curiously, few Americans stopped to celebrate. They found, in fact, that the quality of their lives was declining rather than improving. Their economy, the envy of the Soviet Union, Eastern Europe, and the Third World, was a mess. They were confronted with an industrial infrastructure and transportation system in decay, a corrupt banking system that had cost thousands of people their life's savings, massive unemployment, and widespread homelessness. The Reagan administration, in its effort to expand American military power without asking the American people to pay for it, had run up an incredible deficit, leaving the government without the means to respond to the economic crisis at home or the needs of its less fortunate constituents. Once the nation upon which the world depended for investment capital, the world's leading lender, it had become in 1985 the world's leading debtor, dependent on Japan, and Germany, and Arab oil-producing states. It had to solicit donations from foreign governments to finance the war against Iraq in 1991. It could no longer provide sufficient aid to needy countries abroad or necessary services for its own people. Voter apathy eroded the value of its electoral system. Racism simmered just below, barely below, the surface and boiled up explosively with painful frequency. And as a portent for the future, international tests showed American children far behind most Western European and Japanese children in their mastery of math and science skills.

Some analysts, most notably Paul Kennedy and David Calleo, had suggested that the United States was in decline, that it suffered from imperial overreach, or at the very least a lack, among its leaders, of the political will or courage to ask the people to make the sacrifices necessary to rebuild the nation for their children and their children's children.[20] But the United States had won the Cold War: It was still number one.

20 Paul Kennedy, *The Rise and Fall of the Great Powers* (New York, 1987); David P. Calleo, *The Imperious Economy* (Cambridge, Mass., 1982).

Conclusion: America and the World, 1945–1991

The era herein reviewed began in the closing months of World War II and ended with the disappearance of the Soviet Union. The central thread in the tapestry of the international politics of the time was the Soviet-American confrontation. In 1945, the Soviet Union and the United States, allied in the war against the Axis powers, crushed their enemies and emerged from the war triumphant, each with only the other remaining as a credible adversary. The next forty-five years constituted what John Lewis Gaddis has called the "Long Peace," as the two great empires competed without direct conflict between them.[1] And then the Soviet empire collapsed and was gone.

The period was also striking because of the disintegration of all of the pre–World War II colonial empires, and the appearance of scores of newly independent states in Africa, Asia, and Latin America. As each of these new nations struggled to define itself, to search for some modicum of wealth and power, it contributed another ripple to the tides of world affairs, sometimes barely perceptible, often so evident as to force one or both of the great powers to change course. There was too much turmoil in the world for any country, even one as powerful as the United States, to exercise hegemony. And along the way the locus of power shifted, as Chinese military strength developed, and as Japan, South Korea, and the ASEAN states demonstrated their economic vitality. The reemergence of Japan and Germany as major forces in the world and the solidifying of the European Community were also important currents precluding superpower complacency.

Ideologically, anticommunism was the engine that drove American action, just as hostility to what they perceived as capitalist

1 John Lewis Gaddis, *The Long Peace* (Oxford, 1987).

imperialism energized Soviet leaders, few of whom still dreamt of a socialist utopia. As Soviet power grew in the 1950s, 1960s, and 1970s, so did American fears of communism. With the opening of Soviet society in the late 1980s, even ideologues like Reagan were prepared to cooperate with the former "evil empire." With the collapse of the Soviet state in 1991, American leaders lost their compass, and sailed bewildered, in search of a new heading. What remained of the Soviet hierarchy, in Russia and other former Soviet republics, had a surer sense of what it sought: the course to capitalist development. An era that began with Stalin's rejection of Bretton Woods, of the invitation to participate in GATT, the IMF, the World Bank, ended with his heirs begging for membership, at a time when aspirants to lead the United States were talking of abandoning the liberal international economic order.

And, perhaps most incredibly, a time that began with the United States as the greatest economic power the world had ever seen, extending its largesse to former enemies as well as allies, using its enormous wealth to buy friends in the struggle against the Soviet Union, ended with the United States as the world's largest debtor nation. Embattled American diplomatists, assigned to protect uncompetitive industries, devoted their energies to persuading Japan to limit its exports to the United States, and to demanding that the Japanese open their doors to imports. And the president was reduced to begging other nations to finance his foreign policy goals.

How does one explain the menacing posture the United States and the Soviet Union adopted toward each other in the late 1940s and sustained until the late 1980s? The answer has three parts, found by pursuing three intersecting lines of inquiry. First, there was the determination of American leaders to accept what they saw as the responsibilities of power, to lead the world, to create a new world order. Second, was the qualities of the two states, the excesses of civil society in one (the powerful-state, weak-government pattern in the United States) and the absence of it in the other (the all-powerful Stalinist government). Third was the "security dilemma."

Without the American determination to provide world leadership, it is difficult to conceive of a Cold War. Had the United States chosen to pursue a version of the "continentalism" advocated by some intellectuals in the 1930s or the autarky advocated by others in the 1960s, the dynamics of the postwar world would have been very different. But a generation of American leaders had concluded that it was American shirking of responsibility after World War I that had allowed for the temporary ascendency of Adolf Hitler and the Japanese militarists, for the Great Depression, and for World War II. Conscious of Santayana's dictum about those who forget the past being doomed to repeat it, they learned the lessons of the historians and began to apply them in the mid-1940s.

Their goal was to create a world order conducive to the interests of the United States, in which the wealth and power of the United States would grow, in which the values Americans treasured would be carried around the world. Specifically, they planned for a liberal international economic order based on free trade and stable currency exchange rates that would provide prosperity for all peoples. The world they envisaged had no place for militarism; military power would be largely irrelevant. The kind of international system of which Richard Rosecrance has written, where economic prowess rather than brute force prevails, is close to what they had in mind, although it was American economic prowess, not German or Japanese that they envisaged.[2]

The Bretton Woods agreements were designed to implement that vision. The agreements were unquestionably intended to serve the long-term interests of the United States, but it also was widely believed, at home and abroad, that the United States was taking a responsible and generous position that would benefit those nations that participated in the system, that accepted American hegemony.

The Bretton Woods agreements are also useful as an illustration of the strong-state, weak-government notion. They were designed by the men who controlled the apparatus of government in 1944 not only to serve American interests abroad but also to preempt special interest groups of the sort that often prevent the leadership from pursuing its conception of the national interest. The executive

2 Richard Rosecrance, *The Rise of the Trading State* (New York, 1986).

branch of the government in 1944 was committing the United States to a particular economic regime before the opposition (primarily protectionist and functioning primarily through Congress) could act. In wartime, the executive tends to have much greater leeway to impose its will, and students of contemporary American affairs will note how often the executive attempts to simulate wartime conditions to claim powers it could not otherwise exercise.

The Soviet decision not to participate in the Bretton Woods system was not perceived at the time as a serious blow. The British were the key foreign players in the world economy. But when it came to strategic planning, which President Roosevelt controlled more closely, it was evident that the Soviet Union was important. Between the United States and the Soviet Union there had been a generation of enmity, largely ideological, but the two nations had no vital interests in conflict. They shared an interest in pacifying Germany and Japan and Roosevelt had few reservations about conceding to the Soviets a sphere of influence in Eastern Europe.

The issue of the Soviet sphere in Eastern Europe provides another illustration of how the structure of the American government placed restraints on even a strong president and, equally important, how the brutality of the Stalinist system precluded an acceptable solution. Roosevelt had no problem resolving the matter of conflict between the Polish right to self-determination and the Soviet right to security in favor of the Soviets. The Poles had done little to commend themselves in the 1930s. They had flirted with Hitler, persecuted Jews, and seized a part of Czechoslovakia after Munich. Soviet power was essential to victory over the Nazis and would be essential for maintaining world peace after the war. But because of the nature of the American political system, Roosevelt needed some help from Stalin. He needed Soviet gestures toward the cherished principles of self-determination and he needed to have Soviet influence in Eastern Europe generally and in Poland in particular to be exercised magnanimously (as the Americans would exercise theirs in Germany, Italy, and Japan, which were, after all, defeated enemies). But, just as the exigencies of the American system demanded a benign Soviet domination of Poland, the exigencies of the Stalinist system precluded it.

At the end of the war, Soviet suspicion of American intentions, combined with awareness of superior American power and the memory of Western hostility to the existence of the Soviet state, drove Stalin and his colleagues to take steps to enhance their security. These steps aroused apprehension in Washington in 1946, as the security dilemma – the notion that an increase in one state's security automatically decreases that of another – began to affect strategic thinking. Initially divided in their estimates of Soviet intentions, American leaders, troubled by Soviet behavior, reached a consensus on the need for policies to demonstrate the nation's will to protect its interests. These policies were perceived as threatening by the men in the Kremlin. Although each state conceived of its own actions as defensive, each was alarmed increasingly by the maneuvers of the other. Every wary step triggered a response that heightened the sense of menace felt in both capitals.

After the 1946 elections, Truman's foreign policy advisers emphasized the collapse of European power and the importance of the United States filling that vacuum. They saw the disinclination of Congress and the American people to concern themselves with world affairs, the desire to demobilize and consume, as the principal obstacles to assuming the responsibility of world leadership – a conflict between the perceptions of the international relations elite and popular pressures (again the strong-state, weak-government paradox). They also warned of the unexpected difficulty of Europe with postwar recovery. Marshall, Acheson, Harriman, Will Clayton, and Kennan did not fear Soviet attack on the United States or Western Europe but rather the collapse of Western European societies unable to recover from war damage, subverted by local Communists.

Their task was get a hostile, budget-cutting Congress to finance the reconstruction of the economies of America's competitors in order to oppose an imperceptible threat. They had to persuade the American people to make new sacrifices after so recently persuading them that joining the United Nations would spare them international concerns. They chose to use the idea of a Soviet threat to dominate the world. They did not see such an attack coming; they were not preparing for war. But they saw the Soviets as expansionist, opportunistic, reaching beyond their security needs. The Middle East, specifically Greece, and Western Europe were in danger of being subverted by indigenous Communist forces. Only the United States could stop them, if it had the will.

This, of course, is the context for the Truman Doctrine and the Marshall Plan. In the weak-government paradigm, the president's authority is contested constantly by Congress, especially when the two branches of government are controlled by different parties. Certainly this tension is what the framers of the American Constitution intended as a check on executive power. In practice, congress members who have been elected on the basis of issues peculiar to their home districts respond more readily to the demands of domestic special interest groups than to the imperatives of foreign policy. To focus congressional attention on foreign affairs and attain their objectives, the president and his retainers may contrive an international crisis. Often in domestic affairs, almost always in foreign affairs, a sense of crisis will result in legislative deference to the president, to an enchancement of executive power, to an imperial presidency. In 1947, the Truman administration misled Congress and the American people by exaggerating the Soviet threat, in order to enable the president to gain congressional and public support for aid first to Greece and Turkey and then to Western Europe.

There may have been no other way to get money from the Republican-controlled Eightieth Congress. Truman and his advisers obtained the funding they wanted and provided the foundation for an extraordinary level of material prosperity for all who accepted American hegemony. In the process, however, they strengthened forces at home hostile to the New Deal and to the dream of social democracy, and they gave renewed hope to the supporters of Chiang Kai-shek.

And once again the security dilemma came into play. Although the Marshall Plan may have been conceived defensively, to protect Western Europe from possible communist subversion, it was perceived by Stalin as a threat. He responded "defensively," by consolidating his control over Czechoslovakia and the rest of Eastern Europe, provoking new fears in the United States. With memories of the grand alliance fading rapidly, there seemed no way either the Soviet Union or the United States could enhance its security without undermining that of the other.

In June 1948, Soviet imposition of the Berlin blockade increased anxieties. Stalin was trying to prevent the creation of a German state capable of challenging Soviet dominance in Eastern and Central Europe, of reversing Soviet gains since 1945. This confrontation was unlike earlier disagreements between the Soviet Union and the United States. American action was not merely irritating; it was fraught with danger. Stalin consequently risked more in trying to deflect the Americans from their course. He failed and had to acquiesce in the inevitable revival of German power, supported by the United States.

American leaders, denying any animosity toward the Soviet Union, perceived the confrontation differently. They had conceded the requirements of Soviet security and offered the Soviets a role in the new international economic order. The Soviet response had been hostile, aggressive, ominous. The men in Washington suspected the Soviets of attempting to dominate the Eurasian landmass; they had to be stopped before they threatened the security of the United States. The problem of perception was complicated by the Stalinist system. It was difficult to trust the Soviet government, because it was closed, secretive, brutal toward its own people and the others it dominated – because of Stalinism.

After the Berlin blockade, relations between the United States and the Soviet Union were clearly adversarial. And yet the two countries were not quite enemies. They had avoided bloodshed, and no critical issues remained to divide them. None of their vital interests were in conflict. American security and that of its allies were assured by the preponderance of American power. The United States was uninterested in pressing its advantage any further, nor is there any evidence to indicate that Stalin feared an American offensive against his Eastern European buffer. The division of the European continent may not have satisfied the leadership in Washington or Moscow, but it was bearable. A return to the level of amity achieved during the war years, permitting attention to pressing domestic problems, was conceivable. But it did not happen.

Stalin was ready to consolidate his gains, accept the status quo of 1949, and promote peaceful coexistence. His maneuvers had stiffened American resolve and increased rather than lessened the danger to his regime. War with the United States had no appeal to him. But even peaceful competition meant the Soviet Union would strive for equality with the United States, demand respect as a superpower, remain mistrustful of American intentions, and compete for control of the periphery.

The structure of the international system, nominally bipolar, continued to frame Soviet-American relations. By 1949, the two governments had gained considerable experience contending with each other. In Europe, the United States had drawn the line and Stalin had accepted it as consistent with the existing correlation of forces. Continuing Soviet efforts to compete for power and influence, however, and the decline in America's relative power as the rest of the world began to recover from the impact of the war, proved intolerable to Truman's advisers. They were profoundly troubled as they watched decolonization and pressures for it loosen Western control over the periphery, and they determined to prepare for the worldwide struggle to come.

The principal obstacle to American preparedness, as perceived by Dean Acheson and Paul Nitze, had been Truman's determination to hold down defense spending. The president's parsimony was supported by Congress and public opinion. Change followed the Soviet A-bomb test in 1949. The loss of the nuclear monopoly forced the United States to reconsider the size and deployment of its conventional forces. In January 1950, Truman approved the development of the H-bomb and the review of policy that emerged as NSC-68, both with the intent of maintaining American superiority.

With evidence that the Soviets had acquired a nuclear capability, a new cycle of anxiety began. Soviet leaders could not accept a permanent American monopoly of nuclear weapons. Perhaps their apprehension over the Marshall Plan was unjustified, but there was nothing unreasonable about their fear of Germany or of NATO, or about their decision to arm against the threat they perceived. But increments to Soviet power and improvements in Soviet security threatened American security and interests. Certainly the Soviet acquisition of nuclear power constituted such a threat.

The United States and the Soviet Union engaged in a systemic rivalry after World War II. To paraphrase the historian Melvyn Leffler, both sides acted prudently.[3] Friction was predictable as they

3 Melvyn P. Leffler, *A Preponderance of Power* (Stanford, 1992).

competed. The principal surprise was probably the extent to which
the United States asserted its interests across the globe, in the
Middle East, and ultimately in Africa and Southeast Asia as well.
This is easily attributable to a sense of mission, Wilsonian internationalism, or perhaps, more simply, a conviction that the time had
come for the United States, as the world's greatest power, to behave
responsibly and benevolently, to create and oversee the new world
order. The United States was, after all, far and away the world's
greatest power. It alone could afford the short-term sacrifices necessary to gain broad acceptance of its hegemony.

One problem with the Pax Americana was the circumscribed role
it allowed the Soviet Union. Contempt for the Soviet system, for
Stalinism, contributed to American unwillingness to contemplate
partnership. The historic experience with the Stalinist regime precluded trust. But the Soviets were far too strong to tolerate American dominance any longer than forced to.

The fact that the competition became hostile and evolved into the
Cold War is attributable principally to the nature of the Soviet
regime – a powerful and vicious dictatorship, a ruthless totalitarian
state that terrified its own people and all who came under its control, a closed society whose secretiveness precluded verification of
agreements. Like most revolutionary regimes, the Soviet Union was
slow to learn the value of traditional diplomatic procedures, of
civility in discourse. Communication was difficult, and suspicion
was always close to the surface.

But the American political system also contributed mightily to
the problem. To serve the national interest as they conceive it, the
president and his foreign affairs advisers appear to have two choices.
First, and apparently the choice of Roosevelt, Johnson, Nixon, Reagan, and Bush, they can ignore congressional and constitutional
restraints and do what they think right, being as devious as necessary to get the job done. Or, second, they can persuade Congress and
the people of the wisdom of the course chosen. The latter approach
also allows two further choices. The president can tell the people the
truth, as Jimmy Carter promised to do, or he can tell them something "clearer" than the truth, as Dean Acheson had Harry Truman
do, and as he believed all great teachers do. In this context, articu-

lating something clearer than the truth meant magnifying the Soviet threat, and the Soviet role in events with undesirable outcomes – to the delight of anti-Communist ideologues who then argued, if the Soviet threat was so great, why had Truman not done more. The exaggerated view of the Soviet threat took root, came back to haunt Truman, Acheson, Kennan, et al., and seems to have been internalized by some of the mythmakers themselves.

The security dilemma, ostensibly a product of the systemic rivalry, was aggravated by the American sense that the United States posed no threat to anyone, was acting in the best interests of all, and that any state, specifically the Soviet Union, that enhanced its own military position, was preparing to take hostile action. Kennan occasionally, unlike most others, was able to conceive of Soviet actions as defensive responses to the disposition of American power.

In the years when the United States enjoyed a monopoly or a preponderance of nuclear power, Stalin's natural prudence was reinforced by a disinclination to invite the use of such weapons against the Soviet Union. Truman and Eisenhower were unquestionably willing to resort to nuclear blackmail against the Soviets or the Chinese, but recommendations for preemptive strikes against one or the other of the Communist giants emanated primarily from the lunatic fringe and never received serious consideration in the White House. The United States enjoyed the status quo: It would not start a war against a major power. Its historic traditions militated against (although they did not prevent) acts of aggression, as did the image it hoped to convey to the rest of the world.

As the Soviets developed their nuclear capability and the necessary delivery systems, civilian theorists in Moscow and Washington concluded that war was unwinnable. Khrushchev understood that Leninist concepts of international relations were irrelevant in the age of the hydrogen bomb, that the bomb did not observe class principles. The initiator of a nuclear war, whether it ultimately won or lost, would have to endure a retaliatory strike of unacceptable magnitude. All of its cities might be destroyed in a few hours, perhaps in a matter of minutes, with scores of millions of almost immediate deaths. Avoiding war, deterring an enemy strike, rather than fighting became the mission of Soviet and American strategic forces. The

Soviets did not actually have a second strike capability until the 1960s, but Eisenhower was also a prudent man. Subsequent Soviet-American summitry and then arms control negotiations, promoting a sense that the two nations could resolve their differences peacefully, helped preclude direct confrontation.[4]

It must not be forgotten, however, that the Soviet-American Cold War was responsible for millions of deaths. Walter LaFeber noted that 21.8 million people died of war-related causes between 1945 and 1990, most of them as surrogates for one or the other super-power or at the receiving end of arms provided by one of the super-powers.[5] The Korean War was probably the most dangerous of the wars on the periphery. Civil strife escalated into an international conflict and very nearly a world war. Approving Kim Il Sung's design for attack was Stalin's most serious miscalculation of the postwar era. Truman's decision to send American forces across the thirty-eighth parallel was equally misguided.

For Americans, Vietnam was the most grievous of its many inter-ventions in the Third World, bringing incredible misery to the Vietnamese people, weakening further an already faltering American economy, and undermining the willingness of many Americans to support further adventure in the guise of exercising the responsibility of world leadership. In Afghanistan, for the first time, Soviet troops were bloodied as they tried to control an unruly neighbor. But for every American or Soviet soldier that was killed in combat, perhaps as many as two hundred Africans, Asians, Central Americans, and Middle Easterners died in these wars. Millions more suffered human rights abuses in the Soviet empire and in countries like Chile, El Salvador, Guatemala, Iran, and South Korea where the United States supported brutal regimes as bulwarks against communism.

Almost always internal or regional issues precipitated the struggle in the Third World, one or the other superpower intervened, posing a perceived challenge to the credibility or resolve of the other, and intensifying the misery of the local people. Rarely did these conflicts

4 See Gaddis, *The Long Peace,* and especially Robert Jervis, *The Meaning of the Nuclear Revolution* (Ithaca, 1989).
5 Walter LaFeber, *America, Russia, and the Cold War, 1945–1990,* 6th ed. (New York, 1991), 335.

threaten the vital interests of either the Soviet Union or the United States. The superpowers simply would not tolerate indigenous challenges to the status quo unless the challengers were likely to align with their side. With less risk of provoking a nuclear exchange, intervention was always tempting. More often than not the superpowers underestimated the autonomy of countries like Cuba, or Israel, or Korea, or Vietnam and feared the machinations of their major adversary. Washington and Moscow developed elaborate rationales, like the notorious "domino theory," to explain why it was necessary to expend lives and dissipate their wealth in some distant benighted land.

And then it all came to an end – not the turmoil in the Third World, for sure, but the will and capacity of the superpowers to attempt to control the world. The Americans, staggering since the late 1960s, held on longer. The Soviets, after a furious flurry of activity in the late 1970s, collapsed in the mid-1980s. Changes in Soviet society, Gorbachev's reforms, modifications of Soviet military doctrine and, more important, Soviet military posture, provided the United States with a desperately needed respite. The Americans no longer had the financial means necessary to respond to every test of their resolve and the collapse of the Soviet Union allowed them to claim victory before their own society was strained beyond bearable limits. Finding a credible enemy, a potential threat so grave as to sustain the enormous military establishment of the United States, was not conceivable in the 1990s. So weakened was the victor that even with Soviet support, the United States needed German and Japanese money, Saudi and Kuwaiti funds, to underwrite its forces in operations against Iraq in 1990 and 1991.

Much of the change on the international scene was related only marginally to the Cold War. Most significant was decolonization, the end of the European empires and the emergence of scores of new nations, each seeking to modernize as rapidly as possible, to gain a share of the wealth and power so long enjoyed exclusively in the metropoles. World War II was the catalyst, weakening the imperial powers, awakening the colonials. In some instances, Cold War tensions affected the pace and the price of winning freedom and attaining its rewards. Sometimes the Cold War helped Third World peoples like the Egyptians who, in the absence of superpower competition, might have been ignored, but who were able to manipulate the anxieties in Moscow and Washington to their advantage. Sometimes, superpower-supported internal strife delayed development, as in Angola, or brought widespread misery and death, as in Vietnam and Afghanistan.

Another disruptive legacy of World War II was the state of Israel, an effort to do justice to the Jewish people, victims of the world's earlier indifference and persecution, who had suffered horribly at Hitler's hands. But the Jewish return to their ancient homeland displaced thousands of Palestinian Arabs who did not move aside voluntarily. The Palestinians and their Arab neighbors fought war after war against the Israelis, and again both sides manipulated the superpowers. The Soviets, eager to disrupt the British position in the Middle East, contributed to the victory of the Jewish settlers with a critical shipment of Czech weapons in 1948. Beginning with an arms deal with Egypt, the Soviets shifted sides in the mid-1950s and supplied the radical Arab states with sophisticated military equipment and advisers until 1990. In the 1960s, the United States, after an initial effort to remain aloof, was drawn by primarily domestic political considerations into becoming Israel's principal backer. As the Soviets aided the Arabs, Israel was seen increasingly as an American surrogate against Soviet surrogates in the region. The end of Soviet assistance to the Arabs in 1990 soon diminished the intensity of American support for Israel, but Arab-Israeli tensions continued without the backdrop of the Cold War.

At the end, Germany and Japan had reemerged as major forces in the world, the nations of Eastern Europe had regained their freedom, some of the Soviet republics seceded from the Soviet Union, and the rest struggled to define their new identities. Ethnic tensions long suppressed by communism exploded into civil strife reminiscent of the early years of the twentieth century. The Cold War was over, but the world would not know peace.

The United States in the 1990s was a land very different from what older Americans remembered of 1945. The lot of minorities –

Catholics, Jews, African Americans, Hispanics, and Asian Americans — and of women was greatly improved. There remained enormous room for progress, but American society was vastly more open, unimaginably more open than it had been in 1945. Some of the change had been set in motion by the ideals for which Americans had professed to be fighting in World War II. Some — for example, the improved status of Catholics in American society — might be attributed to the Cold War, as the Catholic church had long been in the vanguard of anticommunism, and Cardinal Spellman of New York and Senator Joseph McCarthy of Wisconsin provided Catholic folk heroes in the anticommunist crusade. The election of John F. Kennedy to the presidency in 1960 put an end to the Catholic issue in American politics.

The distribution of wealth in America left much to be desired and seemed to be heading in the wrong direction in the 1980s and early 1990s. Much of the maldistribution — the fact that the most affluent 1 percent of the American people controlled more of the nation's wealth than did the bottom 90 percent — was simply in the nature of the capitalist system. But the enemies of New Deal efforts to redistribute wealth more equitably among the American people had succeeded in using the Cold War to crush progressivism in the United States. And the Reaganomics of the 1980s had used defense spending, the rebuilding of American military power for the Cold War, as a means of manipulating the federal budget to enhance the fortunes of the already very rich.

When historians of the twenty-first century look back on the Cold War era, at its impact on the world in which they live, they are less likely to be struck by the death and destruction facilitated by the superpowers than by the influence of American culture, the success of the American model. The obvious manifestations will be the McDonald's, Pizza Huts, and Kentucky Fried Chicken franchises found all over the world, the blue jeans and rock and roll. More significant will be the computers and fax machines that facilitate global interdependence. And not least will be the heightened concern for human rights, the hope for governments that rule by law — governments of the people, by the people, and for the people — and illusions about the miracles that a market economy will bring.

Of course, the United States of the 1990s had been influenced noticeably by its intense encounters with the outside world during the Cold War years. The percentage of Asian Americans had risen greatly, as increased contact had brought Koreans, Vietnamese, and Thais, as well as Indians, Pakistanis, and Chinese, in large numbers to the United States. The new immigrants contributed enormously to the broadening of American culture – to conceptions of art and food and beauty. They staffed the nation's hospitals and universities, as well as its groceries and restaurants. To a country fearful of losing the work ethic, they brought new vitality.

Economically, the interdependent liberal world order, facilitated by the leadership and foresight of Americans in the 1940s, had come into existence. The United States no longer had the wealth with which to dominate that order, and many members were temporizing about meeting their obligations – but there were as many nations outside clamoring to get in. Learning to share power with Japan, the European Community, even ASEAN, proved difficult for the United States, but there were no viable alternatives.

Politically, militarily, the United States in the early 1990s was more secure than at any time since World War I. Terrorism would continue, was indeed unstoppable, but however angrily, Americans could tolerate that level of violence. The global concerns of the Cold War era, justified by the existence and threat of the Soviet Union, were shrinking rapidly. Interest in black Africa, South America, South Asia, rarely intense, all but evaporated. But there was no returning to the Atlanticism of pre–Cold War American leaders. People like Dean Acheson, George Ball, and George Kennan had tried to focus American attention and power on Europe, the Middle East, and Japan, seeing little of importance in the rest of the world. They calculated that with control of sufficient oil and with the industrial power of Western Europe, Japan, and the United States, the United States would prevail in any competition short of nuclear holocaust. In the 1990s, men and women who thought like Acheson, Ball, and Kennan would include the need to attend to all of East Asia, noting the resurgence of China and the economic power of Taiwan, Hong Kong, ASEAN, and South Korea.

Given the quality of the leaders they chose in the 1960s, 1970s, and 1980s, men who abused the nation's power and mishandled its economy, the American people had much for which to be grateful in the 1990s. They had nonetheless survived. There were no external dangers. Most of them were eating. They were no longer the wealthiest people in the world, but the top was still within reach if they were willing to work for it and were able to find leaders who would demand the appropriate sacrifices. And despite the many failings of the United States, there was no doubt that the world, for all its misery, was a better place than it would have been without American resistance to Joseph Stalin's vision.

Bibliographic Essay

Perhaps the most important point to be apprehended by the student of the history of international relations in the Cold War era is that the documentary record is incomplete, that American and British archival material is being released thirty years after the events at best. Moreover, there is evidence indicating that the integrity of the American record has been compromised. Other materials, Chinese and Soviet for example, are being released very selectively, often to privileged nationals. Little was seen by Western scholars before the mid-1980s – and not much more has been seen since. Finally, most of what we know about the late 1960s and thereafter is provided by participants who are never disinterested, journalists, and those who write "contemporary history," an oxymoron if there ever was one.

A second point worth noting is that enormously important work, much of it theoretical, has been done by political scientists and political economists. In particular the work of Robert Gilpin, Robert Jervis, Peter J. Katzenstein, Robert O. Keohane, Stephen D. Krasner, and Jack Snyder provides valuable guides to an understanding of what happened and why – and what is likely to happen tomorrow. See, for example, Gilpin, *The Political Economy of International Relations* (Princeton, 1987); Jervis, *Perception and Misperception in International Politics* (Princeton, 1976); Katzenstein, ed., *Between Power and Plenty* (Madison, 1978); Keohane, *After Hegemony* (Princeton, 1984); Krasner, ed., *International Regimes* (Ithaca, 1983); Snyder, *Myths of Empire* (Ithaca, 1991).

The standard survey of American foreign policy since 1945 is Walter LaFeber, *America, Russia and the Cold War,* the 6th edition of which was published in 1991. Interesting overviews of the entire era, alluding to Henry Luce's vision of an "American Century," can be found in Thomas L. McCormick, *America's Half-Century* (Baltimore, 1989), and William Pfaff, *Barbarian Sentiments: How the*

262

American Century Ends (New York, 1989). And every issue of *Diplomatic History* has a new and often important contribution to some episode from the American involvement in world affairs after 1945.

1. At War's End: Visions of a New World Order

Robert Dallek, *Franklin D. Roosevelt and American Foreign Policy, 1932–1945* (New York, 1979), remains the most useful introduction to FDR's thoughts on world affairs. The quest for a liberal international economic order can be followed from the 1920s through the 1940s in Michael J. Hogan, *The Marshall Plan* (Cambridge, 1990). Richard N. Gardner, *Sterling-Dollar Diplomacy,* expanded edition (New York, 1969), and Alfred E. Eckes, *A Search for Solvency* (Austin, Tex., 1975), are important to an understanding of the Bretton Woods agreements. The British perspective is most accessible in the relevant chapters of Roy F. Harrod, *The Life of John Maynard Keynes* (New York, 1951). Gabriel Kolko, *Politics of War* (New York, 1968), offers the least flattering evaluation of American ends leading up to Bretton Woods.

John Lewis Gaddis's classic *United States and the Origins of the Cold War, 1941–1947* (New York, 1972) captures Roosevelt's sinuous path toward the goal of maintaining the Grand Alliance after the war. Herbert Feis, *The China Tangle* (Princeton, 1953), is still the best introduction to American problems with wartime China. See also Michael Schaller, *The U.S. Crusade in China, 1938–1945* (New York, 1979). The most balanced account of Chiang Kai-shek's wartime diplomacy is John W. Garver, *Chinese-Soviet Relations, 1937–1945* (New York, 1988). Two very different efforts to read Stalin's mind are William O. McCagg, Jr., *Stalin Embattled, 1943–1948* (Detroit, 1978), and William Taubman, *Stalin's American Policy* (New York, 1982). Gar Alperovitz, *Atomic Diplomacy: Hiroshima and Potsdam,* expanded and updated edition (New York, 1985), is the best-known indictment of Truman's use of the atomic bomb against Japan, but see J. Samuel Walker, "The Decision to Use the Bomb: An Historiographical Update," *Diplomatic History* 14 (1990): 97–114. Roosevelt's decisions on with whom to share the bomb's secrets and from whom to withhold them can be followed in Martin J.

Sherwin, *A World Destroyed* (New York, 1975). Two excellent volumes on the subsequent importance of nuclear weapons are Gregg Herken, *The Winning Weapon* (New York, 1980), and Robert Jervis, *The Meaning of the Nuclear Revolution* (Ithaca, 1989).

2. Origins of the Cold War

The American domestic context is portrayed vividly in Eric Goldman, *The Crucial Decade – and After, 1945–1960* (New York, 1960), and with more concern for women and minorities in William Chafe, *The Unfinished Journey* (New York, 1986). H. Bradford Westerfield, *Foreign Policy and Party Politics* (New Haven, 1955), remains the best account of how partisan politics contributed to the shaping of the Soviet-American relationship. The single most important study of Truman's foreign policy is Melvyn Leffler's magisterial *A Preponderance of Power: National Security, the Truman Administration, and the Cold War* (Stanford, 1992). Deborah Welch Larson, *Origins of Containment* (Princeton, 1985), provides a fascinating psychological study of how the policy toward the Soviet Union developed. Foreign economic policy is traced by Robert A. Pollard in *Economic Security and the Origins of the Cold War, 1945–1950* (New York, 1985). Richard M. Freeland argues persuasively the relationship between *The Truman Doctrine and the Origins of McCarthyism* (New York, 1972). Joyce and Gabriel Kolko offer a densely written but otherwise engaging Marxist analysis in their *Limits of Power* (New York, 1972). Joseph M. Jones, *The Fifteen Weeks* (New York, 1955), is the standard work on the evolution of the Truman Doctrine and the Marshall Plan by a participant.

The Wise Men (New York, 1986) by Walter Isaacson and Evan Thomas is a highly readable examination of the thought and interactions of six major policymakers, but Dean Acheson's own *Present at the Creation* (New York, 1969) is still essential. There are too many books about George Kennan whose own elegant writing and occasional profundities have led historians to exaggerate his importance. See, for example, Walter L. Hixson, *George F. Kennan: Cold War Iconoclast* (New York, 1989), and Anders Stephanson, *Kennan and the Art of Foreign Policy* (Cambridge, Mass., 1989). The most recent is

Wilson D. Miscamble, *George F. Kennan and the Making of American Foreign Policy, 1947–1950* (Princeton, 1992).

Lawrence Kaplan's *NATO and the United States* (Boston, 1988) is particularly helpful on the origins of NATO. European perceptions and activities are best explored with Geir Lundestad, "Empire by Invitation? The United States and Western Europe, 1945–1952," *Journal of Peace Research* 23 (1986): 263–77. See also Alan S. Milward, *The Reconstruction of Western Europe, 1945–1951* (Berkeley, 1984), and Anton W. dePorte, *Europe Between the Superpowers*, 2d ed. (New Haven, 1986). Wolfram F. Hanrieder, *Germany, America, Europe: Forty Years of German Foreign Policy* (New Haven, 1989), offers a wealth of information and insights for the entire postwar period. Marshall D. Shulman, *Stalin's Foreign Policy Reappraised* (New York, 1966), suggests Stalin was seeking to retreat from confrontation on the eve of the Korean War.

Marc S. Galliccio, *The Cold War Begins in Asia* (New York, 1988), looks at American fears of Soviet influence in East Asia in 1945. Steven I. Levine, *Anvil of Victory* (New York, 1987), explains the American response to Communist successes in Manchuria in 1946. The major works on relations with China are Dorothy Borg and Waldo Heinrichs, *Uncertain Years: Chinese-American Relations, 1947–1950* (New York, 1980), and Nancy B. Tucker, *Patterns in the Dust* (New York, 1983). See also Robert J. McMahon, "The Cold War in Asia: Toward a New Synthesis," *Diplomatic History* 12 (1988): 307–27, for a superb overview, especially of work at variance with the prevailing Tucker-Cohen thesis. For Japan, see Michael Schaller's *The American Occupation of Japan* (New York, 1985), John Dower's *Empire and Aftermath* (Cambridge, 1979), and Carol Gluck's discussion of the issues and literature, "Entangling Illusions – Japanese and American Views of the Occupation," in Warren I. Cohen, ed., *New Frontiers in American–East Asian Relations* (New York, 1983), 169–236. The early American involvement in Southeast Asia is most accessible in Gary Hess, *The United States Emergence as a Southeast Asian Power, 1940–1950* (New York, 1987). See also Robert J. McMahon, *Colonialism and the Cold War: The United States and the Struggle for Indonesian Independence, 1945–1949* (Ithaca, 1981), on Indonesia.

3. The Korean War and Its Consequences

Bruce Cumings, *The Origins of the Korean War,* 2 vols. (Princeton, 1981, 1990), is essential reading for the serious student of the war. James Matray, *The Reluctant Crusade* (Honolulu, 1985), and Burton I. Kaufman, *The Korean War* (New York, 1986), are more accessible. Rosemary Foot, *The Wrong War* (Ithaca, 1985) and *A Substitute for Victory* (Ithaca, 1990), are major contributions to understanding American strategy during the war and in the peace negotiations. Allen S. Whiting's classic *China Crosses the Yalu* (Stanford, 1960) should be supplemented by Zhang Shuguang, *Deterrence and Strategic Culture* (Ithaca, 1993), which relies heavily on recently released cables exchanged between Mao and Stalin. In recent conferences in Moscow, Washington, and East Lansing, Russian scholars have been forthcoming about Soviet complicity in the North Korean attack, but Nikita Khrushchev's memoir, edited by Edward Crankshaw and translated by Strobe Talbott as *Khrushchev Remembers* (Boston, 1970), is all we have in print at this time.

Three important articles are Okonogi Masao, "The Domestic Roots of the Korean War," in Akira Iriye and Nagai Yonosuke, eds., *The Origins of the Cold War in Asia* (New York, 1977), 299–320; James I. Matray, "Truman's Plan for Victory: National Self-Determination and the Thirty-eighth Parallel Decision in Korea," *Journal of American History* 66 (1979): 314–33; and Robert Jervis, "The Impact of the Korean War," *Journal of Conflict Resolution* 24 (1980): 563–92.

4. New Leaders and New Arenas in the Cold War

Eisenhower "revisionism" was a growth industry for historians in the late 1980s and early 1990s, as archival material for the 1950s was declassified. Richard A. Melanson and David Mayers, eds., *Reevaluating Eisenhower* (Urbana, Ill., 1987), is a convenient place to start. Ronald W. Preussen, *John Foster Dulles* (New York, 1982), is the best of the current biographies. Richard H. Immerman, ed., *John Foster Dulles and the Diplomacy of the Cold War* (Princeton, 1990), contains a number of superb essays. Immerman's own book, *The CIA in Guatemala* (Austin, Tex., 1982), is a very good account of how Eisenhower got things done, as is Fred I. Greenstein, *The Hidden-Hand Presidency* (New York, 1982). Burton I. Kaufman, *Trade and Aid: Eisenhower's Foreign Economic Policy* (Baltimore, 1982), delivers what it promises.

Warren I. Cohen and Akira Iriye, eds., *The Great Powers in East Asia, 1953–1960* (New York, 1990), includes the perspectives of British, Chinese, Japanese and Soviet, as well as American scholars. The Chinese essays are especially interesting. Akira Iriye and Warren I. Cohen, eds., *The United States and Japan in the Postwar World* (Lexington, Ky., 1989), has substantial material on the 1950s, from Japanese and American scholars, economists and political scientists as well as historians.

Robert J. McMahon is thoughtful as always in "Eisenhower and Third World Nationalism: A Critique of the Revisionists," *Political Science Quarterly* 101 (1986): 453–73. On the Eisenhower administration and Castro, see Richard E. Welch, Jr., *The Response to Revolution: The United States and the Cuban Revolution, 1959–1961* (Chapel Hill, 1985). Stephen Rabe, *Eisenhower and Latin America* (Chapel Hill, 1988), is cast more broadly. Diane Kunz, *The Economic Diplomacy of the Suez Crisis* (Chapel Hill, 1991), provides a fresh approach to a battered subject. The single most important volume on the Suez crisis is W. Roger Louis and Roger Owen, eds., *Suez 1956* (New York, 1989). John C. Campbell, *Defense of the Middle East* (New York, 1960), is still useful for understanding the designs of the Eisenhower administration in the region. Howard Palfrey Jones, Eisenhower's ambassador to Indonesia, relates the pathetic tale of being undermined by Washington and especially the CIA in his efforts to woo Sukarno in *Indonesia: The Possible Dream* (New York, 1971). George M. Kahin, *Intervention* (New York, 1986), is excellent on Indochina.

Useful works on the Soviet side include Adam Ulam, *Expansion and Coexistence* (New York, 1974), William Zimmerman, *Soviet Perspectives on International Relations, 1956–1967* (Princeton, 1969), and Bruce D. Porter, *The USSR in Third World Conflicts* (Cambridge, 1984), as well as *Khrushchev Remembers*, cited earlier.

5. Crisis Resolution

Thomas Paterson, ed., *Kennedy's Quest for Victory* (New York, 1989), is the best place to start the study of the early 1960s. Warren I. Cohen, *Dean Rusk* (Totowa, N.J., 1980), is more revealing than Rusk's own story, *As I Saw It* (New York, 1990). See Gordon Chang, *Friends and Enemies* (Stanford, Calif., 1990), for some especially provocative suggestions on Kennedy's policy toward China.

The Berlin crisis has not received as much recent attention as has the Cuban missile crisis. It can be studied in Philip Windsor, *City on Leave* (London, 1963); Jean Edward Smith, *The Defense of Berlin* (Baltimore, 1963); Robert M. Slusser, *The Berlin Crisis of 1961* (Baltimore, 1973); Jack M. Shick, *The Berlin Crisis, 1958–62* (Philadelphia, 1972). See also the relevant portions of Alexander L. George and Richard Smoke, *Deterrence in American Foreign Policy* (New York, 1974), and Wolfram F. Hanrieder, *Germany, America, Europe: Forty Years of German Foreign Policy* (New Haven, 1989).

The history of the missile crisis has benefited enormously from a series of conferences involving American, Cuban, and Soviet participants. It is apparent the world was even closer to nuclear war than we had imagined previously. See James G. Blight and David A. Welch, *On the Brink* (New York, 1989), and Raymond L. Garthoff, *Reflections on the Cuban Missile Crisis,* rev. ed. (Washington, D.C., 1989).

6. America's Longest War

An unusually wide range of documentation has been available on the war in Vietnam since the "Pentagon Papers" were first published in 1971. The U.S. Department of State Historical Office subsequently accelerated publication of the relevant volumes of the *Foreign Relations* series.

George Herring, *America's Longest War,* 2d ed. (New York, 1986), remains the single most valuable book on the war in Vietnam. In *On Strategy* (Carlisle Barracks, Pa., 1981), Harry Summers explains how the war could have been won. Other recent books of interest include Gabriel Kolko's dense *Anatomy of a War* (New York, 1985) and

Timothy J. Lomperis's *The War Everyone Lost — and Won* (Baton Rouge, 1984). Marilyn B. Young, *The Vietnam Wars, 1945–1990* (New York, 1991), is a powerful statement by a leading historian and antiwar activist. Lomperis, *Reading the Wind* (Durham, N.C., 1987), is a valuable analysis of the fictional and memoir literature.

7. The Rise and Fall of Détente

The single most valuable book for the Nixon, Ford, and Carter years is Raymond L. Garthoff, *Détente and Confrontation* (Washington, D.C., 1985). Although ruthless editing might have produced a better book at half the length, it is a gold mine of information provided by a thoughtful midlevel participant. Henry Kissinger's two-volume memoir, *The White House Years* (Boston, 1979) and *Years of Upheaval* (Boston, 1982), is self-serving but nonetheless essential reading. William Hyland, *Mortal Rivals: Superpower Relations from Nixon to Reagan* (New York, 1987), is a useful study by another midlevel participant.

The complex character of Richard M. Nixon is deciphered only in Garry Wills, *Nixon Agonistes* (Boston, 1970). Good critical accounts of the Nixon-Kissinger years are provided by the journalists Tad Szulc, *The Illusion of Peace* (New York, 1979), and Seymour Hersh, *The Price of Power* (New York, 1983), the latter probably a trifle severe for the taste of most readers.

Zbigniew Brzezinski, *Power and Principle* (New York, 1983), is informative, especially of the author's efforts as national security adviser to usurp power once reserved for the secretary of state. For ego, the memoir rivals Kissinger's — but lacks the self-deprecating wit that was always Henry's charm. Instead of Carter's memoir, look to Gaddis Smith, *Morality, Reason and Power* (New York, 1986), for an understanding of Carter's foreign policy efforts. Cyrus Vance tells his own story in *Hard Choices* (New York, 1983).

Given the limited documentation available, Soviet-American relations are covered surprisingly well. Robert S. Litwak, *Détente and the Nixon Doctrine* (Cambridge, 1984), neatly indicates the contrasting expectations each side had of détente. Joseph S. Nye, Jr., *The Making of America's Soviet Policy* (New Haven, 1984), contains several useful essays. Harry Gelman, *The Brezhnev Politburo and the Decline of Détente* (Ithaca, 1984), is vintage Kremlinology. The Soviet thrust in the Third World characteristic of the late 1970s is analyzed nicely in Rajan Menon, *Soviet Power and the Third World* (New Haven, 1986), and Jerry Hough, *The Struggle for the Third World* (Washington, D.C., 1986). David Holloway, *The Soviet Union and the Arms Race,* 2d ed. (New Haven, 1984), focuses on the other critical issue in Soviet-American relations in the 1970s.

For Sino-American relations, see Harry Harding, *A Fragile Relationship: The United States and China Since 1972* (Washington, D.C., 1992). John W. Garver, *China's Decision for Rapprochement with the United States, 1968–1971* (Boulder, Colo., 1982), is interesting and suggestive. See also Michel Oksenberg, "A Decade of Sino-American Relations," *Foreign Affairs* 61 (1982): 175–95. The Chinese perspective is offered in David Shambaugh's fascinating analysis of the views of China's foreign policy elite, *Beautiful Imperialist* (Princeton, 1991). William B. Quandt, *Decade of Decisions: American Policy Toward the Arab-Israeli Conflict, 1967–1976* (Berkeley, 1977), and Gary Sick, *All Fall Down* (New York, 1985), are excellent on Arab-Israeli relations and the collapse of the American position in Iran respectively. On Iran, see also James A. Bill, *The Eagle and the Lion* (New Haven, 1988). Oksenberg, Quandt, and Sick all served on the National Security Council. For economic issues, especially the collapse of the Bretton Woods system, Joanne Gowa, *Closing the Gold Window: Domestic Politics and the End of Bretton Woods* (Ithaca, 1983), and Robert Gilpin, *The Political Economy of International Relations* (Princeton, 1987), are most helpful.

8. In God's Country

The journalist Lou Cannon has been studying Ronald Reagan for a very long time and his *President Reagan: The Role of a Lifetime* (New York, 1991), is the most knowledgeable and the best-balanced biography. Another journalist-cum-historian, Don Oberdorfer, has written a valuable portrait of Reagan's metamorphosis from apocalyptic horseman to Gorbachev's partner in the quest for peace. See his *The Turn: From Cold War to the New Era: The United States and the Soviet*

Union, 1983–1990 (New York, 1991), based heavily on interviews with George Shultz. See also Michael Mandelbaum and Strobe Talbott, *Reagan and Gorbachev* (New York, 1987), and Talbott, *Deadly Gambits* (New York, 1984). A very thoughtful, accessible overview of the Reagan years is Robert W. Tucker, "Reagan's Foreign Policy," *Foreign Affairs* 68 (1989): 1–27.

The Soviet side of the 1980s is approached most easily through Seweryn Bialer, *Politics, Society, and Nationality Inside Gorbachev's Russia* (Boulder, Colo., 1989), and Seweryn Bialer and Michael Mandelbaum, *Gorbachev's Russia and American Foreign Policy* (Boulder, Colo., 1988). See especially articles by Robert Legvold and Bialer. The articles in Marshall D. Shulman, ed., *East-West Tensions in the Third World* (New York, 1986), are also helpful – see the essays by Elizabeth K. Valkenier, Donald S. Zagoria, and Frances Fukuyama in particular.

The historical context for American policy toward Central America is provided by Walter LaFeber, *Inevitable Revolutions* (1984). For a more contemporary focus see Nora Hamilton et al., *Crisis in Central America* (Boulder, Colo., 1988); Mary B. Vanderlaan, *Revolution and Foreign Policy in Nicaragua* (Boulder, Colo., 1986); Robert A. Pastor, *Condemned to Repetition* (Princeton, 1987); and Tommie Sue Montgomery, *Revolution in El Salvador,* 2d ed. (Boulder, Colo., 1990).

Conclusion: America and the World, 1945–1991

In addition to works already mentioned, see Paul Kennedy, *The Rise and Fall of the Great Powers* (New York, 1987); David P. Calleo, *The Imperious Economy* (Cambridge, Mass., 1982); Richard Rosecrance, *The Rise of the Trading State* (New York, 1986); and John Lewis Gaddis, *The Long Peace* (Oxford, 1987).

Index